I0796868

Always Remember provided a place for me to share my story of God's redeeming love and divine plan. Throughout its pages, I hope you will see how he weaves every part of our lives for his glory to equip and inspire future generations.

Shari Rigby, actor, director, writer, founder of a women's ministry group

What an honor to be asked to share my story of God's plan for my life. May it help you to always remember that your life can be an encouragement to others.

Alexandra Boylan, filmmaker, producer, screenwriter

God has graciously blessed me with a decades-long career in TV and film. But that pales in comparison to the honor of sharing Jesus's redeeming love and hope to the world. My deepest heart cry is that readers will always remember who God is—and who they are in him. I can think of no greater blessing!

Nancy Stafford, actor, author, speaker

I pray that *Always Remember* will inspire you, as the apostle Paul says, to always know Jesus and to help make him known.

Shelia Erwin, author, ministry leader, teacher

Always Remember

365 DAYS OF WISDOM FOR LIFE

KIM CRABILL

BroadStreet
PUBLISHING

BroadStreet Publishing® Group, LLC
Savage, Minnesota, USA
BroadStreetPublishing.com

Always Remember: 365 Days of Wisdom for Life

9781424568574 (faux leather)
9781424568581 (ebook)

Disclaimer: This book contains mentions of depression, suicidal ideation, and eating disorders. The information presented represent the writers' opinions and does not constitute medical advice for mental or physical health. Please seek advice from a medical professional for any health concerns.

Cover and interior by Garborg Design Works | garborgdesign.com

Printed in China

25 26 27 28 29 5 4 3 2 1

To
Sophia

May you
always remember
the profound gift you are,
cherished by your mom and dad,
deeply loved by your grandparents
and all who will come to know you.

With all my love,
Gigi

I would like to express my heartfelt gratitude to the contributors of this book. Your invaluable wisdom and insights serve as a timeless gift to all. Each of you has enriched this work with your unique voice, perspective, and profound biblical knowledge, creating a tapestry of truths that will undoubtedly inspire generations to come.

INTRODUCTION

Near the end of a counseling session, I heard myself say, "Now always remember…" to which I added a word of hope to my client until our next appointment.

Why do I do that? I wondered. *Why do I always end that way?* A little four-year-old version of myself came to my mind, sitting on the swing almost daily with my grandfather. He would use our "swing moments" to speak truth into my life, often describing scenarios that I might find myself in, and then saying, "But now always remember…"

For example, one time he said to me, "Kim, I may not always be with you. I may not always have you on this swing with me. You may not always be able to hear my words. But I want you to always remember that I love you, and there's someone who will always go with you, and his name is Jesus. I want you to always remember that, Kim." And here I am, sixty years later, always remembering the words of wisdom my grandfather put into my heart and into my thoughts as seeds that grew and illuminated my mind when I needed them most.

My thoughts turned next to all the incredible people I've met along my life's journey, and I recalled many of the "always remember" words that they have spoken and are still speaking. And so this book was born: a collection of wise words from friends who, I believe, will speak into your life and will inspire you to speak your own godly wisdom into the lives of generations to come.

I hope you'll always remember that you matter, that you are loved, and that no matter what anyone may say and no matter what darkness may come upon your life, there is someone who loves you beyond anything you could ever imagine, and he is always with you, and his name is Jesus.

Kim Crabill

January

THOUGHTS MATTER!

For as he thinks in his heart, so is he.

PROVERBS 23:7 NKJV

"There's just something special about you!" Have you ever thought about the words that have gotten you through life? What kept you from giving up? What words echo in your heart, inspiring hope that something good lies just beyond your current struggle or your latest mistake? "You are special," spoken to me as a child by someone I loved and trusted, illuminated some of my darkest days and helped me reach many of my brightest moments. And I can't tell you how many times these words helped me battle my own negative thinking.

Here's the truth: thoughts matter. What you believe today is guiding you to who you are becoming tomorrow. I pray this book becomes like a trusted friend you rush to sit with each day to fill you with God's hopeful truth and empowering thoughts. And even if no one ever told you before, I pray that throughout each page, you hear the words that help you always remember what your heavenly Father says each day: "There's just something special about you."

Dear Father, help me each day to remember your words of Isaiah 43:4, that I am precious in your sight!

Kim Crabill, TV host, author, ministry leader,
Christian counselor

MORE THAN GETTING BY

"I came that they may have life and have it abundantly."

JOHN 10:10 ESV

So many Christians today seem to be worn out. When you ask how they're doing, they say "Just making it" or "Getting by," giving the impression that they are barely surviving. What about you, friend? What is your answer when someone asks how you're doing? This life has a way of consuming our mental and emotional energy. News stations thrive on the negative, and gossip abounds on every side. It all robs us of our peace and joy, leaving weariness in its place.

But God is a God of *abundance*, and when you receive that abundance, it changes how you think and how you live. You are no longer "getting by." Instead, you are more than a conqueror, loaded with daily benefits. This truth should put a spring in your step and a smile on your face. Always remember that the God you serve has provided everything you need to live joyfully in his abundance. If you choose to focus on that fact today, you will find yourself soaring with eagles, high above the others who are barely making it.

Lord, thank you for your joy that I can experience no matter the circumstances or the news.

Kim Crabill, TV host, author, ministry leader, Christian counselor

SEEK GOD'S MERCY AND GRACE

Let us confidently approach the throne of grace to receive mercy and find grace whenever we need help.

HEBREWS 4:16 NET

Am I the only one who feels the Christian life is difficult? You see, I love Jesus, and I so want to represent him well in this world, but I don't always operate out of the gifts he has given me. I don't always lean on his power and, instead, try to do things in my flesh, knowing I will fail when I do! Oh, those days bring such grief to my sinful heart when I realize the tremendous grief I have caused my loving Father.

I need to always remember that my High Priest, Jesus, sympathizes with my weakness because he was tempted in every way that we are (Hebrews 4:15). Does this mean he was tempted to do things in his flesh and was tempted not to use his gifts for good works? Yes! He was tempted, but, unlike me, Jesus didn't sin. The beautiful truth is that I can still approach the throne of grace confidently, knowing I will find his mercy and grace there. And friends, so can you.

Lord, thank you for your mercies that are new every morning.

Carmen Pate, Roses and Rainbows advisory board member, author, speaker, Bible teacher, mentor of women

A DEPENDABLE GUIDE

"I am the Lord your God, who teaches you what is good for you and leads you along the paths you should follow."

Isaiah 48:17 NLT

While sipping your coffee or tea each morning, do you contemplate the day ahead of you and the decisions you need to make? I know I do. Some decisions, like what outfit is appropriate for the day or what to make for dinner, won't matter much beyond today. But what about the weightier things, like how to deal with a family crisis, where to tighten your spending, what college is best for your kids, or what church you should attend?

Whatever lies unanswered before you, always remember that your Creator God invites you to call on him when you need direction. He promises to guide you, advise you, and watch over you. You don't have to make your decisions alone. He loves to reveal the steps you need to take one day at a time. How comforting it is to realize you serve a God like that! What confidence it should instill within you as you walk through this day with him!

Thank you, Lord, that I can depend on your guidance every day.

Kim Crabill, TV host, author, ministry leader, Christian counselor

A DROPPED BALL?

"My ways are higher than your ways, and my thoughts higher than your thoughts."

Isaiah 55:9 NLT

What are you supposed to do when, by all appearances, God has dropped the ball in your situation? You've prayed for weeks, months, or maybe years. You spent many long night hours staring into the dark as you wavered between hope and fear. *God, please work things out and give me my heart's desire*. Then the answer comes—a resounding *No*. What bothers you most is that you know he could have done what you asked, but he chose not to. How do you cope with the sting of rejection?

I have been with you in this land of bewilderment more than once. I know it's hard to see beyond the hurt and confusion you feel today, but always remember that no matter how it looks in the moment, Jesus has not failed you. What appears to be a mistake on his part is only a small portion of the bigger, beautiful plan he has for your life. For now, know that he loves you, and trust that one day it will all make sense.

Lord, help me to trust your goodness and love even when I don't understand your ways.

Esther Carpenter, author

GLORIOUS PRESSURE

We are hard pressed on every side, but not crushed.

2 Corinthians 4:8 niv

Are you feeling the pressure of having too much on your plate today? Are you afraid to even look at the long list of things you must accomplish for fear that your emotional health will buckle under the weight? Does it help to know that you are not the only thing in life that feels pressure? Grapes must be crushed to make wine. Diamonds form in the dark under great pressure. Olives must be pressed to release the oil we covet so much.

The next time you feel the pressure is too much and worry that its weight will crush you, keep in mind that in the darkness of the struggle, a powerful transformation is happening to you too. Trust God in the process today, my friend, and don't lose hope. Always remember that, although the trials you are facing may be difficult, they have all been filtered through the hands of our loving heavenly Father. He allows only what is for our good and his glory.

Lord, help me look to you for strength when the pressure of life overwhelms me.

Kim Crabill, TV host, author, ministry leader, Christian counselor

A FEATHERY REFUGE

He will cover you with his feathers,
and under his wings you will find refuge.

Psalm 91:4 NIV

Do you understand that you aren't meant to carry life's painful secrets on your own, yet you find yourself in that place anyway? Shame. Guilt. Embarrassment. Regret. These are just some of the reasons we don't want to discuss the heaviness of our hearts.

You might be keeping a secret today (perhaps one you've held for decades), and its weight has affected how you feel about yourself, others, and even God. But, my friend, don't let your hurts isolate you. Always remember first and foremost that God loves you. His love brings with it a peace he wants to share with you. You can find refuge in him today. Even before you become brave enough to tell a friend, you can talk to God about anything that's in your heart. He has a place for you, warm and secure, under his wings. He wants you to stay there until you find the healing you crave. Talk to him today. Let him cover you with his feathers.

Lord, help me remember that I always have a place of loving safety under your wings.

Kim Crabill, TV host, author, ministry leader,
Christian counselor

BUSLOADS OF GRACE

By grace you have been saved, through faith—and this is not from yourselves, it is the gift of God—not by works.

EPHESIANS 2:8–9 NIV

I had just graduated and moved to New York City. I was headed to an audition when I read these words in a Campus Crusade discipleship book: "If our relationship with God was dependent on our own good works, we could never have assurance. We would never know if we had done enough to please God." There it was in black and white: salvation is a gift from God. Yet I had spent my life frantically trying to earn acceptance and prove my worth at home, at school, and at work.

Sadly, I realized I was doing the same thing in my faith walk with God. I wept and poured out my heart to God on that bus. He tenderly showed me that he didn't want me to try harder; he wanted me to trust him more deeply. He invited me to rest on his finished work on the cross. My relationship was secure because he had done it all. Always remember, there is nothing you can do to earn your salvation. It is God's gift to you. Rest!

Lord, help me to remember the cross where your love and mercy meet. Thank you for your amazing grace.

Candace Kirkpatrick, actor, speaker, talk show cohost

A READY ANSWER

He has given us his very great and precious promises.

2 Peter 1:4 NIV

A frustrated mother once asked her disobedient daughter, "Who do you think you are, young lady?" Her words make me think of how we hear the same question on a spiritual level as well. Can you relate? Do you ever hear in your head, *Who do you think you are?* The trouble is, we often hear these words when we're trying to do the right thing and live in obedience before God. Yet our heavenly Father would never raise such a question at a time like that.

So who is it who's speaking to you? It's the enemy, our accuser, that's who. When you hear this condemning question in your head, do you have a ready answer for him? If not, here are a few: *I am God's child* (1 John 3:1). *I am forgiven* (Romans 8:1–2). *I have great purpose* (Jeremiah 29:11). *I can do all things through Christ* (Philippians 4:13). Friend, I want you to always remember that this is who you are. This is what God thinks about you. It is a solid truth to stand on every day.

Lord, thank you for giving me love, forgiveness, purpose, and such a beautiful identity in you.

Kim Crabill, TV host, author, ministry leader,
Christian counselor

A SHARP FOCUS

We must keep our eyes on Jesus.

HEBREWS 12:2 CEV

I do not love standing in front of a mirror. Yes, I know it is a necessary part of life. If we want our hair to look perfect, if we want to hide our wrinkles and blemishes, we need some time in front of a high-focus mirror. But I'm glad we don't have to stay there all day. It isn't good for us to focus on ourselves too long.

This concept applies to our spiritual lives too. We need to spend time in Scripture so we can see blemishes that need our attention. But it's important not to fall into the trap of focusing on ourselves, our faults, and our flaws. C. H. Spurgeon once said, "It is ever the Holy Spirit's work to turn our eyes away from self to Jesus, but Satan's work is…trying to make us look at ourselves instead of Christ." My friend, always remember to focus on Jesus, not yourself. He alone can replace your flawed spirit with his pure and peaceable one. Focusing on Christ will always bring you the greatest joy.

Lord, help me to focus on you and not on my shortcomings.

Kim Crabill, TV host, author, ministry leader, Christian counselor

PLOTS AND PERSECUTION

Hide me from the conspiracy of the wicked,
from the plots of evildoers.

PSALM 64:2 NIV

Can you recall a time in history when people were more pitted against one another? When the culture "cancels" believers for speaking up and defending their beliefs? Does it seem like every family has a member no one is speaking to? Rather than being surprised, be ready! Spiritual attack and persecution may very well come from the people in your circle. As you experience opposition, recognize it for what it is, and don't lash out against others. Instead, get mad at your real enemy—Satan. You may even derive a curious comfort from the fact that he always hits those who are making spiritual progress.

King David was well acquainted with persecution. Many plotted against him—some from his own household. Always remember that, as believers, we will not go unopposed: "In fact, everyone who wants to live a godly life in Christ Jesus will be persecuted" (2 Timothy 3:12 NIV). That warning came from an expert!

Dear Lord, please build character in me so that I can stand up to persecution, victorious in you.[1]

Pat Boone, actor, singer, songwriter, author

---

1 Adapted from *Pat Boone Devotional Book*, published by Bible Voice, Inc. Used by permission from Mr. Boone.

SCARS OF PURPOSE

"Flesh gives birth to flesh, but the Spirit gives birth to spirit."

John 3:6 NIV

My eyes blinked open and saw the red numbers of a wall clock glaring overhead. The time was later than I expected. I was told that the procedure would take only about sixty minutes, but almost half the day had passed. *Why?* I gradually absorbed the news that I had suffered a life-threatening hemorrhage and had been operated on to find the source of the bleeding.

There was a lot of shock and grief in those first few days after the emergency, but there was also a profound sense of awe. God was so close to me that it felt like my eyes were open for the first time ever. Through my own body breaking and blood spilling out, I felt as though I had been born again with Christ. He gave me a new life and vision. In an instant, God transformed the worst moment of my life into one that erased all fear of death and filled me with purpose and love. Always remember that he can use our darkest times to give us new life.

Merciful God, thank you for always being ready to transform my bleeding wounds into scars of purpose. You lovingly give me new life when I least expect it.

Maggie Winzeler, women's wellness writer, business owner

ABIDE AND THRIVE

"Abide in me, and I in you."

John 15:4 ESV

Do you ever struggle to stay close to Jesus? You want to abide in him as John 15 says, but so many things out there distract you: a full day's activity, too many commitments, or the damaged relationship you are trying to repair. Maybe think of it this way: When a good friend comes into town for a few days and wants to stay with you, don't you rearrange your schedule as much as possible to accommodate them?

Abiding in Jesus is like that. You can choose to make room for him, and the coolest thing is that he is only a prayer away. One breath of *Jesus, help me* is all you need to bring yourself into proximity with him. My friend, always remember that as you stay close to Jesus, he'll exchange your distractions for his own qualities of love, patience, and peace. Through thick and thin, happiness and sadness, failures and triumphs, he will always be there. He wants you to rest as you abide in him.

Lord, thank you for providing a way for me to stay close to your heart and rest in you.

Kim Crabill, TV host, author, ministry leader, Christian counselor

WHEN YOUR LIFE SEEMS DARK

"I create the light and make the darkness. I send good times and bad times."

Isaiah 45:7 NLT

Don't be surprised when God leads you on a dark, troubled path. He may call you to uncomfortable situations. When I was a young believer, I didn't understand the troubles that God allowed in my life. So I would run to him, crying out in desperation and sometimes anger. But I learned a valuable lesson that I hope you will always remember: it is the darkness that makes us long for God's light.

We recognize our need for God in times of trouble and will seek his help and comfort. That is exactly what God desires! When things are going well for us, we may forget God, who gives us all good things. So doesn't it make sense that God, who loves us most and desires we stay close, would allow us to walk a troubled path? It is not because God is cruel but because he is good! He knows that when we recognize our total dependence on him, we are ready to press on to the great things he has in store for us.

Lord, thank you for taking me through the darkness from time to time so I better appreciate your goodness and light.

Carmen Pate, Roses and Rainbows advisory board member, author, speaker, Bible teacher, mentor of women

AN ATTITUDE OF REST

"My Presence will go with you, and I will give you rest."

Exodus 33:14 NIV

Have you ever felt like your strength was gone, yet you had no choice but to keep going? I'm talking about the times when you just wanted to curl up in bed and sleep for a while, but your to-do list was too long. You knew rest was coming but it wouldn't be today. I have found that, many times in my life, the strength I thought I did not have was more of an attitude problem than a lack of physical strength.

If this is you today and you feel like you just have too much to do, I hope you will always remember that God is within you, and he will give you strength to keep going. No matter how much your journey feels like an uphill battle, now is not the time to give up. Choose instead to be the kind of person who gives in to God, leaning on his strength and allowing him to equip you with whatever you need for this day. Your day of rest will come.

Lord, on days when I struggle with an attitude of weariness, give me your gentle strength.

Kim Crabill, TV host, author, ministry leader,
Christian counselor

AN EVER-CHANGING YOU

Anyone who belongs to Christ has become a new person. The old life is gone; a new life has begun!

2 Corinthians 5:17 NLT

I love the story of Joseph and his brothers in Genesis 37–50. It's a story of great highs and terrible lows. Deep emotion, family stress, hurt, and shame are all found on its pages. Hated by his brothers and sold into slavery, Joseph was dragged from a prison to a palace before his brothers again stood before him. He could have been bitter. He could have sought revenge.

But instead, Joseph gave his brothers a chance to show they were not the same men who'd abandoned him years ago. My friend, are you grieving a past hurt, or maybe you need to tell someone you are sorry for causing them pain? Whatever the issue, always remember you are not the same person today, and neither are they, so consider forgiveness. You are a new creature in Christ. Jesus is in the process of changing you and making you more like him. This truth will set you free.

Lord, help me to remember that forgiveness is the way to freedom.

Kim Crabill, TV host, author, ministry leader, Christian counselor

BELIEF THAT TRANSFORMS

Remember now your Creator in the days of your youth.

ECCLESIASTES 12:1 NKJV

I was living in Hawaii and enjoying everything a twenty-something could desire: a Waikiki condo, zany friends, and a convertible. I had put God on the far back shelf of my life and was content to leave him there. Then came *the letter*. Dad didn't write often, and when he did his letters were short, casual. At the bottom of this letter, however, he wrote, "Remember now your Creator in the days of your youth." My dad has no recollection of adding that Bible verse to his letter. But it turned out to be an "always remember" moment for me.

The next day I bought a Bible and started reading. Over the next week, I came to believe—really believe—what I'd heard all my life: "that Jesus is the Christ, the Son of God, and that by believing you may have life in his name" (John 20:31 ESV). I will always remember that move from mentally assenting to who Jesus is to believing in "life in his name," which is nothing like plain old life.

Dear God, thank you for remaking me when I strayed from you. Truly, life with you is never "plain."

Sue Kline, writer, editor, writing coach

ARE YOU OK?

Surely your goodness and love
will follow me all the days of my life.

PSALM 23:6 NIV

Seven little words from God were a driving force in my life: *You're not OK, but you can be*. They weren't audible words, but I've learned to recognize his voice, and I knew beyond any doubt that it was he. And while some days I feel more OK than others, those words helped me see that when I don't feel OK, God is the one to run to.

What about you, my friend? Do you feel OK today, or are you struggling to be OK? Regardless of how you feel, let me remind you that God cares about every detail of your life. He is the faithful one who keeps his promise to heal broken hearts and restore lives. Even when you don't feel OK, always remember that God is still good. You can trust his goodness despite your circumstances. He is good even when life is not. If you are not OK today, keep going because maybe tomorrow you will be.

Lord, thank you for your goodness and that I can always count on you to meet my needs.

Kim Crabill, TV host, author, ministry leader,
Christian counselor

ARMS OF RESCUE

He lifted me out of the slimy pit.

PSALM 40:2 NIV

When I was a little girl my grandfather and I would often take long walks together. I would run ahead and serenade him with my songs; I loved being his little princess. One day, busy with my princess act, I wasn't watching where I was going, and I fell into a big pothole in the road. My delight turned to tears as I surveyed my scrapes and scratches. My grandfather rushed to me, took me in his strong arms, and wiped my tears, telling me I would be OK.

My friend, sometimes in life you will experience unexpected potholes that steal your joy. It may be a wrong choice you made, an unwanted phone call, or maybe a misunderstanding with a friend. I want you to always remember that there is no pothole so deep that God won't come running to your rescue. He will reach down, pick you up, and whisper words of reassurance to you. You will never have a problem too big for him to redeem. He will right your world. His arms are always strong enough to rescue you.

Lord, thank you for the assurance that you will always come to my rescue.

Kim Crabill, TV host, author, ministry leader, Christian counselor

STRAWBERRY SHORTCAKE

Gracious words are a honeycomb,
sweet to the soul and healing to the bones.

PROVERBS 16:24 NIV

Growing up, I often heard younger members of my large family refer to some of the older members by saying, "They have sugar." This loving point of reference marked the reason for their forgetfulness, their sweating, their frequent trips to the bathroom, and a lot of other characteristics I found funny.

My aunt once baked a cake that we kids were not allowed to touch because it was for the adults who had "sugar." That cake was the prettiest kind of cake, a strawberry shortcake. As I grew older, I learned that "they have sugar" was actually a loving way to say they were diabetic. Because of this, I will always remember how the words we use shape us and all around us who hear our words. It's funny to think about now, knowing that the one cake I could not have in childhood would be the one that impacts me the most in adulthood. It is a reminder to choose kind, gracious words in every conversation.

Lord, please grace me with your discernment so that I may choose my words wisely.

Melinda D. Davis, Roses and Rainbows advisory board member, radio network executive

BE HIS CHILD

Let my soul be at rest again.

Psalm 116:7 NLT

"Grow up!" Did anyone ever tell you that? I'm exhausted just thinking of it! But being grown-up doesn't mean that we push down our pain and forge ahead, trying to be what we know we're supposed to be. Maybe the reason the song "Let it Go" resonates with so many people today is because, for our own well-being, we want to let go of things that have weighed us down for too long.

My friend, if this is you, I want you to always remember that our Lord doesn't ask you to shove the pain down or push it away, trying to forget about it. Jesus said, "Come to me, all you who are weary and burdened, and I will give you rest" (Matthew 11:28 NET). Our heavenly Father only asks for our presence, not our perfection. He doesn't want us to pretend anything. He wants us to come just as we are. You don't have to be grown-up today. God has given you permission to just be his child.

Lord, thank you for giving me a place to lay down the baggage I carry. Thank you for rest.

Kim Crabill, TV host, author, ministry leader, Christian counselor

BE LIKE NICK

They were all filled with the Holy Spirit and spoke the word of God boldly.

Acts 4:31 NIV

How do you feel about speaking out for Jesus? Do you hesitate to identify with him in public? If so, I get it. We stand a good chance of being snubbed or openly ridiculed. Nicodemus knew a thing or two about this dilemma. He had skulked through dark city streets to visit Jesus in secret (John 3:1–21). Now, three years later, crucifixion day was over. It had been a day of confusion and horror. Jesus was still hanging on the cross, his body broken and spirit gone, when Nicodemus and his friend, Joseph, showed up in the presence of all their friends to retrieve Jesus' body and give it a proper burial (John 19:38–40).

What had changed this man? Jesus had. And as you spend time with him, you will change too. Whenever you feel timid, always remember that Jesus will give you the courage and the boldness to speak the words he wants you to speak, to do the work that he has called you to do. Be like Nicodemus and live boldly for Jesus.

Lord, help me to live as a bold and courageous representative of you.

Kim Crabill, TV host, author, ministry leader, Christian counselor

HEARTBEAT OF SURVIVAL

Be joyful in hope, patient in affliction, faithful in prayer.

ROMANS 12:12 NIV

Turn back time to many years ago: I awoke from a six-week coma, intubated, disoriented, and in excruciating pain. *Why can't I breathe?* Then I remembered the fire. *Where is my family—my husband and my six sons? Who lived? Who died?* I felt the presence of my husband, James, entering the hospital room. Then I heard the voice of our pastor telling me about the fire's devastation. We lost our home and everything we owned. Our sons had all been burned. Our twenty-two-month-old Benjamin suffered second- and third-degree burns. His twin brother, Amos, didn't make it.

That blow drained every ounce of hope from me. I closed my eyes and surrendered to the death I felt coming. But the thought of my surviving children jolted my motherly instincts, infusing hope that reignited my will to survive. I prayed, asking God to heal and restore my family.

Lord, you are the God of the hills and valleys. In my time of trial, may I always remember that you are my hope of glory.

Justina Page, author, speaker, actor

BELIEVING IS SEEING

"Did I not tell you that if you believed you would see the glory of God?"

John 11:40 ESV

How many times have you heard the words "Seeing is believing?" Jesus puts another view out there for you to consider: "Believe, and then you will see." What is your response? Confusion? Think about it. Do you have a dream that is slowly dying in front of you? Is God withholding something from you for reasons you cannot fathom? You're not alone. Many great men and women of the Bible experienced confusion too. Abraham couldn't understand why God would ask him to give up what he loved most, his son. Moses couldn't understand why God would keep him wandering in the wilderness for forty years. Mary and Martha tried desperately to understand why Jesus didn't come quickly when their brother was dying.

Dear one, you may not understand your situation today, but always remember that God sees a bigger picture than you do. He may be preparing to call forth a miracle on your behalf today. Will you believe without seeing? Begin this day by praying for and believing in your miracle.

Father, give me faith to believe until I see the miracle you will provide.

Kim Crabill, TV host, author, ministry leader, Christian counselor

NO RESERVATIONS

Submit yourselves, then, to God. Resist the devil, and he will flee from you.

JAMES 4:7 NIV

Remember all those if-then scenarios we grew up hearing? If you finish your homework, then you can watch TV. If you eat a good dinner, then you can have dessert. If you save your allowance, then we'll buy that bike together. As believers, we quote the verse that says to resist the devil, and he will flee from you. But just like the if-thens of childhood, James 4:7 is conditional. In order for the devil to flee, we must submit to God and resist the devil. What does that even mean? We say, "Of course I submit because I know God is superior." But do we submit to his will, or do we have ideas of our own?

Do we pray, *Thy will be done*, or do we have our own if-then scenario: *Lord, if you just do this one thing, then I promise from now on I'll...*? Do we read about praying blessings over our enemies but add our own, "Except for so and so, because he..."? Submitting to God takes humility. Obedience. Subservience. All those words we just love. But if we're not fully submitted as Christians, we're not fully protected in spiritual warfare.

Is there any area of reservation in my heart, Lord? If so, show me. I want full protection from the enemy.[2]

Pat Boone, actor, singer, songwriter, author

2 Adapted from *Pat Boone Devotional Book*, published by Bible Voice, Inc. Used by permission from Mr. Boone.

BETTER TOGETHER

Then all of them were encouraged and their spirits improved.

ACTS 27:36 AMP

Have you ever looked around you and wondered if you're the only one? The only one to be searching for answers? The only one trying to make sense of your circumstances? The only one fighting some type of battle? Everyone you see at church or the office looks like they have it together. Even the folks at the mall show no signs of struggle or worry on their faces.

Ah, my friend, but looks can be deceiving. First Peter 5:9 tells us that the whole family of believers throughout the world is going through the same type of suffering you are. Every person around you is fighting some kind of battle. Always remember that when God drew you to himself, he drew you into a family too. You are not alone. There is always someone who understands your struggle—who is ready to support you in the battle to resist your enemy and stand firm in your faith. Reach out!

Father, thank you for giving me the family of believers who support me in my walk of faith.

Kim Crabill, TV host, author, ministry leader,
Christian counselor

BEWARE THE TWIST

Take...the sword of the Spirit, which is the word of God.

EPHESIANS 6:17 NIV

Have you ever looked for a verse to use as leverage to get what you wanted or to condone your actions? Perhaps you felt uneasy about a decision and wanted to justify it, so you searched for a verse that would build your case. That's a dangerous game, but one we are all tempted to play. Satan used it on Jesus, in fact, which should caution us even more. One of his challenges to Jesus in the wilderness included Scripture. Satan said, "The Scriptures say, 'He will order his angels to protect you'" (Matthew 4:6 NLT).

The verse Satan quoted was the truth, but he used it out of context. My friend, beware of twisting God's words to make them say what you want them to say. Always remember that the only way to have peace in decision-making is to follow what you know God is telling you to do. Choosing any other option leads to trouble. Be like Jesus and keep your eye on what's at stake. He will always guide you right.

Lord, give me a sense of holy awe as I read your words and treat them with reverence.

Kim Crabill, TV host, author, ministry leader,
Christian counselor

ORDER FROM CHAOS

God is not a God of disorder but of peace.

1 CORINTHIANS 14:33 NIV

I spent my early years split between two households. When my mom was doing OK emotionally, I lived with her. When she struggled, I moved in with my grandmother. For many years, my mother and I lived in my grandmother's garage. One room. No carpeting. No plumbing. Life was dysfunctional and semi-chaotic. But as an adult, God brought order to my life, just as he can do for anyone who surrenders the chaos to him. During a difficult scenario, it is important for us to admit that we cannot handle it by ourselves and need the Lord's strength.

As I look back on those early years, I am thankful because they taught me humility. They showed me how to adjust to ever-changing situations. I am grateful for grandparents whose help taught me to always remember that God will create order in our lives when we bring our chaos to him. Where is chaos rearing its ugly head in your life? Ask God to manage the scenario. It's his nature to restore what is out of order.

Lord, I give you all the current and past dysfunction in my life. I trust that you will create order out of chaos.

Lisa Burkhardt Worley, film producer,
ministry founder/leader, radio/TV host

BOLD FAITH

"God will give you the right words at the right time."

MATTHEW 10:19 NLT

Sometimes sharing your faith can be really intimidating, right? You feel God nudging you to speak about the hope you have in him, and you want to be obedient, but you don't know how those around you are going to react. In such moments it's important to remember that when God asks you to share your faith, he will give you the words to speak. I love the saying, "Because Jesus lives in you, demons cannot defeat you, haters cannot silence you, people cannot break you, money cannot buy you, trials cannot stop you, and temptations cannot silence you." It has given me courage more than once.

The temptation to keep silent when we are prompted to share our faith is one we all face, but I hope you'll always remember that what God is asking you to do will take you to places you can't imagine. You never know who is on the brink of giving up, wondering if life is worthwhile. You have everything they need to find their way back to life and hope. So speak up and be blessed.

Lord, give me the boldness to share my faith when I feel you prompting me to do so.

Kim Crabill, TV host, author, ministry leader, Christian counselor

BRAINS AND THE BIBLE

Do not conform to the pattern of this world, but be transformed by the renewing of your mind.

Romans 12:2 NIV

I recently listened to a neuroscientist talk about the positive and negative patterns in our brains. Statistics prove that positive thinking diminishes negative brain patterns. This got me thinking. If you can change negative brain patterns by positive thinking, imagine what the powerful Word of God can do! Sometimes we fall into a mindset of negative thinking. Maybe the world's problems rub off on us, or we visit with a friend who always sees the glass half empty, and before long we are walking in a rut of negativity. If you recognize that trait in yourself, remember that it is a rut you can crawl out of.

Paul encouraged the Roman Christians to let God renew their minds so they wouldn't conform to the pattern of the world they lived in. My friend, I want you, too, to always remember that you needn't conform to the world and its ways. You can be renewed by digging into the transforming Word of God.

Lord, thank you for your living and powerful Word that changes my life.

Kim Crabill, TV host, author, ministry leader, Christian counselor

TAKE CARE OF YOU

Love your neighbor as yourself.

MATTHEW 22:39 NIV

Do you ever think about this: that loving yourself is part of the second greatest commandment? Many times, we seem to think that loving others is the important part, and we forget the part about loving ourselves. But self-care is so important. There are so many occasions when I have not thought about caring for myself. For example, at times I've spoken negative words over myself, not realizing that what I speak about myself is just as important as the words I speak about and to others. It took time for me to learn that obeying the second commandment means I need to care for myself.

As I began to take care of myself, realizing it was OK and not prideful, I saw a big difference in my health and life. As we take care of ourselves and love ourselves, we are able to love others better. Let's meditate on this verse to see what God has to say about loving your neighbor as yourself. Always remember to take time to care for yourself as God directs.

Father, show me ways to love myself as I love others.

Chris Luppo, TV producer, media consultant, speaker, author

February

BUILDING YOUR BOAT

"I will instruct you and teach you."

Psalm 32:8 NIV

Do you hear God's voice telling you exactly what he wants you to do? There is no doubt about your assignment, and you are willing. You just have no idea where to begin. I imagine Noah felt the same way when God told him there would be a flood and that he must build a boat. Noah had probably never seen a flood, and he had certainly never built a boat like the one God commanded. He had no blueprint with detailed instructions. His assignment was certainly an overwhelming one. How was he going to pull it off?

God, however, didn't leave Noah to figure it out on his own. God did something much better. He came alongside Noah, saying, "This is how you are to build it" (Genesis 6:15 NIV). Step by step, listening to God's instructions, Noah built that ark. Always remember that God will do the same for you. One step at a time, he'll provide directions for anything he asks you to do. With his help, you can accomplish all that he has in mind for you.

Lord, thank you for being a "hands on" God who shows me how to carry out your orders.

Kim Crabill, TV host, author, ministry leader,
Christian counselor

BUSY WITH THE BEST

You can make many plans,
but the LORD's purpose will prevail.

PROVERBS 19:21 NLT

Are you familiar with the saying, "If the devil can't make you bad, he'll make you busy"? Well, my friend, I'm afraid there's more truth to the statement than we want to admit. Think about it. Being busy can make you feel important, distract you from the pain you carry, and make you say yes to every opportunity that comes along. But it can also prevent you from embracing the work God has in mind for you. When Nehemiah was sent to rebuild the wall of Jerusalem, his enemies tried to distract him. But he kept his focus on the work God had given him.

Always remember that God has custom-designed work for you to do that will fulfill his purpose for your life. You don't have to be pain-free or perfect—just available. Are you free to embrace his opportunities, or are you in bondage to too many other demands on your time and energy? What do you need to cross off your to-do list so that you are free to be a blessing?

Lord, help me to slow down and say yes only to the opportunities you have in mind for me.

Kim Crabill, TV host, author, ministry leader,
Christian counselor

WANNA WEAR MY SHOES?

"If you pour yourself out for the hungry and satisfy the desire of the afflicted, then shall your light rise in the darkness."

ISAIAH 58:10 ESV

During one of the darkest times in my life, I cried in the dark with a broken heart. I wondered if God was hearing my prayers for relief and if he understood the pain I was in. Eventually I got up, forced myself to brush my teeth, and took a shower. While the water washed over me, I heard my grandmother's voice saying, *Always remember, someone would love to be in your shoes.*

That truth resuscitated me. I had thrown myself a pity party that lasted entirely too long. I washed my hair, cleaned up, and did an inventory check: I had food, shelter, clothes, good health, and people who loved me. I began to move with a sense of purpose for the first time in weeks. I searched online for a place to volunteer. While serving, I realized God was with me and hearing me. He had already planted something inside of me that could be activated: my grandmother's wisdom. I served myself back to joy!

God, help me understand that no matter how bad things seem, there is always someone who would love to trade places.

Maura Gale, speaker, actor, author, podcaster

GOOD GROWTH

These trials will show that your faith is genuine. It is being tested as fire tests and purifies gold—though your faith is far more precious than mere gold.

1 PETER 1:7 NLT

Did you know that right this moment, God is using your experiences, both good and bad, to develop your character? That's right. He has a calling on your life, my friend, and just like fire tests the purity of gold or silver, he is using your current reality to test your heart and make you more like him. Every experience you face in life serves God's good purpose. Each test is designed to develop your endurance because endurance is what strengthens your character, and strong character results in a confident hope in him. The situation you see as a problem, God sees as potential for developing your character.

What problem or trial stands in the way of your plans for success? Whatever is happening today, whether good or bad, always remember that God will use every part of it for his good purpose. So keep going and rejoice, because you never know which part of your situation will eventually bring about the good work that he wants to do in your life.

Lord, give me patience to endure the trials that will bring out your good work in me.

Kim Crabill, TV host, author, ministry leader, Christian counselor

CHERISHED

For no one ever hated his own body, but [instead] he nourishes and protects and cherishes it, just as Christ does the church.

Ephesians 5:29 AMP

Do you believe that Jesus cherishes you today? We hear so often that Jesus loves us that we almost become desensitized to the truth of it. The word *cherish* gives a different slant to the common idea of love. It means to protect and care for, to hold dear. Jesus holds you close to his heart. In his mind, you are his treasure. Your whole world will begin to change as you accept the truth that Jesus loves you unconditionally.

His protection and care are far superior to any you will find on earth. And the best part of all is that he will never change his mind about you. My friend, always remember that no matter what mistakes you make, no matter how many times you fail him, Jesus will never walk away from you. He will never give up on you. He loves you as much on your worst day as he does on your best day. Let your heart be rocked by this truth today!

Lord, how thankful I am that you cherish me today, holding me close to your heart.

Kim Crabill, TV host, author, ministry leader, Christian counselor

GRRRRRRR!

Be angry and do not sin; do not let the sun go down on the cause of your anger. Do not give the devil an opportunity.

Ephesians 4:26–27 NET

Wait, what? The Bible tells us it's OK to be angry? So it's OK to tell off our boss—and to stop talking to everyone we disagree with? Probably not. Anger based in righteousness is that which gives us emotional energy against evil. Jesus expressed anger at the hypocrisy of the Pharisees, and he overturned the tables as moneychangers transformed the holy temple into a retail free-for-all (Matthew 21:12–13).

But always remember, Jesus' fury was quick and controlled; it stemmed from a holy hatred for sin and sacrilege, *not* from hurt feelings. What if we directed less anger at people and more at unrighteousness and lies? What if we were mad at the enemy as he destroys lives rather than at the neighbor who rubs us the wrong way? Let's get mad as Jesus did—over injustice. Let's allow our anger to provoke action rather than reaction.

Father, I confess that most of my anger has been destructive. Rechannel and control this emotion in me so it might become a tool against the forces of evil and never against people.[3]

Pat Boone, actor, singer, songwriter, author

3 Adapted from *Pat Boone Devotional Book*, published by Bible Voice, Inc. Used by permission from Mr. Boone.

CHOOSE YOUR GUIDE WELL

You will guide me with Your counsel.

PSALM 73:24 AMP

Abraham made a surprising choice when he got to Egypt. After trusting God enough to uproot his wife, extended family, servants, and herds to go to a new land, he now made a big decision without seeking God's help. Afraid for his life because of his beautiful wife, Abraham went into protective mode and chose to deceive the Egyptians. He made a real mess of things (see Genesis 12). How much better it would have been if, instead of resorting to human reasoning, he had stayed before God asking, *Lord, why did you bring me here? What lesson am I to learn?*

I hope that Abraham's choice will help you to always remember to seek out the lesson in your trial rather than turning to self-protective thinking. Every difficult situation allows you the opportunity to become a student of God's guidance. Don't miss that opportunity, my friend!

Lord, help me always to seek your counsel and guidance in life's difficult situations.

Kim Crabill, TV host, author, ministry leader, Christian counselor

ALL THEIR HEART

"They will return to me with all their heart."

JEREMIAH 24:7 NIV

The prophet Joel described a time when grain and drink offerings were no longer part of the daily offering because of the locusts' destruction (Joel 1). The priests and the people grieved. Still today, we have allowed many of mankind's ways, worldly or fleshly things, to take our hearts on a detour away from God's presence. We can tend to lean into the world's wisdom, expecting change to arrive, only to find that the spiritual locusts have left nothing for a daily sacrifice.

But God faithfully guides us saying, *Now that you have tried it all and there is nothing left in your hand for you to offer, bring yourself to me instead.* Always remember that he wants your *whole* heart. He is the only one who can make the change.

Father, thank you for giving me a heart to know you. Remind me frequently that I am yours and you are my God.

Charlene Baktamarian, ministry president, executive producer, TV host

CHOSEN!

Even before he made the world,
God loved us and chose us in Christ.

EPHESIANS 1:4 NLT

Remember the days in grade school when it meant the world to be chosen—for drama, sports, music, or entrance into the popular kids' group? To be chosen meant everything. To be rejected was the end of the world. What about today, my friend? Do you still sit on the sidelines, longing to be chosen? Have you been passed over at work or at church or been denied an invitation to the party?

Not being chosen can make you feel inferior or unloved and unneeded, but there is one who will always choose you—not because of your good looks, abilities, or skills, but because he created you carefully and precisely for his own purposes, and he loves you fiercely. Always remember that in God you have great value. Even though he may not always provide the job you want or the skills you wish for, he has a better plan in mind, and he wants to use you. That is far better than being chosen for any earthly activity or party.

Father God, thank you for creating and choosing to use me in your kingdom.

Kim Crabill, TV host, author, ministry leader,
Christian counselor

COLLATERAL DAMAGE

All my ways are known to you.

Psalm 119:168 NIV

Do you find yourself caught in the crosshairs of a conflict that isn't yours? Perhaps you're involved simply by association and have no choice but to live with the consequences. You feel the effects of a house divided or a treasured relationship severed but are powerless to fix it. So you sit alone, surrounded by your losses, weeping because there's nothing you can do to restore the broken pieces of your life. You are just collateral damage. Oh, dear friend, if you find tears running down your face as you whisper, "This is me," may I remind you that all is not lost?

Always remember that your way is not hidden from the Lord. The chain of events leading up to your situation may not make any sense to you, but rest assured, they did not surprise God. Jesus is with you in everything you experience. Give him your broken dreams and relationships. He will transform them into a thing of beauty in his time. He can heal even the collateral damage done to your heart.

Lord, thank you for redeeming the broken pieces of my life and bringing healing to my heart.

Esther Carpenter, author

CONVERSING WITH GOD
(PART ONE)

Pray in the Spirit on all occasions with all kinds of prayers and requests.

EPHESIANS 6:18 NIV

Prayer can sometimes feel lofty, mystical, and unattainable, but really, prayer is just talking to God about whatever is on your heart. You can tell him what makes you happy, what confuses you, and what makes you angry. He can handle any question or emotion you bring to him. He will listen because that is what a friend does, and he wants to be your very closest confidant.

The Psalms are a collection of prayers offered to God by people who experienced all sorts of uncertain or problematic situations. Their cries for help, mixed with praises and thanksgiving, were a kind of sacrifice that sent a sweet and pleasing aroma into the heavens. God desires this same relationship with you. Always remember that giving God a few minutes of your undivided attention will bring you closer to him. Pick a psalm and try praying it to God today. Prayer really isn't that difficult after all, is it?

Thank you, Father, for providing the privilege of intimate friendship with you.

Kim Crabill, TV host, author, ministry leader,
Christian counselor

CONVERSING WITH GOD
(PART TWO)

"My sheep know my voice, and I know them."

JOHN 10:27 CEV

Yesterday we talked about how prayer is simply talking to God about everything that concerns you. Your friendship with God will also thrive when you take the time to listen. This may feel a bit mystical and unattainable, but it's not as hard as you might think. You already know that deep friendships consist of two-way conversations. Just as God loves to listen to you, he is also delighted when you take the time to listen to his response. He may have directions or plans he wants to reveal to you.

Jesus taught his disciples about listening in the story of the Good Shepherd, stating that his sheep know his voice (John 10:1–16). As you quiet your heart in talking with him, you are better able to hear him. If you want to know what God has in mind for you, always remember that you will need to take time to both talk to God and listen for his answering voice. Give him your undivided attention today and see what happens. He may surprise you with the sweetest conversation ever.

Thank you, Father, for making it possible for me to hear your voice and to follow your leading.

Kim Crabill, TV host, author, ministry leader,
Christian counselor

ONE DAY AT A TIME

"Blessed are those who mourn, for they will be comforted."

MATTHEW 5:4 NIV

In 2021, I lost my youngest sister to COVID-19. I miss her deeply, and despite being a student of God's Word and worshiping him daily, I was confused, hurt, and left with a lot of questions. *Why her? Why so soon?* It was hard to come to terms with her death. I had pictured us growing old together. But through the Spirit, I heard these words: *One day at a time.*

Each day I gain strength with acceptance and a deeper understanding of truth. I am learning to receive God's grace to live "one day at a time" so that I may understand the fullness of his blessings. He is always with me and has also surrounded me with a spiritual village, friends and family who pray for me and remind me of God's love and healing power.

Lord, thank you for seeing me in my grief. I pray for comfort and that you will speak understanding to me through your grace.

Melinda D. Davis, Roses and Rainbows advisory board member, radio network executive

CONFIDENT HOPE

You have been my hope, Sovereign LORD,
my confidence since my youth.

PSALM 71:5 NIV

Humans love to reminisce, don't we? We remember what our mothers told us when we were kids—we retell inside family jokes, we speak fondly of family no longer with us. Just as often, though, we rehash our biggest hurts and traumas. David, the "apple of God's eye" (Psalm 17:8 NIV), also looked back on his youth and called to mind adversity, even calamity. Each time he called to the Lord, he seemed confident God would come through again. Was he confident because he was God's favorite?

Always remember, David's confidence arose from his hope in God, not in his own perceived favoritism. Because David had kept a close relationship of trust and intimacy with God since childhood, he based his appeals on the blessings he'd already received. When we stop to consider all the times God has provided for us, we find a new confidence in our current situation. Hope wells up in our spirit. Rather than ruminating on our troubles, we can refocus on the times when God stepped in, when we prayed and our prayers were answered. The Lord is our hope!

Lord, I place myself and my concerns in your loving hands again, believing you will act on my behalf. I trust in you.[4]

Pat Boone, actor, singer, songwriter, author

---

4 Adapted from *Pat Boone Devotional Book*, published by Bible Voice, Inc. Used by permission from Mr. Boone.

DECLINABLE INVITATIONS

Let the peace of Christ rule in your hearts....And be thankful.

COLOSSIANS 3:15 NIV

Wouldn't it be wonderful to wake up tomorrow without a care in the world? No uncertainty. No stress. Nothing in your heart other than peace and joy. But how realistic is that? If you're like me, you're tempted to worry before your feet even hit the floor in the morning. However, there is hope when you realize that tucked in with each temptation to worry is a personal invitation to walk in faith with God. Fear doesn't come from God, and each time you are tempted to fret, he is there to assure you of his faithfulness.

Worries and fears are a part of life, but you don't have to be stuck in them. Always remember that you can choose to decline those invitations. You can choose to release each worry and fear to the power of prayer and take hold of a spirit of thankfulness. Your thanksgiving declares that no matter what your current circumstances are, you believe that God is actively working out more for your life than you can imagine.

Lord, when worry and fear try to rule my thoughts, help me to replace them with thankfulness.

Kim Crabill, TV host, author, ministry leader,
Christian counselor

DELIVER ME FROM DOUBT

For the word of God is alive and powerful.

HEBREWS 4:12 NLT

When the going gets rough, what do you do with the discouraging voice that says, *What's the use?* or *God doesn't care*? That, my friend, is the familiar voice of doubt. It is a troublesome companion, always showing up at the wrong moment, draining you of energy and the ability to do the work God has called you to do. The good news is that you can defeat the voice of doubt with the truth of the Word.

When doubt whispers, *God doesn't care*, you can remind yourself to "[cast] all your cares on him, because he cares about you" (1 Peter 5:7 CSB). When doubt leaves you feeling lost and uncertain about what to do, you can "ask God who gives [wisdom] generously" (James 1:5 NIV). If doubt is nagging you today, always remember that God has given you his Word as your weapon. You can take captive all those crippling thoughts (2 Corinthians 10:5) and replace them with life-giving, power-inducing ones that spur you on to action. Silence doubt today with the promises of God.

Lord, thank you for giving me the tools I need to live victoriously in Jesus.

Kim Crabill, TV host, author, ministry leader, Christian counselor

AVOID THE SHORTCUT

"'Love the LORD your God with all your heart, all your soul, all your mind, and all your strength.'"

MARK 12:30 NLT

"Clean your room before you go outside," said my mother. I could hear my friends playing, and I was eager to join them. I decided to take some shortcuts by throwing toys into the closet and sweeping things under my rug. I shoved both clean and dirty clothes into my dresser drawers and ran downstairs to join my friends. However, my mother stopped me at the front door. Needless to say, I failed her inspection and had to stay inside to clean my room properly. If only I had cleaned it right the first time.

That day, I realized that doing things halfway not only wastes time but also deprives us of the expected reward. This is especially true when it comes to the Lord. If we offer him a portion of our lives while sweeping sin and compromise under the rug, we forfeit a deeper, more intimate relationship with him. Always remember that God is looking for us to offer him clean hands and a pure heart.

Lord, may I never take the shortcut. May I always approach you with a surrendered heart, fully willing to follow you to the expected reward.

Myshel Wilkins, speaker, worship leader, recording artist

DISTORTED CONCLUSIONS

I was senseless and ignorant....Yet I am always with you; you hold me by my right hand.

PSALM 73:22–23 NIV

"If only." The words are spoken with longing and regret. "If only I hadn't done that." "If only you would have been there." "If only you would help me." Did such words cross your lips recently? Do you hear a hint of accusation in your voice? The children of Israel spoke some "if only" words to Moses while in the wilderness. They were thirsty, and it made them angry. "If only we had died in the LORD's presence with our brothers!" (Numbers 20:3 NLT). Their words sound silly to us, but their lack caused their thinking to become distorted.

It's the same with you and me. When we feel God has let us down, we draw the wrong conclusions. We miss the right perspective. Whenever you face a situation that fills you with longing and regret, always remember that God is not done with your story. At just the right time he will bring you out of the confusion and turn your "if only" into a miracle that will showcase his glory.

Lord, when regret clouds my judgment, bring me back to rest in your hope.

Kim Crabill, TV host, author, ministry leader, Christian counselor

TO KNOW HIM

I want to know Christ—yes, to know the power of his resurrection.

PHILIPPIANS 3:10 NIV

My determined purpose is that I may know Jesus more deeply and more intimately, recognizing and understanding him. Spending time with him allows us to see the wonders of his person. Time in prayer causes us to know him progressively, increasingly, little by little. We can also know him more intimately through his Word. How wonderful to experience his love and strength moment by moment!

But there is more to the above verse from Philippians. It continues, "and the fellowship of His sufferings." Wait, what does that mean? Since when is suffering a part of knowing him? Jesus sometimes allows suffering in our lives to burn away what binds us, what keeps us from walking with him. Just living in this broken world can bring suffering. He allows us to suffer so that others see his glory. Depending on him in our suffering grows our faith and takes us deeper with him.

Always remember: When you know him, you are never alone. In joy or in suffering, you always have Jesus!

Jesus, thank you that I can know you.

Shelia Erwin, author, ministry leader, Bible teacher

DON'T GIVE AN INCH

Take up the shield of faith, with which you can extinguish all the flaming arrows of the evil one.

Ephesians 6:16 NIV

Some days, it seems like all my efforts end in disaster. Like I'm trying to take down a stone wall with a dinner fork. Sound familiar? The presentation won't come together or the chapter I'm writing won't take shape. My plans were a flop. My work didn't get done. You get the picture, right? There just isn't enough of you to go around, and discouragement sets in. But what if the wall before you isn't a physical one but a spiritual one? What if the enemy is behind the blocked project, the disrupted plans, the overwhelming workload? If you sink into discouragement, you let him win the battle.

God has provided his armor so you can stand firm against the strategies of the devil. Don't flee in despair and weariness. Stand your ground and fight! Always remember how great your God is, and he has supplied you with all you need to stand, fight, and win. What a good feeling it will be when the battle is over and you find yourself on the winning side!

Lord, thank you for giving me all that I need to stand strong in you, especially on difficult days.

Kim Crabill, TV host, author, ministry leader, Christian counselor

DON'T REJECT THE TRANSPLANT

You were bought at a price; do not become slaves of human beings.

1 Corinthians 7:23 NIV

Do you ever struggle to know what pleases God? Maybe someone in your life is demanding certain things from you, stating, "This is how a Christian behaves." Your relationship with God becomes stressful rather than joyful. You begin evaluating your life based on your performance, and grace is a distant object in your rearview mirror. The early Christians grappled with this issue too. Some insisted that Jesus' followers keep the Old Testament law, but Paul preached that a change of heart produced by God's Spirit is what pleases the Lord (Romans 8:3–4).

Receiving the gift of salvation is like undergoing a heart transplant. When you receive your new heart from Jesus, you will desire to live in obedience to him, to follow his example of love and compassion for others. Always remember that a life based on performance is not the way of God. Choose instead to live free in Christ Jesus. Your obedience to him will allow you to hold on to peace. Don't reject your heart transplant. It was purchased for you at the highest price.

Lord, thank you for the freedom to live in obedience to you alone.

Kim Crabill, TV host, author, ministry leader, Christian counselor

DO YOU LOVE ME?

"You are precious to me. You are honored, and I love you."

ISAIAH 43:4 NLT

She stared at the ceiling, an intense longing and extreme vulnerability in her eyes, and whispered eight very important words: "But how do I know he loves me?" This is the heart cry of every person born into the world, the burning question through which we siphon the events of our lives and our interactions with others. Do you know what I mean? Do you struggle to understand your place in an earthly relationship? Maybe your ears hear words of affirmation, but your heart rebels at the sound because those words don't always match the actions behind them.

Our earthly relationships will never be perfect because we, as humans, are incapable of granting perfect love to each other. But while earthly relationships are faulty and sometimes fickle, God offers you a love that will endure forever. I hope you will always remember that the God who created you loves you more than any human being ever can. He will give you confidence and discernment as you work through the emotions of unsettled earthly relationships.

Lord, thank you for providing a love that will never fail me—no matter what I encounter in this life.

Esther Carpenter, author

DON'T SWEAT THE CURVES

Trust GOD from the bottom of your heart; don't try to figure out everything on your own.

PROVERBS 3:5–12 MSG

There's a street in San Francisco called Lombard Street, also known as the crookedest street in the world. Its eight sharp, hairpin curves seem rather perilous but were built to slow the traffic down, making the steep hill safer to navigate. Are you walking that kind of road today? Are there so many twists and turns and hairpin curves that you wonder if you are making any progress?

If so, my friend, don't be discouraged! Even though you can't see where your life is headed, you have a heavenly Father who does. He asks you to rely on him rather than on your own understanding because only he has the power to remove the obstacles that get in your way. Whenever the path you are walking starts to resemble Lombard Street, always remember that your only job is to trust. God knows how to smooth out the hairpin curves and make your way straight. So don't sweat the curves. Relax, knowing he will keep his promise to guide you every step of the way.

Father God, I trust you to guide me through life and into an eternal destiny with you.

Kim Crabill, TV host, author, ministry leader, Christian counselor

GOD'S WILL FOR YOU

Rejoice always, pray continually, give thanks in all circumstances; for this is God's will for you in Christ Jesus.

1 Thessalonians 5:16–18 niv

I've had so many conversations with friends—and with myself—about what I should be doing with my life. What I am really asking is this: What is God's will for my life? What job should I be doing? Where should I live? How should I spend my time? What activities should I have? Whom should I spend my time with? All are important questions that need prayer and, sometimes, the help of godly counsel.

I found that, in its simplest form, God tells us his will for us. He wants us to rejoice always, pray continually (throughout the day, not just upon waking or going to sleep), and give thanks to him in *all* circumstances, even when we go through challenging situations. God is concerned with every aspect of our lives but always wants us to focus our eyes on him. Always remember that a close relationship with him is his will.

Dear God, thank you for the wisdom found in your Word. Help me to live out your will for my life.

Ella Hartt, Roses and Rainbows advisory board member, songwriter, singer, storyteller

DUMP IT

Cast your cares on the LORD and he will sustain you.

PSALM 55:22 NIV

What if there were a place where you could dump all your hurts, worries, mistakes, and everything that is bothering you today? There is! God invites you to bring everything that is worrying you and cast it onto him. How easily we forget that there's someone who cares that much for us! God sees it all. He sees what we are worried about, the trouble we face, and the fear that wants to control us. He doesn't want us to carry all those things.

My friend, I hope you'll always remember that you don't have to go through life carrying all those hurts, fears, and worries. God has offered to take them all from you if you let him. So be encouraged! You have a place where you can go and say, *God, I know this is bigger than me. I know that you can handle it. I'm giving it to you.* Then rest and let him take care of you.

Lord, how I love you for your broad shoulders and your willingness to bear my burdens.

Kim Crabill, TV host, author, ministry leader,
Christian counselor

THE POWER OF SURRENDER

"If you try to hang on to your life, you will lose it. But if you give up your life for my sake, you will save it."

MATTHEW 16:25 NLT

A well-loved pastor of mine once said something very profound: "You only meet Jesus in one of three ways: in desperation, in surrender, or in eternity." At the time I heard this, I was working with addicts seeking recovery, and I wanted so badly to understand why many chose to remain in their suffering rather than sincerely move toward change. When we are unwilling to repent, the Lord often uses our circumstances to move us into submission. The more we resist, the more painful it gets. It's almost like he is saying, *We can do this the easy way or the hard way. Your choice.*

Always remember, there is incredible power in surrender, and when we finally seek him in humble repentance, he will meet us with his grace.

Dear Lord, help me to submit to You. Help me want to change anything that separates me from Your love.

Melissa Huray, author, podcast host

ENOUGH ALREADY

He gives power to the weak and strength to the powerless.

Isaiah 40:29 NLT

Do you ever struggle with feelings of inadequacy? Maybe you face a project that is above your skill level, or you signed up for a class you thought you could sail through, but now you're in over your head. You feel embarrassed or defeated. You're not enough. Join the club. I doubt there is one person alive today who hasn't dealt with this issue. The world is waiting to tell you that you are not good enough. The enemy pronounces you unfit. If you aren't careful, those same thoughts will take root in your mind, bringing you to the same conclusion.

Then Jesus comes and whispers softly, *But I am enough.* Friend, I want you to always remember that when you feel most inadequate, Jesus is there. He will give you what you need to meet inadequacy with victory. You can boast today, not in your own ability, but in the One who makes you able to be enough.

Lord, thank you for your love and grace that provide everything I need for the task at hand.

Kim Crabill, TV host, author, ministry leader, Christian counselor

SEEKING PEACE

Do not be anxious about anything, but in everything by prayer and supplication with thanksgiving let your requests be made known to God. And the peace of God, which surpasses all understanding, will guard your hearts and your minds in Christ Jesus.

PHILIPPIANS 4:6–7 ESV

At age twenty-four, I had a new graduate degree and began working in a rehabilitation center. One day, the facility director called me to his office and explained why something I had done was not acceptable. My eyes filled with tears. The director said, "You do not cry." I took a deep breath and held in the tears until I returned to my office. Years later, I don't remember what got me into trouble, but I never forgot being told not to cry. I do not cry in a professional setting.

I am now the one explaining why a behavior is not acceptable. I try to cover those meetings in prayer so they do not come to tears but instead are teachable moments. Anxiety does not help anyone. I try to always remember to seek peace in everything I do

Lord, help me always remember to seek your peace.

Barbara Parker, women's ministry leader, educator, audiologist

March

DIVINE APPOINTMENTS

We are God's handiwork, created in Christ Jesus
to do good works.

EPHESIANS 2:10 NIV

What comes to mind when you hear someone say you are created to do good works? Some of us have an aversion to the "good works" mentality because of unpleasant past experiences. Others love the idea that there's something tangible they can do for God. Where does this idea land with you today? If your spirit immediately grows defensive upon hearing the mention of good works, let me encourage you to consider a new perspective.

What if today you just took time to look at the faces around you? What would you see? A discouraged coworker? A heartbroken child? A weary cashier or a lonely widow? Always remember that the good works God asks of you are often no more than taking your eyes from yourself to notice another who needs a reminder of God's love. Consider doing this today. Those encounters may very well be divine appointments prepared by God specifically for you.

Lord, help me to see our "good works" as being your hands and feet today, sharing your love with others.

Kim Crabill, TV host, author, ministry leader,
Christian counselor

RIGHTEOUS OR REBELLIOUS

Righteousness exalts a nation,
but sin condemns any people.

PROVERBS 14:34 NIV

When you're watching the news or scrolling through social media, do you consider America to be righteous and exalted? Righteousness—right standing with God—is a principle as fundamental as the law of gravity. Why do we, as believers and as a Christian nation, keep ignoring it? Always remember that just as righteousness exalts, sinfulness brings reproach, shame, and dishonor.

We live in a time of individual and collective rebellion, and unless we reevaluate our principles, returning to the pursuit of right standing with God, we will no longer be "one nation, under God"—no longer a light to the world. This begins with individual commitment. What made us righteous and exalted as a country started with people who had personal and passionate determination. And we can resuscitate righteousness again.

Righteous Lord, thank you for the blessing you've bestowed on our nation. Convict us of our need to pursue righteousness as a people. Bless those who cry out against sin and who spotlight the good to encourage us. Help me to be an example of your righteousness.[5]

Pat Boone, actor, singer, songwriter, author

---

5 Adapted from *Pat Boone Devotional Book*, published by Bible Voice, Inc. Used by permission from Mr. Boone.

FAITH OVER FEAR

Say to those with fearful hearts, "Be strong, do not fear; your God will come."

ISAIAH 35:4 NIV

Do you consider yourself to be fearful? Most of us would answer no to that question because it doesn't sound like something a godly person should admit to. But let's face it: we all have fears in life, don't we? Loneliness. Rejection. Failure to measure up. And more. You don't need to be ashamed of your fears, but neither do you need to let them cripple you.

While on earth, Jesus loved to heal hearts and calm fears. More than once, he admonished his disciples with the words "Don't be afraid" (Matthew 10:28; 28:10; Luke 12:32; John 14:27). His favorite words to needy souls seemed to be "Your faith has made you whole" (Matthew 9:22, 29; Mark 10:52; Luke 17:19). Whatever the situation you are facing today, don't let fear overtake you. Always remember that God has replaced your identity as a fearful person with a beautiful new one called a person of faith. Allow your heavenly Father to help you take a step past the boundary of your fear and into a new possibility of faith.

Lord, thank you for giving me the power to face my fears and trade them for faith.

Kim Crabill, TV host, author, ministry leader, Christian counselor

FAMINE 101

"Be still, and know that I am God."

Psalm 46:10 NIV

Remember how in Genesis God instructed Abraham to go to a promised land where he would receive lots of blessings? But when he got there, it was not what he had envisioned? The land was in the throes of famine. Perhaps this is you. Maybe you walked into a job or a marriage with certain expectations, and once you got there, you were met with disappointment. What are you going to do now?

You could do like Abraham and run away from the situation, but think with me for a minute. If Abraham had stayed in Canaan, he would have learned to trust God in new ways. In going to Egypt, he met the very emptiness he was running from, he deceived the Egyptians, and he denied God the chance to meet his needs (see Genesis 12 and 20).

My friend, maybe you are in a personal famine of sorts today. Always remember that God has put you there for a reason. You may feel a little lost, but he has not forgotten you. He makes no mistakes. Just be still and trust God. He is taking you somewhere greater than you could ever imagine.

Lord, help me not to run from hard times but to face them head-on with you.

Kim Crabill, TV host, author, ministry leader, Christian counselor

JESUS FIRST

"Cursed are those who put their trust in mere humans, who rely on human strength and turn their hearts away from the Lord."

Jeremiah 17:5 NLT

I have spent much of my life looking "out there" for answers. Experts, gurus, prodigies—they surely must know something I don't! Because of a childhood abandonment wound, I spent a lot of time tethered to humans for security. From scholars to sages, once they ultimately failed or showed their humanness, I was left empty and still searching. I had to stop looking to people, who are just as fallible as I am.

Always remember to turn to Jesus first. He holds the keys and power to unlock every door, overturn every obstacle, and liberate every prison. He wants to be your best friend, closest confidant, and most trusted advocate. You can trust him to lead you to the right people and places, but the journey must start with him.

Lord, help me to trust you in all things. As I put you first today, lead me to the right path.

Melissa Huray, author, podcast host

FIGHT OR FLIGHT

"Go, and the LORD be with you."

1 SAMUEL 17:37 NIV

When anyone mentions giants today, the story of David and Goliath usually comes to mind. A huge man who defied God needed to be confronted and destroyed. Maybe you wince a little because you know there is a giant before you that needs to be taken down too. Where did David get that kind of courage?

God had anointed David to be king years before David ever wore the crown. During that time, David faced other obstacles before his encounter with the giant Goliath, such as battling lions and bears to defend his sheep. He could have chosen to run rather than fight, but those previous battles gave him the courage and confidence he needed to defeat Goliath. Those experiences also came to his aid once he entered his ultimate role as king of Israel. What do you fear today? What might you lose if you give in to those fears? If you are tempted to run rather than fight, always remember that you serve the same God that David did, and he will help you to conquer your giant too. Face that giant in the name of your God.

Lord, give me the courage I need to fight my battles in your name, the Lord Almighty.

Kim Crabill, TV host, author, ministry leader,
Christian counselor

I LOVE YOU MOST

See what sort of love the Father has given to us: that we should be called God's children.

1 John 3:1 NET

Mom Baker had sixteen grandchildren, but I was her favorite—or so I thought! As family and friends gathered around her bed just after her passing, we shared memories. Each grandchild expressed their certainty that they were her favorite. My grandmother loved every person as though they were the one she loved most. If she knew you were going to visit, she made your favorite food. She dropped everything to listen to every word you had to say. She gave you the best hug as she told you to remember how much she loved you. Her house was always filled with people who believed Mom Baker loved them most.

Isn't that like our Savior? Always remember that he loves you as though you are the only person, and he died on the cross for your sins to prove it! He's preparing a room for you right now, and one day he will come and take you home. Yes, he loves everyone, but just as my cousins and I each believed our grandmother loved us the most, you can always choose to believe Jesus loves you most.

Lord, help me to love others as you have loved me: with unconditional, sacrificial love.

Carmen Pate, Roses and Rainbows advisory board member, author, speaker, Bible teacher, mentor of women

GIFT OF WORDS

An encouraging word cheers a person up.

PROVERBS 12:25 NLT

My granddaughter told me how someone at school was unkind to her and how bad the other child's words had made her feel. I looked at her and said, "Oh, but Cohen, you had something to give her!" I reminded her that she was a gift just waiting to be unpacked, that God had packed love, kindness, and goodness inside her for her to give away.

"But Gigi, I don't understand. I don't see any wrapping paper on me."

"It's like a surprise and you unwrap it by being good and kind when someone else is not."

"Gigi, you mean I can be a gift just by being good and kind to someone?"

"Yes, you sure can."

She was delighted! "Well, I can't wait until the next time I have the chance to be nice to someone!"

Always remember that God has packed us with good things. And many times, the delivery is when we least expect it.

Lord, thank you for the gift of kind and beautiful words that I can use to bless others.

Kim Crabill, TV host, author, ministry leader, Christian counselor

GOD'S GIFT OF MOTHERS

Mary Magdalene went to the disciples with the news: "I have seen the Lord!"

JOHN 20:18 NIV

Sometimes I marvel at how my motherhood experience has alternated between life and death through the course of five pregnancies: life, death, life, death, life. For me, this journey of motherhood and loss has made the Christ story come fully alive. I have felt like both Mother Mary and Mary Magdalene in my lifetime. I have grieved over the loss of children and had the privilege of discovering new life and hope. Motherhood and womanhood are not easy roles, so it's beautiful to see in the Bible how God cared for women. Jesus honored his mother and appeared to Mary Magdalene first after his resurrection.

Seeing our Lord's loving heart for women makes me grateful for the mother figures in my own life. Take some time today to thank those who have cared for you, taught you, and nurtured you throughout your life. Imitate God's heart to see and appreciate what those women have done for you and others in their lives. And if you are a mother, always remember that God sees every unique struggle you go through.

Dear Lord, thank you for your kind and tender heart. Make me see and value others in the way that you do.

Maggie Winzeler, women's wellness writer, business owner

GO AHEAD AND GIGGLE

A happy heart is good medicine
and a joyful mind causes healing.

PROVERBS 17:22 AMP

Did you know that finding a reason to giggle can glorify God? A friend of mine once endured indescribable hurt and devastation that were unjustly placed on her and her family. Days of agony and sleepless nights took their toll, but in the middle of it all, she determined to protect herself and her family by finding reasons to laugh together. We all find ourselves in seasons where laughter doesn't come naturally. On those days, it's good to remember that a cheerful heart is good medicine.

Research shows that laughter reduces stress, increases pain tolerance, accelerates your energy, and more. It is good medicine for sure! Beyond all that, being able to laugh in stressful or sorrowful times proclaims to those around you that you believe in a God who's able to use your situation for good. If you're struggling to laugh today, always remember that God is at work in you. He is using each of your circumstances to accomplish far more for you than you could ever ask. So why not giggle a little?

Lord, when my body is weary and my mind is stressed, remind me to laugh a little.

Kim Crabill, TV host, author, ministry leader,
Christian counselor

GO FISH

"If you love me, you will do what I have said."

JOHN 14:21 CEV

It is so embarrassing when you are skilled at something and yet you fail miserably. You want to find a dark corner to hide from all the eyes and the questions they hold, don't you? Peter would certainly sympathize with you. He was a pro at fishing, but one night the fish didn't cooperate. As the sun rose, an exhausted Peter started rolling up his nets in defeat until Jesus showed up and said, "Launch out into the deep" (Luke 5:4 NKJV). Peter hadn't caught a single fish, but he obeyed Jesus anyway. It was time to go beyond his fishing smarts and acknowledge God's power. The result was an immediate, boat-sinking catch.

Jesus calls you to launch out into deep water too. Don't shut his voice down just because, like Peter, you failed earlier. Go beyond your feelings and discover what his power can do for you. Always remember that it is worth it to obey Jesus. Saying yes to him will allow him to work freely in your life. Your obedience will be rewarded in ways you can't imagine today.

Lord, help me remember that it's always worth it to obey you even if it makes no sense.

Kim Crabill, TV host, author, ministry leader, Christian counselor

UNIQUELY GIFTED

Encourage one another and build each other up.

1 Thessalonians 5:11 NIV

My parents had to make a tough choice. They decided to place me in first grade when I was only five years old. Though I was a little young, they knew I would turn six by late October, the age when most kids started school. Throughout all my years in school, I struggled. My third-grade teacher advanced me to the fourth grade when she could have held me back. The stigma of not passing would have been devastating to me, and she knew that. She always encouraged me, and it made a difference. I not only graduated from college with a bachelor's degree, but I am now a published author and speaker.

When the writing gets tough and the speaking engagements get scary, I have a dear friend who reminds me, "Remember, you are gifted!" Friends, always remember that God has gifted you like no one else. Don't let the naysayers discourage you as you walk in what the Lord is leading you to do. As you walk in your gifts, it will bring you great joy!

Lord, help me to remember that you have gifted me and that "I can do all things through Him who strengthens me" (Philippians 4:13 NASB).

Kathleen Hardaway, author, speaker

GRACE FOR MISTAKES

"My grace is sufficient for you, for my power is made perfect in weakness."

2 CORINTHIANS 12:9 NIV

You just wanted to be helpful. But somehow, somewhere things went wrong, and the anticipation of being a blessing was turned into an emotional letdown for you. A slip of the salt container, perhaps, and the homemade soup your ailing friend requested became inedible, leaving you to settle for a to-go order from the local deli. Or you volunteered to host the meeting at your house and had to call in sick at the last minute, causing extra stress for the group.

Instead of making someone's day easier by your helpfulness, you made things more difficult. Your best efforts were not enough, and in your moment of humiliation, you are tempted to believe that *you* are not enough either. Let me assure you that you are not defined by a few mistakes or failures. We all make our fair share of them. Always remember that you are not a failure until you quit trying. There will always be grace available for the times when you are not enough. Now, go volunteer your time and efforts and dive into the labor of love.

Lord, thank you for the fact that I am not defined by the mistakes I make.

Esther Carpenter, author

SHOES GOD PROVIDES

For shoes, put on the peace that comes from the Good News.

EPHESIANS 6:15 NLT

Have you ever felt like life was pushing you around? You've looked at your day planner: your to-do list is manageable. Then the phone rings or there is a knock on your door, and in a split second, your well-laid plans disintegrate. One interruption isn't so bad; with a little adjusting, the week's work is salvageable. But when it happens day after day, your messed-up schedule makes you want to give up in defeat.

Well, my friend, now is the time for you to strap on your shoes of peace. As part of the armor of God, these shoes will help you stand firm against the enemy when he tries to keep you from doing the work God has called you to do, the same work that is written in your planner. Don't let Satan defeat you. Always remember that God will prevail, so put on those shoes and embrace his spirit of peace while dealing with the disruptions and interruptions of your day. As you stand fast in peace, your mind will be able to make whatever adjustments this day calls for.

Lord, thank you for the shoes of peace that you provide so I can stand fast each day.

Kim Crabill, TV host, author, ministry leader, Christian counselor

GOD WINKS

"You are the God who sees me…I have now seen the One who sees me."

Genesis 16:13 NIV

"How well do you play football?" It was the director of the faith-based crime drama *Vindication* calling. "One of the actors can't make this shooting schedule, and I need to rewrite this episode."

"You're kidding me!" I responded.

"No, I'm not. Go film a highlight reel and get it back to me within a half hour." And that is how my character had one of the funniest episodes in the entire series.

Growing up, I played football for years with my brother and the guys. I loved it. Still, the editor of my resume had said, "Take that off. No one will hire you to play football."

I have experienced the Lord's goodness and mercy over and over again, redeeming so many of my broken parts, but when the director rewrote this episode, it was a huge "God wink." I still tear up when I think of how God not only redeems our hurts and sorrows but also celebrates those things that give us joy. On the football field, I felt him saying, "Candace, I see you. Always remember that."

Thank you, Lord, that you are El Roi, the God who sees. Thanks for knowing and loving me so intimately.

Candace Kirkpatrick, actor, speaker, talk show cohost

AND LEAD US NOT…

When tempted, no one should say, "God is tempting me." For God cannot be tempted by evil, nor does he tempt anyone; but each person is tempted when they are dragged away by their own evil desire and enticed.

JAMES 1:13–14 NIV

Granola or donut? Exercise or sofa? Maybe those are easy choices for you. How about this one: remain bitter toward ones who hurt you or pray for them? We are surrounded by temptations every day. But always remember: God's plan in allowing us to be tempted isn't to torture but to teach, to bring us to new levels of maturity in him.

The garden of Eden in Genesis was the perfect place with perfect companionship with God, yet right in the middle was the tempting forbidden fruit. God wasn't tempting Adam and Eve, but he wasn't shielding them from Satan's design either. Was it so he could laugh at and punish them? No! It was so his children would *choose* his way and grow spiritually stronger. What the enemy meant for evil resulted in increased strength for God's people. Daily temptations—opportunities to sin—shrink before us when we rise above them. And as we resist temptation, God's rich rewards are our victory.

Teach me, Lord, to learn from temptations, so that each victory moves me toward you.[6]

Pat Boone, actor, singer, songwriter, author

6 Adapted from *Pat Boone Devotional Book*, published by Bible Voice, Inc. Used by permission from Mr. Boone.

EPIPHANY

He put a new song in my mouth, a song of praise to our God.

Psalm 40:3 NASB

As I returned to the United States after living in Europe, I did not know the next step in my business career, but I clearly knew I needed to make a living. Previously I had been an executive in retail. One day I was driving, not thinking about work at that moment, when God's presence filled the car. It was an epiphany moment in my life! I knew beyond a shadow of a doubt it was God who spoke clearly to my heart: "Suellen, you need to get into television." My immediate response was "I don't know anything about television."

Soon thereafter, in obedience to the Lord, I stepped out in faith and entered the field of media. I went from a small television show to a nationally syndicated show with millions of viewers. Along the way, I ran a television station and then a television network. With each step, I saw God's faithfulness and his call upon my life. Always remember to trust in Jesus, and he will open doors in your life.

Heavenly Father, thank you for your guidance. Help me to trust you to open doors for me to be light in this dark world.

Suellen Roberts, media influencer

HELP A FELLOW TRAVELER

A friend loves at all times, and a brother is born for adversity.

PROVERBS 17:17 ESV

Have you ever found yourself deep in a problem that you couldn't get out of on your own, and then a friend or stranger came along and lent you a hand? It made all the difference in the world, didn't it? Are you paying it forward? Are you intentionally looking for ways to help meet needs in the lives of those around you?

If you see someone struggling today, don't hesitate to help. Don't worry that you may be unqualified or that your offer of help won't be well-received or that your efforts won't make a difference. A friend loves all the time, especially in adversity. Always remember that anytime you stop to help another, you will receive the greater blessing. The hands and feet of Jesus are badly needed in this world, so reach out and bless someone today, expecting nothing in return. The satisfaction of helping a fellow traveler get to where they need to be will likely be all the reward you need.

Lord, thank you for friends who meet my needs. Help me to do the same.

Kim Crabill, TV host, author, ministry leader, Christian counselor

LIFE AND DEATH WORDS

The tongue has the power of life and death,
and those who love it will eat its fruit.

PROVERBS 18:21 NIV

The power of life and death are in the tongue. God calls us to pray for one another—to speak life over one another. There is power in unity, and there is power in prayer. Through prayer we can ask for deliverance from all that hinders us. We have the power to pray and speak out against those generational curses that bind us. We can pray the words in Isaiah 54:17 for our families: that no weapon that comes against these family members will prosper. In that way, we stand in the gap for those who may not know *how* to pray.

We are called to stand for our loved ones, to forgive and to *stand*. The Word tells us in Ephesians 6:13, "having done all, to *stand*" (NKJV; emphasis added). God hears our prayers. Prayer produces miracles, signs, and wonders. I have seen its power and will always remember that, in Christ, our words and our prayers can change lives.

Lord, help me to be mindful of how I use my words because they have power and matter greatly.

Destiny Yarbrough, minister, executive TV producer, digital media producer

HOLY INK

Every day of my life was recorded in your book.

Psalm 139:16 NLT

Have you ever picked up a pen and found the ink cartridge was dry or perhaps missing entirely? This has happened to me more than once, and I've used it as a visual in many of my conferences. I hand out pens with the ink cartridge removed so that the conferees receive only an empty shell of a pen. Why? Because I want them to understand that God is still writing their stories.

Your story is a work in progress too. It's tempting to try to write it by yourself with a dry cartridge, but instead, let God's Word be the ink that flows through you. Let him write your story as he would have it to be. And friend, always remember that the Lord doesn't waste anything that happens in your life. He will use it as the ink in your pen. The valleys and the mountaintops will remind you and others of his faithfulness. God is the author of every great story. Let him finish what he has started.

Lord, write your own story of my life using the ink of your Word.

Kim Crabill, TV host, author, ministry leader,
Christian counselor

HOPE FOR SMOLDERING WICKS

"A smoldering wick he will not snuff out."

MATTHEW 12:20 NIV

Do you feel like a candle today, with a wick so low that you can barely even flicker? You used to love Jesus. Your candle burned brightly, and you shared your light with others who needed it. Then life dealt you some confusing blows, leaving you to second-guess your walk of faith and reducing your fire to a barely smoldering wick. Some days you aren't sure you are on the right path anymore. You have nights when you don't feel Jesus anywhere around you.

Have I wandered beyond his reach? Is my faith too small to matter? If you are struggling with thoughts like these, my friend, I want to remind you that Jesus will never extinguish a smoldering wick. If he sees any desire toward himself in your heart, he will reach out to you. Always remember that Jesus understands your human frailty, and he loves you with a tenderness you cannot possibly fathom. Reach back to him and let him turn your smoldering wick into a brightly burning flame.

Lord, thank you for the promise that no matter how weak my faith is, you will nurture and fan its flame.

Kim Crabill, TV host, author, ministry leader, Christian counselor

TRUST ME

When I am afraid, I put my trust in you.

Psalm 56:3 ESV

Recently my healthy, athletic husband noticed an infection. Within a few hours he was in septic shock. From the ICU, I called prayer-warrior friends who blasted our urgent need around the globe. Larry's amazing doctors were valiant, but it took a while to identify the bacterial culprit. And the presser drugs used to save his heart and brain constricted blood flow to his extremities. His feet became gangrenous; the doctors came to amputate. I said no. He flat-lined, another result of the pressers, and needed emergency heart surgery. They put him on a ventilator. Doctors said, "He's very sick"—code for "He won't make it."

But God said something else. From the first moment of this ordeal, I felt his powerful embrace and whisper: *Trust me.* So I did. And I repeatedly whispered God's words to Larry. The infection finally broke. Larry came off the ventilator and kidney dialysis. Today he is fully healed and his feet are free of infection. His doctors call him their "walking miracle." They got to witness the power of faith-filled prayers for themselves as much as Larry did. Like me, they will always remember God's words: *Trust me.*

Lord, in my darkest circumstances, help me to always remember your whisper: Trust me.

Nancy Stafford, actor, author, speaker

WHAT JUST HAPPENED?

The one who stands firm to the end will be saved.

MATTHEW 24:13 NIV

Are you sitting here today wondering how things could go bad so quickly? Wasn't it just last week that you were ecstatic, thinking life just couldn't get any better? You know, it's important to remember that God often sends trouble after a time of prosperity to test our motives for serving him. Will we serve him only when things go well? What about when our wealth or reputation is at stake? What will we do then?

By the way, this is the same question Satan posed to God concerning his servant, Job. Satan accused God of having rigged the game by putting a hedge of comfort and blessings around Job, stating that this was why Job served God (Job 1:10–11). No matter how quickly things may have changed, I hope you will always remember that God is using your circumstances for your good and his glory. Everything that happened to Job was simply a test to prove that he was the man of integrity that God knew he was. And it is the same for you and me today.

Lord, give me the determination I need to serve you in hard times as well as good ones.

Kim Crabill, TV host, author, ministry leader,
Christian counselor

HIS PLAN FOR ME

"I know the plans and thoughts that I have for you."

JEREMIAH 29:11 AMP

Serving at our church coffee shop, life seemed perfect. I was married to a godly man and raising my boys, and everything was going according to plan. I was excited about becoming a mother again after the birth of my youngest son. Even though I believed God knew me before I was born, I was working on my plan and not trusting in his.

Then I received heartbreaking news from my doctor: no more children. Confused by the curve ball, I called my mother. As I cried, she lovingly said to me, "'For I know the plans I have for you,' declares the LORD, 'plans to prosper you and not to harm you, plans to give you hope and a future'" (Jeremiah 29:11 NIV). Still today, as I face trials in my life and my plans take unexpected turns, I can hear her reminding me of God's love for me. It soothes my soul, bringing me back to always remember that he is for me. I must keep my eyes on the prize: Jesus. He is my hope!

Jesus, thank you for the plans you have for me all the days of my life. I love you!

Shari Rigby, actor, director, writer, founder of a women's ministry group

JESUS AND OUTSIDERS

The LORD your God is…the great God…
who shows no partiality.

DEUTERONOMY 10:17 NIV

Have you ever been eager to spend time with your friends, but when you walked into the room, the conversation around you suddenly stopped? Did the awkward silence give you the impression that you had been the topic of discussion? Almost instantly, uncertainty replaces your excitement, and any sense of belonging you had before you entered the room morphs into loneliness and isolation. There was a man in Jesus' day who experienced this same isolation. When Jesus chose his disciples, he included an outsider, a choice that I believe was intentional. Matthew was a tax collector, at the bottom of the social ladder.

My friend, always remember that in Jesus' eyes, you are equal to anyone else in the room. Sometimes what we perceive as rejection turns out to be a simple misunderstanding, but when it's not, take your hurt to Jesus. He will be glad to soothe your broken heart. And if you listen closely, you will hear him "rejoice over you with singing" (Zephaniah 3:17 NIV), the love notes softly repairing your damaged heart.

Lord, thank you that in you we are all the same and your great love covers us all.

Kim Crabill, TV host, author, ministry leader,
Christian counselor

IT TAKES THREE

He who finds a wife finds a good thing
and obtains favor from the LORD.

PROVERBS 18:22 ESV

"It takes two to tango," goes the saying. When I was in college, I tried something I had never heard of before. I was a young man and looking for love. But I wanted a special type of love. A lasting love. For this reason, I asked God to pick my wife for me. I was afraid that if I chose her myself, I'd do it for some superficial reason, and it wouldn't last. I prayed and I prayed and left the choice to God. Am I ever glad I did! God surprised me by giving me the woman of his dreams and she is now my wife. Thirty-six years later I am still thanking God for his choice. We have learned that by each of us living for him, we discover how to love each other for a lifetime.

It's vital to bring God into the picture with every human relationship. Always remember, in love—just as in interactions with friends, siblings, coworkers, and everyone else—it takes three: two people and the Father who loves them both.

Father, I invite you to take control of my relationships.

James and Justina Page, pastor and elect lady

JUST ASK

"He will call on me,
and I will answer him."

Psalm 91:15 NIV

Do you ever feel it would be selfish to ask God for his best? Surely, he is too busy answering the requests of others to be bothered with yours. Or maybe you procrastinate approaching God. You want your life in better order before you get too close. Well, consider Daniel, a young man who lived in Israel during a time of captivity. He didn't hesitate to call on God even though his circumstances were far from ideal (Daniel 9:1–23). His people had sinned, and Daniel felt the burden of it. Yet he didn't wait until he felt he deserved to be heard or until the people had a change of heart. No, he prayed because he knew God promised to turn his ear toward anyone who came to him.

The same is true for you, my friend. The God who made you, who breathed life into your very soul, wants to give you his best. Always remember that your God is a merciful God. He has already granted you freedom to come boldly to his throne. So ask! Be prepared to be amazed at what God does.

Lord, thank you that I can bring my requests to you at any time, and you will answer me.

Kim Crabill, TV host, author, ministry leader,
Christian counselor

WAIT FOR ME

You must all be quick to listen, slow to speak,
and slow to get angry.

JAMES 1:19 NLT

He stood in my office doorway and relayed a situation from earlier in the day. Years later, I still recall his poignant words: "I didn't give Jesus a chance to show up." My colleague had stopped to say hello to a bus driver and the students onboard, and he noticed paper, pencils, wrappers, and trash on the floor of the bus. He became angry, and words were exchanged between the driver and my colleague. Both strong Christian men left hurt and confused.

Later, my colleague apologized to the driver for getting so angry. He explained that in the moment, he perceived no effort on anyone's part to keep the bus clean. What he learned from the driver was the bus was late that morning, students needed to get to class, and they had agreed to straighten up when they got back on in the afternoon. Each man had a chance to speak into the situation with a calmer head and heart. We will all have tricky situations and misunderstandings. When we do, always remember to give Jesus time to show up.

Father, help me to listen well, be slow to anger, and invite you into all situations.

Susan Young, educator, speaker, writer

KEEP SWIMMING

I press on toward the goal for the prize of the upward call of God in Christ Jesus.

PHILIPPIANS 3:14 ESV

Give up? Certainly, I've wanted to give up at times. And I understand why you might want to. Sometimes life is just overwhelming. But friend, I want you to always remember that you are not the first to feel this way, and you won't be the last. Take Florence Chadwick, for example. From the time she was a little girl, Florence loved to swim. She particularly loved swimming in the ocean, so she set her sights on swimming the twenty-six miles between Catalina Island and the coast of California.

She swam for hours, and all was well until a thick fog rolled in and she began to doubt her ability. Once that happened, she gave up. Only later did she realize she was just one mile from completing her goal. Maybe you've set your sights on big things, but the fog surrounding you now causes you to consider quitting. Don't give up! You don't know just how close you are to that goal.

Lord, help me to set my sights on you and never give up.

Kim Crabill, TV host, author, ministry leader, Christian counselor

LITTLE VALLEYS

Our present troubles are small and won't last very long.

2 CORINTHIANS 4:17 NLT

Some days are more emotional than others, wouldn't you agree? I mean, have you ever found yourself holding back tears in the grocery store or while walking down the hall to your office? Maybe a smell in the lunchroom reminds you of cookies from grade school, or a lingering scent of perfume takes you back to days with your grandmother. Suddenly, emotion rolls over you, and a lump clogs your throat.

When you have a day like that, my friend, think of it as a little valley you are walking through. We would rather have mountaintops, but I am learning that God allows me to walk through valleys to draw me closer to him and subtly change my perspective. Always remember that when you walk through a valley of any kind, God can use it to teach you something about himself. Yield to the lesson of the valley experience and trust him to use it for good. Some future day, you will look back, and you will understand.

Lord, thank you for using the little valleys I walk through to bring about good in my life.

Kim Crabill, TV host, author, ministry leader,
Christian counselor

YOU [DO] OWN ME

You are a chosen people, a royal priesthood, a holy nation, a people for God's own possession.

1 PETER 2:9 NASB

The chosen part is nice (God picked me). The priesthood part is nice (he gave me a job description). The nation part is nice (I belong). But being God's possession gives me pause. God owns me? Don't we call people who are owned *slaves*? Everything in me cries out against being a slave. Slaves are exploited and vulnerable to all kinds of abuse.

And yet abuse is the last thing God has in mind for those of us who submit to his ownership. Those he owns, he transforms, empowers, sets free from sin (which also wants to own me), and even shares his glory with. Underlying all these acts is his everlasting, unshakable love. Always remember that we're deceived if we believe we can live any kind of abundant life apart from this owner/possession relationship with God.

Worthy God, I surrender to your loving ownership. You alone can renew my life and make it count for your eternal purposes.

Sue Kline, writer, editor, writing coach

April

LONGING FOR YESTERYEAR

Do not say, "Why were the old days better than these?"

ECCLESIASTES 7:10 AMP

Are you feeling unseen and unneeded today? Are you longing for days gone by when you were someone to somebody and life held great purpose? If this is you, always remember these four things. First, your light shines when you know your identity in Christ, so cultivate your relationship with him. Second, accept your reality. No more thinking about what you wish had happened or where you wish you were. Instead, live in the reality of where you are right now.

Third, bring color and relevance back into your life by doing with a spirit of humility the work God has given you today. Your spirit will bloom! Lastly, remember that you have a God who sees you. You may feel unseen or unneeded, but God will never lose sight of you. He knows right where you are.

Lord, help me to lay at your feet the longings for what was and to joyfully embrace what you've given me today.

Kim Crabill, TV host, author, ministry leader,
Christian counselor

M.O.S.T.

Make the most of every opportunity in these evil days.

EPHESIANS 5:16 NLT

Whatever you're facing today, a mind that is set on God can help you make the most of what he wants to do through you. I have an acrostic that I use when I need to recenter my mind on God. I'd like to share it with you.

M: Mindset. Reset your mind today. Forget about the old way of thinking and replace it with whatever God is asking you to do.

O: Open. Open your mind to the possibilities and promises God has placed before you.

S: Seek. Seek the Scriptures as if they were written just for you—because they were!

T: Take. Take the next step. As you go about your day, just do the next thing God asks you to do, whatever it is.

My friend, always remember that God has called you to something specific each day. Step into God's mindset and make the M.O.S.T. of whatever he asks you to do today.

Lord, help me to remember to center my mind on you and to step into your plan for the day.

Kim Crabill, TV host, author, ministry leader,
Christian counselor

YOU ARE VALUABLE TO GOD

"Do not fear, for I have redeemed you; I have called you by name; you are Mine!"

ISAIAH 43:1 NASB

Do you ever feel alone, forgotten, or worthless? Would it help to know that you are in the company of most people? I have found that when I am vulnerable—exhausted, not physically well, or hurt by someone I love—the enemy uses the opportunity to lie to me and reinforce these negative thoughts about myself. It is in those moments you must remind yourself of who you are in Christ Jesus. Don't allow the enemy to beat you up.

You are part of God's royal family. He made you; he redeemed you; he calls you his child because of your faith in Jesus. He knows you by name and has given you a beautiful purpose in this life that the enemy cannot steal. God cares deeply about you. So the next time you are gullible to the lies of the enemy and you feel alone, forgotten, and worthless, always remember God's truth about you. Then straighten your crown and press on like the royalty that you are!

Lord, forgive me when I listen to the lies of the enemy and forget the truth of who you say that I am.

Carmen Pate, Roses and Rainbows advisory board member, author, speaker, Bible teacher, mentor of women

SUPPORTING OUR YOUNG PEOPLE

Do not provoke your children to anger by the way you treat them.

EPHESIANS 6:4 NLT

Do you have a younger person in your life? Many times, people have asked what advice I would offer those pursuing a particular sport. From my experience as a veteran NBA player and an NBA coach, the answer is straightforward: be passionate, stay disciplined, and enjoy the journey. Yet there's a more challenging question for us as supporters, whether we are parents, mentors, or merely friends a few seasons ahead in life: how can we best support the younger generation in their pursuits?

The key is to remember that our role is to uplift, not to add pressure. Athletes (and young people in general) often feel the weight of our expectations, and they strive to please us at every practice and game, on every test or project. They already carry the burden of their own goals and dreams. Let's not add to that load for any young people in our lives. As we cheer them on, let's always remember to offer encouragement rather than criticism. Let's support them in their pursuit of their life goals without becoming the baggage they must carry.

Father, guide me to support young people in their unique paths, allowing them to flourish in their gifts for your glory.

Michael Curry, former NBA player/coach and college coach

MORNING MERCIES

The Lord's...compassions never fail.
They are new every morning.
Lamentations 3:22–23 NIV

I'm a morning person. I love the quietness of a new morning when the world still seems undisturbed and at peace. But even as I enjoy the stillness, my mind's eye often sees beyond the beauty of the morning and into the pain that is consuming many hearts and homes. The aftershock of hurtful words, a devastating diagnosis, piles of bills, fruitless job searches.

Life is full of hurts and worries. But just as the sun comes up every morning, its rays warming your face, so the love and mercy of the Lord shines upon you, warming your heart and reminding you that you are not alone. Always remember that you can put your worries and hurts in their proper place by focusing on the love and mercy God showers on you every day. This is cause for rejoicing. Let it set you on a landing place of hope today.

Lord, thank you for your faithful love, tender compassion, and mercies that are new every day.

Kim Crabill, TV host, author, ministry leader,
Christian counselor

LIFE IN THE FAST LANE

"Call to me and I will answer you and tell you great and unsearchable things you do not know."

JEREMIAH 33:3 NIV

One Easter as our family gathered on the back porch, stories of the past dominated our conversations. I said, "Oh, it seems like yesterday!" I remembered my mom saying the same thing. Why does time seem to move so fast? Do we allow ourselves to get so busy that we lose track of time? We hit the ground running in the morning and crawl exhausted into bed at night. We become so wrapped up in our issues and circumstances that each day fades into the next. When this happens, our prayer life often suffers.

As a result, we live to exist. This is not God's plan for us! He desires for us to live every day sold out to Jesus. From the moment we wake up, he waits for us to connect with him. God wants quality time with his children but will never push himself on us. Always remember that God has a daily agenda for his children, but it is up to us to pray for the day's assignment.

Lord, help me to take a break from life in the fast lane and pray. Please reveal your agenda for my day.

Carla McDougal, ministry leader, author

NECESSARY STORMS

The Lord is good, a refuge in times of trouble.

Nahum 1:7 NIV

Thunderstorms can be pretty scary sometimes. Especially when you're out in the country where there are no city lights. Everything is pitch black when suddenly the sky lights up as a lightning bolt takes a stab at the earth. You count the seconds until you hear the thunder, trying to determine the distance of the storm and your safety. Spiritual storms are a lot like the physical ones. They come shrouded in a darkness we feel in our hearts and minds, tempting us to give in to fear.

But just as physical storms are necessary for our earth to thrive, so it is with spiritual storms. Perhaps the spiritual storm you are facing is exactly what your soul needs to grow. Maybe God has set you aside in the darkness to test and strengthen your faith. My friend, amid your spiritual storms, I hope you'll always remember to praise the Lord. Praising him will get you safely through the roughest weather. And in the morning light, you will see just how much you have grown.

Lord, in the darkest hour of my fiercest storms, help me to remember to praise you.

Kim Crabill, TV host, author, ministry leader, Christian counselor

NEVER TRULY OVER

Christ will make his home in your hearts.

Ephesians 3:17 NLT

What do you do when the party is over? You've just enjoyed a long-awaited reunion with faraway family or friends. The setting was perfect, the connection immediate, and the conversation just what you needed. Now it's over, the miles separate you once more, and you feel a little let down. Jesus' friends must have felt this way as they stared into the blue sky. Jesus was gone, ascended to his Father. They'd had some good times together, but now it was over, and they must have felt depressed and disoriented.

Imagine their delight when they discovered Jesus hadn't really left them! His Spirit showed up and empowered them, and from that moment they felt the life of Jesus beating in their chests. They would never truly be apart from him. It is the same for you, my friend. Although you struggle with partings, always remember that no matter how many miles separate you from your loved ones, you are always connected in spirit. As long as their voices ring in your ears, your visit never really ends.

Lord, thank you for the gift of relationships that span time and distance and remain strong.

Kim Crabill, TV host, author, ministry leader,
Christian counselor

YOUR HUMBLE SERVANT

Humble yourselves, therefore, under God's mighty hand, that he may lift you up in due time.

1 Peter 5:6 NIV

Hundreds of years ago, people ended letters with the phrase "Your humble servant," followed by their signature. Today, Oxford Dictionary defines the words as "ironic and humorous." Very few of us even write letters anymore, but can you imagine ending an email by referring to yourself as a humble servant? No one would choose to be a servant! And isn't labelling yourself as humble a sign of false humility—or worse, weakness? Always remember, humility has nothing to do with weakness.

Humbling ourselves "under God's mighty hand" is having the correct view of our *finite* nature as it relates to an *infinite* God. He is perfect and complete, righteous and all-powerful. What are we in comparison? We're deficient in all those categories. We humble ourselves with the realization of who God is—and of who we are, by comparison. If we ever reach the point where we're truly humble, we can expect exaltation from God. We will become truly useful in his kingdom business.

Almighty God, you are the beginning and the end, the Alpha and the Omega of all that is. Have mercy on me, your humble servant, and show me what humility really is.[7]

Pat Boone, actor, singer, songwriter, author

---

7 Adapted from *Pat Boone Devotional Book*, published by Bible Voice, Inc. Used by permission from Mr. Boone.

EASTER FINERY

He dressed me up in a suit of salvation, he outfitted me in a robe of righteousness.

Isaiah 61:10–11 msg

Because of the first Easter, we who have put our faith in the Lord are beautifully dressed every day. It has nothing to do with where we shop, the size of our budget, or how refined our fashion sense is. It has everything to do with God.

As early as Genesis 3, we see the first hint of what fashionistas we would become. When Adam and Eve disobeyed God, their solution to the shame they felt was to hide behind fig leaves. But human solutions for sin—be they fig leaves or something more sophisticated—are never adequate. Only God can cover our sin, and he chose to cover Adam and Eve with robes formed from the hides of an innocent animal (v. 21). That act points to another innocent: the perfect Lamb of God, whose death on a cross covered our sin once and for all. He went naked to his crucifixion so we could be clothed in beautiful, glowing righteousness. Let us always remember such amazing grace, such abounding love.

Father God, thank you for the new wardrobe you bought for me at an enormous price. May I wear it with wonder!

Sue Kline, writer, editor, writing coach

NOT FAIR

Wait patiently for the LORD. Be brave and courageous.
Yes, wait patiently for the LORD.

PSALM 27:14 NLT

Does life seem unfair to you today? Does it seem as if everyone else is accomplishing what they set out to do, but you are spinning your wheels? In spite of your best efforts to do the right thing and to make the right choices, it all seems to be falling apart. Let me remind you of Job. Like you, he loved God and obeyed him, yet he lost everything. He, too, questioned God's actions and the lack of them. But even though life felt unfair, Job's conduct sent the message that regardless of his circumstances, he had hope in God.

Life may feel hopelessly unfair to you today, but always remember that God is working out a plan that only he can see. Job's story is a reminder that God can redeem the worst situation imaginable. He turned Job's calamity around and restored to him twice as much as he had taken from him. Hold on, my friend, and wait patiently for God's promised restoration in your life. He has a plan!

Lord, when life seems unfair and out of control, give me strength to wait for you with patience.

Kim Crabill, TV host, author, ministry leader,
Christian counselor

NOT ME, LORD!

Strengthen me according to your word.

PSALM 119:28 NIV

Yesterday we talked about the waiting and training process God puts us through before he reveals his plan for us. But what about when the revealed plan looks frightening and completely out of our element? When God told Moses he was to lead Israel out of Egypt, Moses was completely overwhelmed: "Who am I that I should go to Pharaoh and bring the Israelites out of Egypt?" (Exodus 3:11 NIV). Can you relate? When God calls your name, wouldn't you like to answer with confidence, "Here I am, Lord"?

Yet more often, does your sense of not being enough turn your "Here I am" into a "Who am I?" like it did for Moses? If you are struggling with feelings of incompetence, I hope you'll always remember that God often chooses the most unlikely candidates to fulfill his work and mission. He sees past your present to the potential he has placed within you. His ways stretch far beyond anything you could ever imagine. He will go before you, providing all you need for the job he assigns to you.

Lord, thank you for being enough for every situation.

Kim Crabill, TV host, author, ministry leader, Christian counselor

NOT YOUR FAULT

"This happened so the power of God could be seen in him."

John 9:3 NLT

Some of us have felt the hurt of criticism from those who imply that we are going through difficult circumstances because of some sin in our lives. And yes, sometimes sin is the cause of our problems. The Bible does talk about the consequences of sin, but there are also examples of pain or hardship that were not the result of anyone's sin. For instance, the man described in John 9 who was born blind was subject to a lot of speculation. Even Jesus' disciples discussed his case, trying to decide who was to blame, the blind man or his parents.

Jesus squashed their skewed theology, boldly stating that it was neither. Then he made a statement that rocked their world: "This happened so the power of God could be seen in him." I know it's hard to walk the road of misunderstanding and criticism. But always remember that what you suffer has the potential to display the power of God in you. Jesus is your advocate. Let him prove your innocence. One day this heartache will showcase his grace.

Lord, help me to remember that you will use my sufferings to display your power if I let you.

Kim Crabill, TV host, author, ministry leader, Christian counselor

ATTITUDE ADJUSTMENT

Martha was distracted with much serving.

LUKE 10:40 NKJV

Martha was preoccupied with much serving. She was busy doing good things but was missing the most excellent thing. *Jesus* was there, a guest in her home! Martha fell into self-pity, asking, "Lord, do you not care?" She wanted Jesus to make her sister Mary help. Jesus spoke to the heart of the matter: "Martha, Martha, you are worried and troubled" (v. 41 NKJV). Jesus knew what she needed. To seek him first. To talk to him. To spend time with him. To believe that he cared. Jesus was asking Martha to make an attitude adjustment. He reminded her that only one thing is necessary. Mary had chosen the good portion. Mary had chosen Jesus.

We can all get distracted by "doing." Sometimes we're distracted by fear and worry. What a difference it makes when we adjust our attitudes to seeking Christ's kingdom and his righteousness. Always remember that only one thing is truly necessary, and that is Jesus.

Lord Jesus, remind me to check my attitude often and to focus on you so that I do not become anxious or troubled. Thank you that you do care.

Shelia Erwin, author, ministry leader, Bible teacher

PARALYSIS

"I knew that you are a merciful and compassionate God… filled with unfailing love."

JONAH 4:2 NLT

There are Christians in our world who are so afraid of disappointing God that they become paralyzed, doing nothing at all. Maybe this is you. You view God as someone who is seldom impressed and hard to please, who focuses on your mistakes more than your successes. Jesus told the story of a servant who experienced this struggle. The man viewed his master as harsh and difficult to please. When his master gave him some money to invest, he was so paralyzed by possible failure that he buried the money rather than taking a chance on a successful return (Matthew 25:14–30).

Yet, my friend, your heavenly Father is gracious and kind. Don't be afraid of disappointing him, falling flat on your face, or completely messing up when you try to please him. He loves your desire to bring him your best. Always remember that God will never be disappointed as you strive to live for him. He looks way beyond what your hands do and sees the love you hold for him in your heart.

Lord, thank you for being a father who gladly looks beyond my fumbling efforts to receive my gifts of love.

Kim Crabill, TV host, author, ministry leader, Christian counselor

PATIENCE IS A VIRTUE

Patient endurance is what you need now.

HEBREWS 10:36 NLT

Do you struggle with believing that God keeps his promises? It doesn't help that we live in an age of instant gratification. We are not even patient about waiting in grocery lines or for packages to arrive, much less weighty things like test results or a long-awaited job transfer or other unanswered prayers. Let's be honest, my friend. God does not live by our "rush, rush, get-it-done-yesterday" timetable.

But instead of letting doubt and discouragement nag at you today, surrender to what you know to be true about God. Always remember that he is sovereign and wise, perfect in all of his ways, including his timing in your life. Choose to carry on today with patient endurance and calm confidence that God will work things out at just the right time for you. You can trust him. Every one of his promises will be fulfilled.

Thank you, God, for reminding me that you have always kept your promises, and you won't stop now.

Kim Crabill, TV host, author, ministry leader,
Christian counselor

PEACE NOTE

"I have told you these things, so that in me you may have peace."

JOHN 16:33 NIV

Do you ever wake up in the morning feeling overwhelmed and anxious? The stress rolls in like a cloud, blanketing your day before you even get out of bed. Some days I'm not even sure what I'm worried about. Was it something I saw on the news last night? Is it because I know so many friends are hurting, marriages are in trouble, and kids are struggling? I think we should put a note on our mirrors that says, "Note to self: Today when I feel overwhelmed, I will take a deep breath, exhale stress, and inhale peace."

What about that, my friend? If, by chance, you are feeling stressed and overwhelmed, just know that you're not alone. Always remember that the peace God gives is so much better than what the world has to offer. This world is fickle, but God is unchanging, and it's his peace that calms our troubled hearts. Let's rest in God's peace today, shall we?

Lord, thank you for your peace that relieves the stress I feel today.

Kim Crabill, TV host, author, ministry leader, Christian counselor

UNEXPECTED ENDINGS

We know that in all things God works for the good of those who love him, who have been called according to his purpose.

ROMANS 8:28 NIV

Have you experienced any unexpected endings? Getting laid off, fired, or demoted at work? The end of a relationship, divorce, or a friend's betrayal? I have experienced many different unexpected endings through the years. We may blame ourselves, get bitter, become discouraged or depressed. We may feel betrayed and hurt and ask why. I have learned that when one door closes, another will open. That's the hope that God's Word gives us in Revelation 3:7: "What he opens no one can shut, and what he shuts no one can open" (NIV).

So be kind to yourself when a door shuts. Trust in God to lead and guide you to your new beginning. He has shown me that a new beginning can't start until there is an ending. Release and forgive those who hurt you. We can learn from our mistakes and keep moving forward. Always remember that God will turn things around for your good.

Father, I ask you to open new doors and turn things around for good for those who have experienced unexpected endings.

Chris Luppo, TV producer, media consultant, speaker, author

PERSONALITY AND POTENTIAL

"I have prayed for you, Simon, that your faith may not fail."

LUKE 22:32 NIV

Could you use a good dose of encouragement today? Maybe you made a rash decision you can't undo, or, in the heat of the moment, you spoke harsh words that caused someone you love to lose trust in you. If you are frustrated by your bad behavior, remember Peter, the impulsive disciple with a hair-trigger temper. Jesus looked past his faults and recognized his potential. He realized Peter would need encouragement or else he would be sidelined by his future mistakes. He knew Peter's loyalty would be severely tested. And so Jesus expressed his confidence that, though Peter's faith would falter, it would not be fatal.

It is the same for you, my friend. Jesus sees your personality, your weaknesses, and your failings. Always remember that he offers you the same faith and confidence he offered Peter. He knows you, too, will be tested, and he has encouragement waiting in the wings. Your mistakes will make you stronger and equip you to strengthen others from the encouragement you receive from him.

Lord Jesus, thank you for looking past my mistakes, seeing my potential, and praying for me.

Kim Crabill, TV host, author, ministry leader, Christian counselor

WHOSE VOICE?

"My sheep listen to my voice; I know them, and they follow me."

JOHN 10:27 NIV

Can you tell the difference between the voice of Jesus and the voice of the enemy? It's very important, you know, because you are following either one or the other. Jesus said his sheep listen to his voice and follow him. That includes you and me. I challenge you to get into God's Word. Get to know his voice so that you can readily decipher what is of God and what is not. For example, God will always lead you; Satan will try to confuse you. God will offer forgiveness; the enemy will condemn you. God's words will calm and comfort you, but Satan's words will confound and worry you.

Friend, always remember that you can truly know the difference between God's words and the enemy's. If you feel frightened or worried or condemned, take a deep breath, open your Bible, and focus your mind on God's truth. That truth will change you because you are listening to the words of the one who created you and who promises to lead you like a shepherd. There is nothing more comforting than that.

Lord, thank you for the gift of your voice. Help me to follow you every day.

Kim Crabill, TV host, author, ministry leader, Christian counselor

STEP OUT OF THE BOAT

"Come," he said. Then Peter got down out of the boat, walked on the water and came toward Jesus.

MATTHEW 14:29 NIV

Several years ago, I believed God was calling me to make a faith-based film, so I decided to step out of the boat. I gave up my apartment and moved in with my sister to write the script. Then I spent months traveling. One night when I was driving, I had a panic attack, feeling petrified that I had made a huge mistake. I pulled over and prayed, and I saw myself standing with Jesus. He said, *You are doing everything I want you to do. Well done, good and faithful servant.* A peace enveloped the car, and I felt calm and assured.

When the movie came out, I received countless messages that the film was changing lives, and I had many opportunities to share how giving up my home meant nothing to me as I saw what God was able to do with my little sacrifice. This story is a constant reminder that what is impossible for us is possible for God. Always remember: When God says, *Step out of the boat*, do it! Your Father will be there to provide.

Father, thank you for providing for me when I obey and step out of the boat.

Alexandra Boylan, filmmaker, producer, screenwriter

PRAISE WORTH SEEKING

We are not trying to please people but God,
who tests our hearts.

1 Thessalonians 2:4 NIV

Do you live to receive the praise of others? Is the value of your day determined by what they are saying about you? If so, you may have fallen into the peer pressure trap. Desiring the praise of people more than the praise of God is deadly, and none of us are immune. Even Peter was ensnared by peer pressure. When visiting with the gentile believers, he ate food that was unclean according to Jewish law. When some devout Jews showed up, Peter caved under their disapproval and no longer ate with the gentiles.

There is something in each of us that desires acceptance and approval. God put that desire there, but its purpose is to draw us to him, not to entangle us in pleasing people. Always remember that the praise of people is fleeting and lacks the power that God's approval gives. People are fickle. They praise you one day and forget about you the next, but God will never forget you. His praise is the only kind worth seeking.

Lord, give me a heart that seeks your approval over anyone else's in my life.

Kim Crabill, TV host, author, ministry leader,
Christian counselor

A SONG IN MY HEART

My heart leaps for joy,
and with my song I praise him.

PSALM 28:7 NIV

Oh no! Not again! A regular event at my house was gathering around the piano to sing gospel songs and practice for musical happenings at church. Growing up in a musical family with parents who loved to sing meant the whole family had to join in. As a teenager, this was not my favorite Sunday afternoon activity. Year after year we would practice at home, at church, and in the car. My going away to college interrupted our practice routines, but there were always holiday visits to get a few songs in.

Later, as I watched my mom play the piano and sing with my children, I realized what a special musical gift she had. Then as Alzheimer's slowly stole her away, one of the last things she lost was her ability to play the piano and sing her beloved gospel songs. Now that she is gone, I keep her memory close by, always remembering to keep a song in my heart.

Heavenly Father, thank you for my mother's example of using her gift of music to glorify you. I thank you for the song of praise in my heart that she passed down to me.

Gail Lawler, organizational development consultant

DAYLIGHT SAVINGS

Out of the depths I cry to you, LORD.

PSALM 130:1 NIV

Have you had any nights lately when you sensed trouble was near, but you had no idea which way to turn to escape calamity? You lay in the dark, surrounded by your fears, and prayed for the sun to rise because somehow the storm wasn't as overwhelming in daylight. Paul and his shipmates felt that way when they were caught in a storm at sea near the coast of the island of Malta. Sailing blind and knowing they were near rocks that could destroy them, the terrified sailors did what they could and then hunkered down and prayed desperately for daylight.

Daylight brings clarity, dispelling the awful uncertainty of darkness. It also offers a new perspective. My friend, if you are in a stormy darkness today, I want you to always remember that God is with you there. He will keep you safe as you sit tight and wait for the storm to pass. The light of a new dawn will bring you fresh courage and renewed energy. So don't panic. The sun is almost over the horizon.

Lord, when fears overwhelm me and storms threaten to destroy me, help me to remember that you will send help with the dawn.

Kim Crabill, TV host, author, ministry leader, Christian counselor

CURSED

"Cursed is the one who trusts in man, who draws strength from mere flesh and whose heart turns away from the LORD."

JEREMIAH 17:5 NIV

As believers, it's natural to say we're blessed, isn't it? Blessed by the birth of a child, blessed to regain our health, blessed to have a good job. But do we ever say we're cursed? That almost sounds like an old superstitious saying, like telling someone to avoid walking under a ladder. In Deuteronomy 11, God laid out his conditions for blessing and cursing, based on the obedience of his children. God made *his* intentions clear: he wanted to bless them. But the choice belonged to the people.

In Scripture, we see characters who stepped out from under God's umbrella of blessing and protection and into consequences. Always remember, the prerequisite to blessing was not only trust but also obedience, *not* so God could hold us under his holy thumb but for our own good. The prophet Jeremiah reminded us to be as consistent in our commitment to God as God is to us. The world will inevitably lead us astray into "cursed" territory. God uses believers to help us stay on the path as long as our trust rests in him alone.

Thank you, Lord, that your desire is always for my good and your commandments are for my blessing.[8]

Pat Boone, actor, singer, songwriter, author

8 Adapted from *Pat Boone Devotional Book*, published by Bible Voice, Inc. Used by permission from Mr. Boone.

PURPOSEFULLY PLANTED

"This is my commandment: Love each other
in the same way I have loved you."

JOHN 15:12 NLT

Do you ever wrestle with the idea that your life makes no difference to the world? Maybe you feel like your days don't count for much of anything, and you feel empty inside. Life lacks meaning, but you aren't sure what to do to change things. If this is you, my friend, I want to share some words of Jesus with you. Speaking to his disciples, he said, "I have chosen you and I have appointed and placed and purposefully planted you, so that you would go and bear fruit" (v. 16 AMP).

These words are for us too. If you want to find purpose in your life, look for someone you can encourage today. Find a way to lighten someone's load. Lend a helping hand, visit the shut-in, or bring your love with some flowers to the grieving. And always remember that you will not find your purpose by sitting idly by, waiting for some miraculous event. Jesus has appointed and purposefully planted you where you are so you can reach out and serve others. If you do, your days will soon have plenty of purpose.

Lord, open my eyes to see that helping my neighbor is loving you. That's all the fulfillment I need.

Kim Crabill, TV host, author, ministry leader,
Christian counselor

A HOLY PLACE

"He will glorify me because it is from me that he will receive what he will make known to you."

JOHN 16:14 NIV

You have a place in your heart where only you and the Holy Spirit can go. It is a private and intimate place where you can pour your heart out to him and where he can pour into you. When I visit my place with him, I often find myself overwhelmed by his glorious presence. As I think of it, this praise bubbles up in my heart:

There is a place. Yes, a place in you where I run, and I am safe. I am here in that place right now. With you, I feel so loved. Lord, you made this place just for me, and here I can see the beauty of your face. As I hold and cling to you, you hold and cling to me. How I love this place with you where only you and I can go.

Always remember, he is waiting in that place for you to have dialogue with him.

Help me to remember, Lord, that I can always run to you, and you will always be there for me.

Charlene Baktamarian, ministry president, executive producer, TV host

RECOVER YOUR JOY

Always be joyful. Never stop praying. Be thankful in all circumstances.

1 Thessalonians 5:16–18 NLT

Be joyful. The command is everywhere: bookmarks, greeting cards, and home decor. It's the title for numerous books and Bible studies that line the shelves of the local bookstore. But how can you be joyful when challenges are staring you in the face? It may be a big challenge, such as a troubled teen, work stress, or chemotherapy, or it could be an ordinary challenge, like working on being a better friend, being kinder to your family, or juggling competing demands on your time.

If you are burdened with the weight of life's challenges today, God provides a way out, but he asks that you do three things. And what are they? You guessed it, my friend: be joyful, never stop praying, and be thankful in all circumstances. Do you see how all three are related? I want you to always remember that when you are stuck between joy and thanksgiving, the answer to both is to pray. Pour out your heart to God. When you are finished, the odds are that you will feel more joyful. Give it a try today.

Lord, thank you for showing me a way to recover joy and thankfulness in my heart.

Kim Crabill, TV host, author, ministry leader, Christian counselor

HE CARES

"I am with you always, to the very end of the age."

MATTHEW 28:20 NIV

We all have worries. *Am I likable enough? Will my finances balance out this month?* Before worry becomes obsession, imagine Jesus visiting you in a quiet place. He places a hand on your shoulder and in a soft voice says, *I really care about what is happening to you right now. It hurts me that you hurt. I'm here for you no matter what.* You begin to open up and share with Jesus the details of your struggle. He leans forward and says in a caring voice, *I'm really sorry you're going through all this.* You look closer and see tears of compassion filling his eyes.

Then just as you are about to get up, Jesus reaches out and touches your arm. In a tender voice, he says, *I want you to know that I'm your safe place. You can always come to me without fear of rejection. I'll be your closest friend.* Always remember, Jesus isn't an imaginary friend. He is real, and he cares about everything that is happening to you.

Thank you, Jesus, that you care about me and all that is happening in my life. Help me to bring my worries and cares to you each day. I know you are with me.[9]

Josh McDowell

9 Adapted from *#truth: 365 Devotions for Teens Connecting Life and Faith*, published by Barbour Publishing, Inc. Used by permission.

REMEDY FOR REGRET

Weeping may last through the night,
but joy comes with the morning.

PSALM 30:5 NLT

Regret. A little word packed with so much emotion.

"I wish I hadn't done that."

"I wish this hadn't happened to me."

"I wish I had started earlier. Why did I wait so long?"

Because you are a normal human being, you can probably relate to each of these statements. I know I do.

Though it's so easy to focus on the past and the things we wish we had done differently, God doesn't want us to focus on those things. He offers a much better option. Today, instead of focusing on your regret or disappointment, try asking God to redeem your situation, and then let it go. It will free you to focus on today, which is where God wants you to live. I hope you'll always remember that every day is a new day. Don't spend the hours tangled up in the wilderness of regret. Instead, live each moment with intention, in the freedom of Christ. Take advantage of God's blessings and the new opportunities that unfold before you today. You won't regret it.

Lord, help me to keep my eyes focused on the opportunities of today so I'm not derailed by past regrets.

Kim Crabill, TV host, author, ministry leader, Christian counselor

May

BEYOND MUNDANE

Rejoice before the LORD your God in everything you put your hand to.

DEUTERONOMY 12:18 NIV

Do you ever get caught up in the mundane? You slog along dejectedly, feeling life is more of a chore than a joy. You are tired of the same old stuff. The same old worries. The same wearisome work. And the same negative outlook you've had for days. My friend, if you are looking for a way out of the dreary mundane, God's Word gives you one. It is summed up in one single word: "Rejoice." When Israel was preparing to enter the promised land, Moses instructed the people to remember God's laws and to offer appropriate sacrifices to him. Then he told them to remember to rejoice in God's goodness.

The key to overcoming a negative outlook is the same for us today. The next time you feel the heaviness of the mundane weighing you down, follow Moses's instruction to rejoice. It's amazing how a bit of praise can totally renovate your attitude. I hope you'll always remember that choosing to focus on the goodness of God will lighten your mood, your mind, and your day. So rejoice and have a good day!

Lord, even on my most wearisome days, help me to rejoice in you.

Kim Crabill, TV host, author, ministry leader, Christian counselor

LAMP UNTO MY FEET

Study to shew thyself approved unto God, a workman that needeth not to be ashamed, rightly dividing the word of truth.

2 Timothy 2:15 KJV

Again I came home in tears from a young people's Bible study. I loved the Lord but couldn't understand why my spirit grieved every time I gathered with this group. Finally, I stood up and said, "I'm sorry, but I can't do this." I called my dad, a pastor, and shared how the leader was taking verses out of context and twisting them to make his points. I was frustrated with myself because I couldn't quickly find the citations to refute what he was saying. My dad patiently opened up God's Word with me, and we began poring over passages.

He said, "Candace, don't just take my word for it. Examine it for yourself. See if what the leader is saying lines up with God's Word. Always remember that when you became a follower of Christ, God placed his Spirit within you to guide you into all truth." That was the turning point in my spiritual growth. No longer content being a hearer of the Word, I became a Berean (Acts 17:11 NIV), studying and examining the Scriptures daily for myself.

Thank you, Lord, for your Word. Give me always an insatiable hunger for your truth.

Candace Kirkpatrick, actor, speaker, talk show cohost

DEAR LORD

"Why do you call me, 'Lord, Lord,' and do not do what I say?"

LUKE 6:46 NIV

"Lord, have mercy! That was a close call!"

"See you tomorrow, Lord willing."

"We got a sunny day for the party, thank the Lord."

Do you ever think maybe that, as believers, we use the word *Lord* loosely? As one of God's titles, "Lord" implies power, authority, and influence. We're invited to pray to the Lord, even encouraged to call him Father, but are we so convinced of his friendship that we've gotten casual about the relationship? Always remember, when we call Jesus "Lord," we delegate him as Lord of *our whole life*. Jesus Christ wants—and deserves—total commitment of everything we have. He desires our obedience for our own sakes.

Take some time to read through the Gospels, taking special care to note what Jesus really asks of us. Consider how following him may not be an easy task but is really the only intelligent choice we can make. Remember, it wasn't easy for him either.

Jesus, I want you to be Lord of all my life. Teach me obedience and help me to discover its joy and benefits so that I might be counted as one of your disciples.[10]

Pat Boone, actor, singer, songwriter, author

---

10 Adapted from *Pat Boone Devotional Book*, published by Bible Voice, Inc. Used by permission from Mr. Boone.

HOPE'S ROLLER COASTER

"Keep up your courage…for I have faith in God that it will happen just as he told me."

ACTS 27:25 NIV

Are you afraid of the hurt of hope today? You know what I mean, don't you? You've prayed a thousand prayers and cried a multitude of tears over a certain situation with no results. Now there seems to be a glimmer of possibility that things may be turning around. Do you dare to hope, or is this just another false positive, another awful trip on the same emotional roller coaster? When you feel discouraged, you are afraid to acknowledge that glimmer of hope.

Abraham was well acquainted with dashed hopes and emotional roller coasters. God had been promising him a son for more than ten years. Abraham was far too old to father a child, but because God kept promising the impossible, Abraham kept believing. The Scriptures say that "against all hope, Abraham in hope believed" (Romans 4:18 NIV). If hope is feeling elusive today, I want you to always remember that you can trust God to do what he says. Keep on hoping and never give up. God's Word has been trustworthy since the beginning of time. It won't fail you now.

Thank you, God, for keeping your word every single time.

Kim Crabill, TV host, author, ministry leader, Christian counselor

RUNNING WITH JESUS

Let us run with perseverance the race marked out for us, fixing our eyes on Jesus.

HEBREWS 12:1–2 NIV

How did it happen that you are sitting on the sidelines watching the race instead of participating? You started out strong, determined that nothing would keep you from meeting your goal, and you did well for a while. Then the naysayers showed up and moved your gaze from the goal to your surroundings. You became distracted. The early church in Galatia struggled with intruders, too, especially ones that prevented them from obeying the truth of the gospel. Paul became alarmed and challenged them to consider their position. "You were running a good race. Who cut in on you to keep you from obeying the truth?" (Galatians 5:7 NIV).

I'll ask you the same, my friend. Who is cutting in on you? Is it unkind words from a friend, unexpected bills, too much scrolling on social media? I get it. Intrusions happen, but always remember that God has given you a race to run. That means he has specific things he planned for you to do. You can get sidetracked by disappointments and distractions. Or you can keep your eyes on Jesus and finish strong. It's your choice, but I strongly recommend running with Jesus.

Lord, help me keep my eyes on the prize so I can finish strong in Jesus.

Kim Crabill, TV host, author, ministry leader,
Christian counselor

SECOND CHANCES

The LORD spoke to Jonah a second time. "Get up and go."

JONAH 3:1–2 NLT

Are you thinking about quitting? It's such a normal thing to do. Life hands out many hard knocks, and they take their toll on our spirits and emotions. Maybe today you feel full of regret and shame, thinking, *I already quit a long time ago.* My friend, if you have already quit, all is not lost. Do you remember the story of Florence Chadwick (March 29) and how she quit on the last mile of her swim? We felt the angst of her failure, didn't we? But Florence didn't quit entirely.

A month later she swam those twenty-six miles a second time, hoping to succeed. Again, the fog rolled in, and the same exhaustion set in, but this time she wasn't starting from scratch. She was starting from experience, and this time she completed that swim. Friend, wherever you are today, always remember that God is a God of second chances. Look at Adam and Eve, at Jonah and Elijah and Moses. All of them received second chances. You serve this same God, so before you give up completely, consider starting over again today with him.

Thank you, Lord, for the gifts of grace, mercy, and second chances.

Kim Crabill, TV host, author, ministry leader, Christian counselor

GOD'S ANCHOR NEVER FAILS

This hope is a strong and trustworthy anchor for our souls.

HEBREWS 6:19 NLT

Friends, if you find yourself in the midst of a storm, remember this truth: you can trust God to be your anchor because he can do anything but fail! My five-year battle with leukemia seemed to be a perfect storm from the standpoint of my medical team. Everything was working against me—my age, my unusual chromosomes, my failed bone marrow transplant. I knew God's plan might mean he would take me to my eternal home, and I was ready. But instead, God miraculously healed me and gave me more years this side of heaven to tell others of his amazing love and grace.

If your storm has lingered and you feel discouraged, always remember that God loves you, and he will sustain you until you reach the destination that he has determined is best for you, according to his purposes for your life. You will have reason to celebrate and praise the Lord regardless. Hang on to your anchor. He will keep you secure.

Lord, I am so grateful that my storms are controlled by your love, your power, and your plan.

Carmen Pate, Roses and Rainbows advisory board member, author, speaker, Bible teacher, mentor of women

SECRET BURDENS

Carry each other's burdens.

GALATIANS 6:2 NIV

Boy, we sure can hide things well, can't we? I remember how, as a teen, I hid behind beautiful cheerleading uniforms and my Miss Teen Time popularity. No one saw the girl suffering from anxiety attacks. No one guessed that behind my academic achievements and successful career lived a young woman controlled by a severe eating disorder, nor did they suspect the suicidal tendencies that consumed me. They didn't notice the young mother who struggled with feelings of inadequacy and depression every hour of the day. I learned to conceal my secrets beneath a badge of marriage, motherhood, and business. I led community groups and the women's ministry of my southern megachurch.

Friend, I want you to always remember that every person you meet has some trial or heartache they are trying to manage. They pass by you, disguising hurt and pain with business success, expensive cars, luxurious homes, and more. Jesus asks that you come alongside them, acting as his hands and feet on this earth. Only then will you be able to unearth the secrets they carry and help them release their burden.

Lord, give me eyes to see the person who is carrying a heavy burden, and a heart to help them bear it.

Kim Crabill, TV host, author, ministry leader, Christian counselor

SECRET PAIN

Turn to me and have mercy,
for I am alone and in deep distress.

PSALM 25:16 NLT

Dear one, I know you hurt so deeply, yet you sit quietly, afraid to tell anyone about it. I get it. Perhaps your life has been turned upside down, and you don't understand why it happened. You want so badly to share your pain with someone, but maybe you tried that before and the only response was a rebuke or even a suggestion that some sin in your life was the cause of your troubles. So to protect yourself, you've stuffed down your hurt, unable to handle the added criticism and judgment from others.

Oh, my hurting friend, I ache for you, and I want you to always remember that the secret pain and disappointment within you is not meant to be carried alone. Ask God to bring you a discerning soul who will share your sorrow and speak blessing over you, realizing that your situation is not a result of God's discipline. Remember, too, that God wants you to endure because he is about to do something magnificent in your life. He knows your greatest desire is to honor him. Hang in there, my friend, for soon you will discover his ultimate purpose for your pain.

Lord, please use the assurance of your love to comfort every heart that is lonely and distressed.

Kim Crabill, TV host, author, ministry leader,
Christian counselor

SEEK HIS FACE

Look to the Lord and his strength; seek his face always.

1 Chronicles 16:11 NIV

Do you long for God today, or do you long for what he can do for you? It is so easy to become self-focused in our prayers, especially when our hearts yearn deeply for God to act to redeem a painful situation. Hannah is a good example for us to follow. Every year she traveled to the place of worship in Shiloh and prayed for a son. She could have become angry with God when each time her prayer went unanswered, but Hannah kept seeking God's heart (1 Samuel 1).

Maybe you've been praying long and hard about a matter dear to your heart. You long for God to answer, but your many petitions seem to fall on deaf ears. You begin to feel frustrated, wanting to push God away rather than pressing in. Are you seeking his face or his hand, my friend? Always remember that you will find more satisfaction in enjoying his presence than desiring what you can get from his hand. God will answer your request in his own time. For now, keep your eyes on his face.

Lord, forgive me for being so self-focused and often seeking your hand rather than your face.

Kim Crabill, TV host, author, ministry leader, Christian counselor

HANDCRAFTED BY GOD

Should the thing that was created say to the one who created it, "Why have you made me like this?"

Romans 9:20 NLT

Have you ever believed a lie about yourself because of something spoken over you by another? I struggled with low self-esteem and poor body image well into my adult life because of a thoughtless comment made by one of my peers. Never mind my contagious smile and great personality. All I could see were my flaws. I've learned this struggle is a common one. Maybe you can relate to it? If so, let me share something that helped me to change the way I think about myself. The Bible names self-criticism as an act of defiance against God. He is our master Creator. Do I really dare to criticize his work? Do you?

Always remember that God formed you with intention, and you are beautiful in his eyes. He placed within you the ability to carry out a calling and purpose unique to you. No part of you is an ugly mistake. Knowing this, you can declare, "I praise you because of the wonderful way you created me" (Psalm 139:14 CEV).

Lord, help me to see myself as the unique and beautiful vessel you created me to be.

Esther Carpenter, author

SINCERE SERVICE

True godliness with contentment is itself great wealth.

1 Timothy 6:6 NLT

Do you ever wish to have a more prominent place of service? You see others climb the ladder of success, and their fame causes them to have a great reach. Their life looks grand and trouble-free. Meanwhile, people pass you by with no acknowledgment of your presence. Your life and your work are just the same as the other "normal people" who fill this earth.

There is nothing wrong with ambition, my friend, nor is it a sin to wish to do great things with your life. But 2 Corinthians 5 tells us that our focus in life needs to be on keeping a sincere heart before God rather than having a spectacular ministry. Besides, all is not as it appears. I want you to always remember that even the most important person among us suffers from heartaches and thorns. Every life has its bitter side. Be content to serve God where you are. Your sincere service to others may be what takes you from where you are to where you aspire to be. Let God work that out when the time is right.

Lord, when I become restless and impatient, remind me to find contentment and rest in you.

Kim Crabill, TV host, author, ministry leader, Christian counselor

SLOW MOTION PLANS

Be still before the LORD
and wait patiently for him.

PSALM 37:7 NIV

Waiting sure is hard sometimes, isn't it? Maybe you are sitting here this morning thinking, *I know God has shown me a plan for my life. My spirit feels a yearning, and Jeremiah 29:11 speaks directly to that calling. I know God has something for me to do, but I feel like I am in slow motion.* Is that what you are thinking today? Or maybe you've been waiting on God so long that you are second-guessing the plan you thought you heard so plainly. You're discouraged and more than a little frustrated.

If this is you, I want you to always remember that God's plan is one of progression. Nothing is ever wasted while you wait. Even Jesus had to wait and grow until the time came for him to fulfill his ministry. Whatever situation you are in right now, though you may feel overlooked, you are not stuck. God just has you in his preparation process.

Lord, my times of waiting are often difficult but never worthless. Help me to grow and not grumble in the wait.

Kim Crabill, TV host, author, ministry leader,
Christian counselor

HOW CLOSE?

All glory to God, who is able, through his mighty power at work within us, to accomplish infinitely more than we might ask or think.

EPHESIANS 3:20 NLT

I was heading to a new job. The location was far away and new to me. I knew I was traveling down the right street, but I couldn't seem to find the building. I was already nervous with this being my first day, and I now had the added pressure of possibly being late.

I called my contact at the location and asked for guidance and grace. It turned out I was only a few buildings away. All I needed to do was keep going just a little bit farther. Always remember you never know how close you are to your destination, to your breakthrough. Never ever give up! You're closer than you think.

Father, guide me and renew my strength when I get weary. Transform my despair into joy and hope. Fix my gaze on all the promises that await me and that you always fulfill.

Gianna Simone, actor, author, producer

SOUL CLEANING

Create in me a clean heart, O God.

PSALM 51:10 NLT

Have you ever noticed that when you dive into a project, things seem to get much messier before they get better? You empty that infamous junk drawer and stare at the contents strewn across the counter, scratch your head, and begin to sort out the mess.

Some seasons of life resemble cleaning out your junk drawer. You feel rather discombobulated, with pieces of your life scattered all over the place. If you are in such a place today, think of it as God spring-cleaning your soul. When he is reordering your life, always remember that it may look worse before it gets better. Don't be surprised at the bumpy road or the unorganized mess. God knows exactly what he is doing, and he is working in the best way possible to make you what he wants you to be. Embrace the lessons you are learning. Gaze softly upon the pieces of your life that make no sense. In time you will see that God has cleaned it up, putting each piece in its proper place.

Lord, thank you for sorting through my messy life and turning it into beauty.

Kim Crabill, TV host, author, ministry leader, Christian counselor

SPECTACULAR SERVICE

Serve wholeheartedly, as if you were serving the Lord, not people.

Ephesians 6:7 NIV

Do you ever feel underwhelmed, thinking that God isn't using you for much in his kingdom? Perhaps you have a strong desire for a daily ministry, but nothing amazing is happening. What does "being used by God" really mean? Well, my friend, God wants to use you right where you are, but you must know that your service to God probably won't look dramatic or spectacular to you. Most of God's operations occur under the radar, so to speak.

Your cul-de-sac may not seem like much of a mission field. Sharing your tomatoes with your neighbor may lack dramatic flair, but to the person whose life you are touching, your generosity just might mean the world. If you long for God to use you, open your eyes to those around you who need kindness. Be encouraging, helpful, and generous. Always remember that there are no small or great opportunities in God's eyes, only acts of obedience to his calling. I promise that your simple, ordinary actions will be pretty spectacular in the eyes of your recipient and also in the eyes of God.

Lord, give me eyes to see the needs around me and hands willing to give aid to another.

Kim Crabill, TV host, author, ministry leader, Christian counselor

ACCELERATE YOUR LIFE

In every matter of wisdom and understanding about which the king questioned them, he found them ten times better than all the magicians and enchanters in his whole kingdom.

DANIEL 1:20 NIV

I started praying this Bible verse when I had my first job in television. I prayed that I would learn the TV industry ten times faster than all the rest. My boss at the time kept commenting on how fast I was learning everything. I knew it was from this prayer. My boss had ten years' experience in the industry, and I believe that by the end of my first year, he had downloaded his ten years of wisdom and TV experience to me. I learned so much!

I also prayed this over my daughter when she started gymnastics. The teachers kept commenting on how fast she was learning and advancing in gymnastics, and I knew why. It was the prayer of Daniel. When you want to accelerate in an area of your life, praying this prayer and speaking the Scriptures can be life changing. The Lord watches over his Word to perform and complete its purpose. Always remember that praying God's Word is powerful in practical ways.

Father, I pray that we will read and pray your Word over our lives and see great results.

Chris Luppo, TV producer, media consultant, speaker, author

PAIN INTO PURPOSE

In your love you kept me from the pit of destruction;
you have put all my sins behind your back.

ISAIAH 38:17 NIV

When I was twenty, I lost my mother to cancer. I was overwhelmed with grief. Why would God allow this to happen? I was faithful and had prayed, believing God would heal her. Before she died, my mother asked an elder at our church, my godfather, to mentor me, but in my grief, I turned to alcohol instead, and it pulled me away from God. But my godfather stayed beside me through my struggles, and he watched me eventually grow into the woman of God I am today. His advice always points me to Jesus. He told me to always remember that we live in a broken, sinful world full of pain and loss.

We don't understand why God allows certain things to happen, but we know he is sovereign and weaves all things together for good to accomplish his purpose. God didn't heal my mother, but looking back, I see God's hands were working to bring purpose to my pain. Now I find comfort when I turn to Jesus. I have a strong testimony, and my joy was restored. I have a family, a wonderful marriage, and my godfather is still influential in my life.

Father, thank you for bringing purpose to the pain I bring to you.

Alisha Griffin, actor, model, blogger

STRONGER THAN MY ENEMY

There is now no condemnation for those who are in Christ Jesus.

ROMANS 8:1 NIV

Today, as you endeavor to be all that God wants you to be, you'll likely battle negative thinking. You know, thoughts of insecurity or unworthiness. The enemy will try to bring you down with reminders of all that you lack and where you are falling short. He might try to frighten you with the demands of the day and your calling in general. When the enemy fills my thoughts with lies, I've learned to run to 1 John 3:20, which says, "If our hearts condemn us, we know that God is greater than our hearts, and he knows everything" (NIV).

I hope you will always remember that those belittling voices making you feel unworthy are never from God. He never condemns his children. But he will cheer you on and whisper words of encouragement to you. He will establish and settle you. No matter what the enemy is trying to make you believe today, God knows you through and through, and he already proclaims that you are not only good, but you are very good. Whatever he calls you to do, he will bring to completion.

Lord, thank you for giving me all I need to battle the enemy and win.

Kim Crabill, TV host, author, ministry leader,
Christian counselor

STUDY TO WIN

We are more than conquerors through him who loved us.

Romans 8:37 NIV

Have you ever watched a professional football team enter the field, running, shouting, and ready to play? Their excitement is contagious, isn't it? And why are they excited? Because they are prepared for the game. They know their opponents. They studied their films, watched their mannerisms, know their plan of attack and how they are going to score. My friend, today we have a spiritual opponent, and it is so important for us to know his game plan, his voice, and his plan of attack.

The Bible plainly states that the devil is prowling around looking for someone to devour (1 Peter 5:8). We need to be aware of our trigger points so that he is not successful when he comes against us. I want you to always remember that while it is important to know your enemy, it is even more important to know your Savior. It is only through him that you will conquer the Evil One. So keep clinging to the truth, put together a battle plan, and remember that in Christ Jesus, the victory is all yours.

Lord, thank you for the assurance of victory as I follow your leading.

Kim Crabill, TV host, author, ministry leader, Christian counselor

NOT IN MY PLANS

Do not be anxious about anything, but in every situation, by prayer and petition, with thanksgiving, present your requests to God.

PHILIPPIANS 4:6 NIV

Our lives were peaceful. My husband, Don, and I were teachers. We had two beautiful young children. We were in leadership roles at church. We had wonderful plans for our future. Then, at age thirty-seven, Don received a diagnosis of "malignant melanoma, metastatic to the brain." His battle against cancer became my battle too. I was grateful he followed medical protocol even though each procedure brought only a little more time for him to be with our children. The continuous medical appointments and intense rounds of chemotherapy and radiation were exhausting.

Then the day came when the doctors said nothing more could be done. I tried to maintain a façade of strength to encourage Don, but he saw my fear. As he pulled my hand into his, he said, "Tough days are ahead, honey. But always remember the Lord never promised us an easy road. But He *did* promise to always be with us on that road." Those words would prove to be true in the days ahead.

Father, help me to be grateful that you walk painful roads with me. Continue to make me aware of your presence.

Sandra P. Aldrich, author, inspirational speaker

THAT AWFUL, BEAUTIFUL THORN

"My power works best in weakness."

2 Corinthians 12:9 NLT

Do you have something in your life that you consider a thorn in your flesh? I've suffered from migraines for years, and many times I would think, *Lord, I'm trying to do your work here. Can't you take these debilitating headaches away?* I know it sounds rather selfish, but perhaps you can relate. After a while, people start reminding you to just pray it away. They say, "If you have enough faith, he will do it."

Well, friend, it's true, God can take it away, but he doesn't always choose to do so. I hope you will always remember that when God allows a thorn in your flesh, he has a reason for it. Many times, we just don't see the bigger picture. Ask him for wisdom and strength to carry on with what he has asked you to do. Don't fear his plan or your lack of ability. Today, let's place in his hands all the thorns we wish we didn't have to deal with since he has everything under control anyway. And now rest, my friend, in his promise and his love.

Lord, thank you for the promise that you are at work in my weakness.

Kim Crabill, TV host, author, ministry leader, Christian counselor

ONE TRUE HOPE

They will soar on wings like eagles;
they will run and not grow weary.

Isaiah 40:31 NIV

Where are you placing your hope today? Is there something in your mind that says, *Gosh, if I could just have this, my life would be so much easier*? A better-paying job, maybe? Improvement in your marriage? The end of this world's wars? Could you be praying for enough money to pay the bills this week or for a new principal at school to better serve your kids? What is that one thing you long for that you are sure will make you happy and give you the strength to face another day?

Well, friend, there is only one in whom we can truly put our hope today. Isaiah 40 tells us that those who hope in the Lord will receive new strength. I want you to always remember that you do not need to walk around head down and heart sore when God provides the strength to run. So check the focus of your hope, my friend. If your hope is fixed on the Lord, you have all you need to fly like an eagle today.

Lord, help me to remember that you are the one who provides the strength I need every day.

Kim Crabill, TV host, author, ministry leader,
Christian counselor

A PRICE ON YOUR HEAD

God chose the lowly things of this world
and the despised things.

1 CORINTHIANS 1:28 NIV

Carlie grinned as she counted the money from her garage sale. She could hardly believe how strangers from all over town handed her money for toys and books she no longer needed. But her excitement melted when she saw she still had a big box of unsold items. Carlie didn't want that stuff. Worse, others didn't want it, even when it was priced at pennies. Carlie tossed her leftovers in the trash.

Most of us have times when we feel like garage sale leftovers—worth even less than small change. When we let others tell us our value or when we compare ourselves to others, it can leave us feeling puny and weak, ugly and unappealing, even dumb, like stuff that no one wants. When you feel that way, don't despair. You're worth far more than a garage sale leftover. In fact, a huge price has already been paid for you. Always remember, your life has been bought by the valuable blood of Jesus Christ!

Father, thank you for counting me worthy to be called your child.[11]

Josh McDowell and Kevin Johnson

11 Excerpted from *The One Year Book of Josh McDowell's Family Devotions 2* coauthored by Josh McDowell and Kevin Johnson with permission of Tyndale House Publishers.

THE NUMBER ONE PHOBIA

"Now go; I will help you speak and will teach you what to say."

Exodus 4:12 NIV

Do you know what the number one phobia in America is right now? It's public speaking. Are you surprised? Statistics tell us that 75 percent of all American adults have a strong aversion to public speaking. If this is so, then how do we reconcile that fact with the times God asks us to go out and speak of the things he has done for us? Well, if speaking in public is not in your skill set, it won't be easy, but for the sake of yourself and others, you need to share your heart and tell your story. This allows you to be God's voice of hope to others.

If God is asking you to step beyond your comfort zone, always remember that you are not doing this alone. His strength is your strength. He will teach you what to say. Yes, public speaking can be intimidating. Speaking to just one person might be terrifying to you, but as you allow God's power to work within you, he will do greater things than you could ever imagine. Are you ready to see what that looks like?

Lord, thank you for your promise to be with me in whatever you ask me to do.

Kim Crabill, TV host, author, ministry leader,
Christian counselor

THE BEST LOVE LETTER

They delight in the law of the LORD,
meditating on it day and night.

PSALM 1:2 NLT

Does the Bible ever seem, well, maybe too super-spiritual to you? Do you read a chapter and then hear yourself saying, "Wait! I have no idea what that means!" If so, join my company, friend, because that's where I lived for many a year. As a matter of fact, I was afraid to read the Bible. First, I thought it was going to condemn me. Then when I finally began to read, I decided it was going to confuse me. I couldn't figure it out. Finally, my desire for knowledge outweighed my fear, and I dove in. I decided to ask others to help me with what I didn't understand. Before long, my fears had flown away.

If you are hesitant or even afraid to read the Scriptures, let me encourage you to wait no longer. Find a friend to study with you. Two minds are better than one. And always remember that God gave his Word as a love letter to you. Open it and discover his heartthrob within the pages. Its truth will set you free.

Lord, give me eyes and a heart that is open to the love found in your Word.

Kim Crabill, TV host, author, ministry leader,
Christian counselor

PERFECT JUSTICE

The LORD within her is righteous; he does no wrong. Morning by morning he dispenses his justice, and every new day he does not fail.

ZEPHANIAH 3:5 NIV

No one wants others to see them as judgmental, and Jesus is very clear that we are not to judge others. But that doesn't mean we should go skipping through life saying, "You do you." If there were no such thing as judgment day, our Creator would not be who we know he is! The reason for judgment isn't so God can point and condemn; it's because of his own character. Always remember, God is entirely just. Sin must be brought to light and dealt with. Deal with it now, or you must deal with it later.

By choosing to live righteously now, we'll one day rejoice in God's perfect justice. To be casual about sin now results not only in fear of justice but also the terror of God's judgment. Rather than living in fear of condemnation, let's allow our reverent fear of the Lord to bring us to repentance *today.*

Thank you, Jesus, that your justice is perfect and your mercy is beyond my understanding. I could never rid myself of my own sin and failure, but you paid the price for it all.[12]

Pat Boone, actor, singer, songwriter, author

---

12 Adapted from *Pat Boone Devotional Book*, published by Bible Voice, Inc. Used by permission from Mr. Boone.

I LOVE YOU

"I have loved you with an everlasting love."

JEREMIAH 31:3 NKJV

Growing up, I had the joy of having a father who showed his love for me in a variety of ways. From a young age, I would occasionally go to work with him. Before he would start the car, he would pat my leg several times and say, "You know, those are love pats!" and off we'd go. As I grew older, Dad might say it in a letter or by phone: "Always remember, I love you!"

You may not have had the love from your father or your mother that you wish you'd had, and the hurt may run deep. No matter your age, you may continue to struggle with these past hurts. Let me encourage you to keep giving your pain back to the Lord. "[Cast] all your care upon Him, for He cares for you" (1 Peter 5:7 NKJV). Always remember: no one else can love you like your heavenly Father.

Lord, you gave your life for me, and there is no greater love. I give you my hurt. Help me daily to walk in your strength.

Kathleen Hardaway, author, speaker

THE PLEASURE OF YOUR COMPANY

My heart has heard you say,
"Come and talk with me."

PSALM 27:8 NLT

How is today looking for you? When you take time to glance up from your work, do you see a wide-open meadow full of sunshine or the headlight of a train barreling down the track, threatening to flatten you? Maybe you are sitting all alone, unable to engage in the busy life you once knew. Regardless of what your day looks like, do you know that God wants the pleasure of your company? He does! And as you set aside a chunk of time each day to be with him, talking and listening, he will become increasingly real to you.

You don't have to beg God to show up. You don't need the perfect chair or a certain translation of the Bible to read. He is always ready to spend time with you. Always remember that God loves the sound of your voice, whether in moments of quiet time with him or as you run errands, attend meetings, or pull weeds in the garden. No matter where you are or what you are doing, keep the conversation going.

Lord, thank you for always being ready to lend a helping hand or a listening ear when I need it.

Kim Crabill, TV host, author, ministry leader,
Christian counselor

THE PROMISE OF MORE

God will generously provide all you need. Then you will always have everything you need and plenty left over to share with others.

2 Corinthians 9:8 NLT

From what everyone else was saying, you expected more. Finding yourself at the top of the ladder was supposed to be more fulfilling. Your marriage was supposed to bring you more security or be more satisfying. Life did not deliver the "more" you expected, and you grapple with disillusionment and disappointment.

If this is you, my friend, I want you to know that God also offers you more, and it's "immeasurably more" than you can imagine (Ephesians 3:20–21 NIV). He offers more strength for the work he called you to do, more grace for your times of weakness and failure, and more power—power that transforms you into the person he wants you to be so that he can accomplish what he wants to do through you. No matter where you are in life, dear one, always remember that God will never disappoint you with his promise of more. Bring him the good and the bad, your strengths and your weaknesses, and then watch him do so much more in you than you could ever imagine.

Lord, I look forward to seeing you work out the unimaginable possibilities in my life.

Kim Crabill, TV host, author, ministry leader, Christian counselor

DRAW CLOSE TO GOD

Draw near to God and He will draw near to you.

JAMES 4:8 NKJV

It is always God's desire for you to draw close to him. And always remember, when you do, you have the promise that he will draw near to you. Oh, how he desires to have you near, to hold you close. That is why he made a way, through the sacrifice of Jesus, to give you open access to his throne room. I always imagine running to that throne room and crawling up onto the lap of my Abba Father. And his response? He wraps his arms around me and comforts his child with his love.

Let your troubles and sorrows draw you close to God. He will draw near to you with his love, his peace, his comfort, and his joy. You may enter his presence with sorrow and tears, but rest assured that when you leave the throne room, you will have a smile on your face and a song in your heart. You will grow to love God's presence and will soon be visiting the throne room even on the good days!

Lord, thank you for desiring me to be close to you. Remind me to approach you regularly with confidence that you will welcome me.

Carmen Pate, Roses and Rainbows advisory board member, author, speaker, Bible teacher, mentor of women

June

THE RIGHT PLAN

The LORD will work out his plans for my life.

PSALM 138:8 NLT

How many times have you heard the words "God has a plan for you?" We know the statement is true, right? And sometimes we wonder about that plan. I know I did. Here's what I wish someone had told me back then. There is a competing plan for your life, one that is from your enemy. For years, when I knew I wasn't living God's plan, I had no idea that I was falling in line with the enemy's plan to steal, kill, and destroy my life.

Do you find yourself on a destructive path, longing for something better? Or are you seeking God's plan, though you aren't sure what it is? Always remember that God wants to reveal his plan to you. So search for him with all your heart and then watch what happens. It won't be all at once, but little by little, as you stay in a relationship with him, he will make his plan known to you.

Lord, thank you for providing a good plan for every life you create. Help me to follow that plan.

Kim Crabill, TV host, author, ministry leader,
Christian counselor

CATCHING BEES WITH HONEY

A person finds joy in giving an apt reply—
and how good is a timely word!

PROVERBS 15:23 NIV

My grandma passed away at age one hundred seven. She was one of the sweetest people I knew. She didn't have much material wealth, but she was rich with wisdom. When someone was mean to me and I wanted to match their anger, she'd say, "Always remember that you can catch more bees with honey than you can with salt." She knew the importance of using your words and actions for good. Being kind and nice to others, even when you don't feel like they deserve it, is a lesson in self-control.

Grandma's wisdom has been my compass for over fifty years. It has led me in very difficult conversations, when anger could have taken me over. People can say and do things that really get under our skin sometimes, but when we match their anger, our witness gets tainted, and our walk looks lopsided. When we extend grace and love, conviction might fall on the person spewing negativity, and an apology may be forthcoming. However, our extension of kindness is most often a rich reminder for us.

God, help me extend grace and see the purpose in every situation rather than feeling like it's a personal attack.

Maura Gale, speaker, actor, author, podcaster

THE ULTIMATE SURRENDER

"Yet not my will, but yours be done."

Luke 22:42 NIV

I sat by my friend's hospital bed and listened to her tell me what was on her heart. "Kim," she said, "I'm afraid to pray for God's will to be done." I get it, don't you? Aren't we all afraid to release something or someone to God and his will at one time or another? Maybe for you, it's a child or a grandchild. It could be your marriage, your finances, or even your own health.

I think of when the angel reassured Mary, saying, "Don't be afraid...for you have found favor with God" (Luke 1:30 NLT). Mary needed that reassurance because what God was asking of her was a real stretch, wasn't it? God will do the same for you today. When he asks something of you and it feels bigger than you can handle, always remember that the only thing he asks of you is that you trust his plan. You never need to fear praying for his will because he will equip you with what you need to carry it out. And his will should be what we ultimately seek.

Lord, in every situation, help me to submit my will to yours.

Kim Crabill, TV host, author, ministry leader, Christian counselor

THE WEARY WAIT

I trust in you, LORD…"You are my God."
My times are in your hands.

PSALM 31:14–15 NIV

Are you in a season of waiting today? Perhaps you are anxious about a test result that should have been delivered weeks ago and has the potential to completely upend your life. Maybe you are asking God to meet a need for a loved one, and he seems to be ignoring your request. Or could it be that the stress from a pile of unpaid bills is draining you of physical energy and emotional stability? You are so tired of trying to make ends meet. You are tempted to quit praying, but the stakes are too high to give up.

My friend, if you are caught up in the weariness of waiting, always remember that God has not forgotten you. He has a reason for your waiting even though you may not be able to see it. On days when it is hardest to hold on, don't forget that he is holding tightly to you. He knows exactly how long the wait is and will see you safely through to rest.

Lord, please instill in me a trust that will sustain me in the wait.

Kim Crabill, TV host, author, ministry leader,
Christian counselor

SPEAKING HOPE

May the God of hope fill you with all joy and peace as you trust in him.

Romans 15:13 NIV

As I approached the register to check out, I looked into the eyes of hopelessness. I sensed the Lord's heart for this person and began speaking hope. I told her things about her life that I could not have possibly known but by the Holy Spirit. God wanted her to know how he loved her and that he saw her struggles. He did this by sending a stranger to tell her about her life of addiction, prostitution, abuse, and her deep desire to have her children back. The girl cried and was shocked because all of it was true. Though she declined my invitation to church, she did begin to seek God. I went on to mentor her, and today she is addiction-free and has her children back.

Always remember that God has a "woman at the well" experience for each one of us (John 4:1–42). He longs to tell us that he knows all about us—our sins, our regrets, our failings—and yet he loves us and has a good plan for our lives.

Fill me with your joy and peace so that I can overflow with hope by the power of the Holy Spirit.

Charlene Baktamarian, ministry president, executive producer, TV host

THIS IS GOOD?

Everything he does is right and all his ways are just.

DANIEL 4:37 NIV

So often it seems that life just passes you by, doesn't it? You didn't get the promotion or you weren't accepted for the school or the job. Everyone seems to be prospering, and you are still trying to figure out why that's not happening for you. If you feel this way today, my friend, I want you to always remember that many times in life we simply will not have the answers. When you don't understand God's ways, that is the time to trust what you know to be true about him.

The Bible says God's timing is never late and never early. It is always right on time. But what do we do in the meantime? We hold on to something we know: "that in all things God works for the good of those who love him" (Romans 8:28 NIV). It's not easy, but if we choose to believe the truth of that verse, then we can rest assured that good is in store for us. It's like I often say to myself: *If it's not good, then God's not finished.*

Lord, thank you for the assurance that all your plans for me are good.

Kim Crabill, TV host, author, ministry leader, Christian counselor

TIME TO REFOCUS

Let God transform you into a new person by changing the way you think.

ROMANS 12:2 NLT

Are you tired of your current thoughts? Do you find yourself caught up in a pattern of negative thinking, rehashing conversations in your mind? Maybe it's a hurtful comment someone said to you, or maybe it's a response you wanted to make to that comment. Either way, the internal dialogue drains you of energy and keeps your focus in a dark place. It's hard to be joyful when your head is filled with negativity, isn't it? What if you could take those negative thoughts captive and exchange them for positive ones?

The Bible tells us to capture every thought that makes it difficult to follow Jesus' way of living. You can do this by swapping the negative thought for a joyful truth from Scripture. As you do this, the hurtful negativity is soothed and eventually forgotten. Always remember that the way to a joyful life is found by focusing on the truth of God's Word. Today seems like a good time to begin replacing your negative conversations and worn-out lies with beautiful, energizing truths from your heavenly Father, don't you think?

Thank you, Father, for providing a way for me to turn a negative focus into one of joy-filled truth.

Kim Crabill, TV host, author, ministry leader, Christian counselor

WISE DISCIPLINE

Train up a child in the way he should go,
and when he is old he will not depart from it.

PROVERBS 22:6 NKJV

"I'm not your friend, I'm your mother." I don't know how many times I heard those words, but it coincided with the number of times I got into trouble! I still picture my mother sitting across the table explaining why my behavior was bad or how the choice I made would lead to danger or destruction. I was usually crying, telling her she was mean and didn't understand. I was well into my teens before I understood. She wasn't trying to be mean, but being friends was not her goal. As my mother, her mission was to train me to be a caring person of impeccable character. Like my mom's rules and reprimands, always remember that God sends discipline for our good.

I'm grateful my mother chose guidance for me over friendship. I came to respect the hard choices she made to help me become a valuable member of society. We were blessed with enough time that we did become good friends. I often wish I could still sit across from her at the kitchen table to continue learning from her.

Lord, help me to listen for your wisdom and be open to your discipline.

Barbara Parker, women's ministry leader, educator, audiologist

TODAY'S MANNA

My God will supply every need of yours.

PHILIPPIANS 4:19 ESV

Today is your day, one given to you by God himself. Are you living it to the full, or are you fretting about yesterday and how much better it was? Are you worrying about what tomorrow may hold? The children of Israel had this problem too. When Moses led them out of slavery in Egypt, they were happy to go. But when they became hungry in the desert, they begged to go back to Egypt. God provided for them, giving just enough manna for each day. He was teaching them to trust him one day at a time.

He asks the same of you today. Will you focus on today and not worry about tomorrow's provision? Will you leave yesterday and tomorrow in God's hands? Yesterday's manna is gone. Tomorrow will have its own manna. I hope you will always remember to enjoy the manna of today; God's supplies never run low.

Lord, thank you for promising to supply every need I have when I need it.

Kim Crabill, TV host, author, ministry leader, Christian counselor

AND THE ANSWER IS…

"My thoughts are not your thoughts,
neither are your ways my ways."
ISAIAH 55:8 NIV

"Daddy," I told him, in my most encouraging voice, "people who never even met you are praying for your healing!" He smiled. "I'll take all the prayers I can get…just remember that sometimes the answer is no." No was not the answer I sought, but it's the one I got. As any kid who ever asked for a pony knows, sometimes parents say no, and not just because there's no room for a horse in the house. A parental no not only teaches us to wait and appreciate ("When you've proven you're responsible, then we'll get a dog!") but also sets healthy boundaries ("No, you can't get a tattoo/go to a coed sleepover/smoke cigars…"). Sometimes a no simply wields authority—the parents' ever-popular "Because I said so."

Good parents—godly parents—say no. Why, then, are we surprised or angry when our heavenly Father says it? Like little children, we don't want to hear "no." We won't always understand. But always remember that our good Father asks us to trust him, his ways, and his answers.

Good Father, help me to trust your plan even when I don't understand it.

Rhonda Jackson, Roses and Rainbows advisory board member, writer

TOO SOON TO QUIT

Our light and momentary troubles are achieving for us an eternal glory.

2 CORINTHIANS 4:17 NIV

Is this the day when life has handed you one too many troubles and you just feel like quitting? We all have days when it would be easy to throw up our hands in surrender and walk away from those financial woes, that overwhelming task, or that difficult relationship. But I want to encourage you: don't quit!

The apostle Paul faced numerous setbacks and difficult situations: ongoing health challenges, more than one prison sentence, hunger, and cold temperatures. I'm sure he was tempted to quit many times, yet his testimony was that all those things he endured were light and momentary troubles. He was determined not to lose heart because his focus was on the eternal.

Whatever you're facing today, follow Paul's example and draw upon the Holy Spirit's strength through prayer. Keep pressing on, my friend, and always remember that every trial you face on this earth is helping you to achieve your eternal destiny. It will be worth it in the end. Don't forsake tomorrow's blessing and eternity's joy by giving up today.

Lord, help me to always keep the eternal perspective central in my heart.

Kim Crabill, TV host, author, ministry leader, Christian counselor

ULTIMATE GOODNESS

He is the Rock, his works are perfect, and all his ways are just.
A faithful God who does no wrong, upright and just is he.

DEUTERONOMY 32:4 NIV

Think about your happiest moments in life: your best meal ever, best vacation, most beautiful sight. In doing so, you're recalling moments of joy, contentment, beauty, and goodness. Where did all those things come from?

Always remember, "Whatever is good and perfect is a gift coming down to us from God our Father" (James 1:17 NLT). He is the originator of all that is good. It's not just that God does things that are perfectly good—*he* is perfectly good by his very nature. He is "the one who is holy and true" (Revelation 3:7 NLT) and "there is no evil in him" (Psalm 92:15 NLT).

Thank you, God, for your goodness. Help me to reflect your goodness in my own life today.[13]

Josh McDowell

---

13 Adapted from *#truth: 365 Devotions for Teens Connecting Life and Faith*, published by Barbour Publishing, Inc. Used by permission.

TRUE VALUE

Everything else is worthless when compared with the infinite value of knowing Christ Jesus my Lord.

PHILIPPIANS 3:8 NLT

What do you value most in life? Is it your religious reputation or your family heritage? Maybe it's your education and the frames on your office wall that proclaim your professional success. All of these are worthy values, but none of them has any true spiritual worth, and they will not satisfy the longing of your soul. Paul was an example of someone who had all these earthly successes, but when he met Jesus, his values changed. His new value was simple. Only one thing mattered: he wanted to know Jesus and become like him.

What about you, my friend? Have your values changed at all since you met Jesus? Have you found the life in him that brings you peace of heart and purpose to your day? I want you to always remember that no earthly success will ever provide the soul-level value that knowing Jesus will. Let him be your first interest and your most valuable relationship. Take time to be with him today and treasure the way he is making you into a new creation—the best kind of value.

Lord, fill my heart with a desire to value a relationship with you above all else.

Kim Crabill, TV host, author, ministry leader, Christian counselor

TRUTH AND TEMPTATION

"'You must worship the LORD your God and serve only him.'"

MATTHEW 4:10 NLT

Do you ever consider going back on your word because it seems God has changed his mind? A lucrative job offer conflicts with a promise you made to stay close to home, or you've agreed to help a neighbor, then your friends plan a weekend trip. You need that quality time with spiritual friends. What then? Let's look back at the temptations of Jesus. In his final temptation, Satan presented Jesus with all the kingdoms of the world. Then he spoke some strangely twisted words. "'I will give it all to you,' he said, 'if you will kneel down and worship me'" (Matthew 4:9 NLT).

Satan's words were a deceptive half-truth at best. But the point is, he was offering Jesus a way around the future suffering of the cross. Satan will offer you things that sound good up front but upon closer inspection, they defy God's plan for you. My friend, always remember to weigh every offer or decision in the balance of what God has called you to do. You can avoid falling prey to Satan's deceptive partial truths by staying in communion with God and the whole truth.

Lord, thank you that you are stronger than the enemy. Keep my heart in tune with yours.

Kim Crabill, TV host, author, ministry leader, Christian counselor

THIS IS A TEST

I saw the dead, great and small, standing before the throne, and books were opened. Another book was opened, which is the book of life. The dead were judged according to what they had done as recorded in the books.

Revelation 20:12 NIV

Do you ever have those dreams where you're back in high school and can't find your classroom—and then, you finally make it to your desk only to find there's a test…that you didn't study for? The book of Revelation gives us a preview of the final accounting, the closing chapters of mankind's time on earth.

Always remember, God isn't going to give us a surprise test! When we compare the brevity of life to eternity, it makes perfect sense to serve God wholeheartedly all our lives, don't you think? God gives us a lifetime of instruction. Don't wait for the perfect time to serve him. Today is the day! This moment is perfect. Commit your ways to him. God's judgment is sure—are you ready to face him in eternity, right now?

Merciful Father, you've chosen to reveal your purposes to me, and I know you will judge every soul. Thank you for giving me opportunities to serve you. I give myself again to you today, totally.[14]

Pat Boone, actor, singer, songwriter, author

14 Adapted from *Pat Boone Devotional Book*, published by Bible Voice, Inc. Used by permission from Mr. Boone.

UGLY IS TEMPORARY

[God] redeems your life from the pit
and crowns you with love and compassion.

Psalm 103:4 NIV

Is there any ugliness in your life that you want to see made beautiful? Maybe a season of ugly circumstances: a relationship you aren't sure how to fix, a job that takes more from you than it gives? Or maybe an unseen burden—a heaviness of heart because of secrets you carry. It's been this way for a while, and you see no hope on the horizon. My friend, if you carry an ugly burden today, don't lose heart. Take your burden to God. Tell him how exhausted you feel from carrying it day after day. He is patiently waiting for you to hand it over to him.

Always remember that, although your situation may not appear beautiful today, God has promised that, at the appropriate time, he will make it so. It's true that you are powerless to change anything, but he has all the power in the world. So don't give up hope. God's blessings are underway, and the best is yet to come.

Thank you, Father, for promising to create something beautiful from my ugly burdens.

Kim Crabill, TV host, author, ministry leader,
Christian counselor

MY PRINCE

His name will be called Wonderful Counselor, Mighty God, Eternal Father, Prince of Peace.

ISAIAH 9:6 NASB

As a recent widow, I kept busy each day. I worked in my office, went to church, and had lunches with friends. However, when the day ended and I was alone, the tears often came. One night I cried out to God to bring peace and joy back to me. I needed him to come into my life and take over. I wanted to stop feeling sorry for myself. I needed his comfort as I grieved. I remember the moment he touched my spirit and brought me out of my desolate, lonely place.

With God's help, I was able to reestablish my life and move away from my loneliness and self-absorption. Giving to others was key for me. As I prayed, God led me to people who had greater needs, and I was able to help them. Always remember, Jesus is our Prince of Peace. He also gave me an earthly prince—my husband, an amazing godly man who inspired, cared for, and loved me.

Heavenly Father, thank you for your Son, Jesus, the Prince of Peace. Thank you for always seeing my needs and filling them with your love.

Suellen Roberts, media influencer

UNEXPECTED BEAUTIES

He has made everything beautiful in its time.

Ecclesiastes 3:11 NIV

Did you know that God makes all things beautiful? That's what he says in Ecclesiastes 3:11. You may be sitting there, saying "I'm not sure about that. Things are not going well for me. I don't see much beauty in my world right now." I understand. Not all things are beautiful in my world either. God doesn't say your life is beautiful at the minute, but he does promise to make it so. Sure, we go through rough patches, and we wander around in the weeds sometimes. But then suddenly, the thicket opens into a meadow full of sunshine.

You know what I mean. I'll bet you can remember a time that felt dark and hopeless. Then without warning, something good happened, bringing joy to your day. God prepared that pleasure just for you, and he has more beautiful things on the road ahead. I hope you will always remember that even though you don't have answers to the situations that hold only sorrow today, God is there, working to create future beauty. Keep going, my friend. There is a beautiful future ahead of you.

Lord, give me eyes to see past my troubles to the beauty you place in my path each day.

Kim Crabill, TV host, author, ministry leader, Christian counselor

I PRAY FOR YOU DAILY

"My prayer is not for the world, but for those you have given me, because they belong to you."

JOHN 17:9 NLT

I never left my great-aunt Velear's home without hearing her say, "Always remember, I pray for you daily." I don't think those words resonated with me as a child, or even as a teen, but when I became a young divorced mom of two, I treasured them. You see, I didn't feel worthy to pray for myself, but I knew this godly woman must have a direct line to God. I experienced the power of her prayers.

As I grew in my knowledge and love for our dear Lord, I began to pray fervently for my own children and now for my grandchildren. And I tell them that I do. My prayers may not mean much to them now, but someday they will. When Aunt Velear went home to our Savior, I felt the void in my life. I miss her dearly, but it is her prayers I miss most. So isn't it wonderful to know that Jesus prays for you? Always remember, his prayers for you will never end. Take comfort in that.

Father, thank you for Jesus, who died, rose again, and intercedes for me every day.

Carmen Pate, Roses and Rainbows advisory board member, author, speaker, Bible teacher, mentor of women

UNKNOWN TERRITORY

"He knows the way that I take; when he has tested me, I will come forth as gold."

Job 23:10 NIV

Have you ever found yourself saying, "But I don't like anything about this, God! This is not what I expected life to be like, and it is not what I had planned." If so, take heart! You are not the first one to say those words, and you won't be the last. Often in life, I have found myself in places I never thought God would take me, and quite honestly, the unknown territory caused a lot of anxiety, worry, and even anger.

If you are wandering in unknown territory, bewildered by your situation, here's something to consider. What if, instead of asking God to change your circumstances, you would ask him to change you? My friend, even if you are in the last place you ever thought you would be, I hope that you will always remember that God is using it for your good. He knows where you are and what he is doing. This place you are in just might be bringing out the gold in you.

Lord, help me to allow our hard times to bring the changes you want to see in my life.

Kim Crabill, TV host, author, ministry leader, Christian counselor

MY LIFE WORK DEFINED

To him who is able to do immeasurably more than all we ask or imagine…to him be glory.

EPHESIANS 3:20–21 NIV

Campus Crusade for Christ (now CRU) had recently expanded their ministry to Boston University when I came there in 1968 as a journalism major. Eventually, I came to Christ through their work. That's when I first met Bill Bright, the Crusade founder, during one of his visits to BU. In my senior year, I needed to choose a topic for my term paper from something current in the news. A few months earlier, the June 21, 1971, edition of *Time* magazine had done a front-page piece on the Jesus Movement. I convinced my journalism teacher to allow me to make that the topic of my term paper.

I asked Bill for an interview when he was back in town. He agreed and sat with me for an entire hour. His answer to one of my questions—"How did you accomplish all this?"—became the definition for my life's approach to work: "At Crusade, we do things in such a way that only God can get the credit, never man." That one statement still resonates in my heart. It held words I will always remember.

Father, let me decrease so Christ can increase in me.

Joe Battaglia, author, producer, broadcaster

CHECK YOUR CALENDAR

Although Jesus loved Martha, Mary, and Lazarus, he stayed where he was.

JOHN 11:5–6 NLT

Is your candle burning at both ends today, causing you to be too busy to enjoy life? How many activities did you add to your calendar because you didn't want to make someone angry? How often did you say yes because you felt guilty saying no? What did you agree to do just because you've done it every other time you were asked? My friend, if you find yourself run ragged today trying to fulfill the priorities of others, I have a way out for you.

Jesus was never pressured by other people's priorities. He loved Mary and Martha deeply, yet he didn't run to their aid just to please them. His daily steps were determined by one priority: his desire to please the Father. Jesus' example is a good lesson for us today. Always remember that you can take your daily calendar to him. Ask him to show you what needs to disappear from your to-do list. Ask him if there is anything he wants you to add. Then surrender your day to him to use as he sees fit!

Lord, slow me down so that I can fulfill your plans, not mine.

Kim Crabill, TV host, author, ministry leader, Christian counselor

TRUSTWORTHY

"Whoever comes to me I will never drive away."

JOHN 6:37 NIV

Has anyone broken your trust lately? Trust is difficult to repair, especially when it's been broken by someone close to you: a family member, a friend, or, hardest of all, a spouse. Whenever I think of betrayal, I'm reminded of Jesus. He experienced a level of betrayal that you and I cannot fully grasp. For three years, Jesus and his disciples had traveled everywhere together. Then all in one night, Judas turned him over to his enemies to be killed, the rest of his friends took off running, and Peter swore that he didn't even know Jesus.

When Jesus rose from the dead, he could have found new followers, but instead he came back around to personally comfort and reassure his friends of his love. No wonder he tells us to love each other as he loves us. When hurtful memories assault you, and you don't know whom to trust, always remember that it is safe to trust Jesus. He has never broken a single promise. People sometimes let you down, but Jesus never will. You can trust him—I promise.

Lord, thank you for being the unchanging, never-ending, always-loving Father that you are.

Esther Carpenter, author

UNPOPULAR CHOICES

Am I now trying to win the approval of human beings, or of God?

GALATIANS 1:10 NIV

What should you do when you feel in your heart that God wants you to do one thing but everyone around you is saying you should do it their way? Well, I think there is a great example for us in God's Word that will shed light on this issue. Jesus found himself in just such a predicament. He was busy doing what God had sent him to do up in Galilee when he got a message that his friend Lazarus was dying. His disciples wanted him to go to Lazarus immediately, but God had revealed a different idea to Jesus.

My friend, there are times when you will want to listen to the convincing voices of those around you. In those times, you need to always remember the principle Jesus lived by. You are not following people but God. God does not always ask you to do the popular thing, but he will always ask you to do the right thing. Don't be pressured by other people's opinions. Walk steadily with God, obeying his voice, and maybe those around you will be challenged to do the same.

Lord, speak clearly to my heart and teach me to follow only you.

Kim Crabill, TV host, author, ministry leader, Christian counselor

WRESTLING WITH IRRELEVANCE

[We are] God's instruments to...tell others of the night-and-day difference he made for you—from nothing to something, from rejected to accepted.

1 PETER 2:9–10 MSG

The above passage shaped my understanding of God's purposes for me forty years ago. It came back to me with force recently after I read an article about feeling irrelevant after retirement. It was as if God were saying, *Child, always remember that whatever else is making you feel irrelevant on any given day, you still have the highest calling imaginable: tell!*

How often have we heard that we need to "retool" to stay relevant? Did the fisherman Andrew retool before he ran to find his brother Simon and announce, "We've found the Messiah" (John 1:41 MSG)? No, he met Jesus, and he knew what to do next: tell someone! That telling could be a full-blown Damascus Road testimony. More likely, though, it's a conversation over coffee about loneliness during a pandemic, joy over a child's achievements, or worry about a medical scan. But those comparatively smaller happenings come with an added invitation: "See what a difference it makes to have a loving God walk with you through such stuff!" That's relevance for you!

Lord, I am humbled and deeply thankful to know that the stories of how you are at work in my life will never be irrelevant.

Sue Kline, writer, editor, writing coach

LIGHT IN THE DARK

Even the darkness is not dark to you;
the night is bright as the day,
for darkness is as light with you.

PSALM 139:12 ESV

Have you ever cut off all the lights and sat in total darkness? That is what depression feels like. You're unable to see anything around you. Even when you look into the mirror, you can't see who you truly are. If life has brought you to a point where there is too much sadness, I want you to know you are not alone. Although you may not feel him, Jesus has a firm hold on your hand. He promises to work for your good everything you face in life.

Others have traveled this road with him and found their way back to a joyful life, and you will too. Although it may be hard to imagine now, better days are coming. You will get through this. Always remember, my friend, that God's plan is more beautiful than your disappointment or despair. He can bring you safely from the darkness into his soul-warming light. Be patient in the sadness. Hold on to God's promises. Thank him because he has not forsaken you. Trust God to bring something beautiful from this darkness.

Lord, give me faith to believe that you will bring me safely through the darkness.

Kim Crabill, TV host, author, ministry leader,
Christian counselor

VACATION OR CONVERSATION?

"Let me teach you...and you will find rest for your souls."

MATTHEW 11:29 NLT

Are you in need of rest today? Are the external stressors of life and the internal struggles of worry and care weighing you down to the point of exhaustion? A week's vacation sounds like what you need. Or maybe a day at home alone in peace to work on your favorite hobby, with no interruptions or expectations—just some time away from your burdens. But is that truly the rest you need?

Vacations do not bring the rest we crave; only Jesus can do that. He doesn't want you to bring your burdens to him so he can erase them. No, he wants to reverse them. He would much rather turn them around and give them a purpose. If you are tired and burdened today, I want you to always remember that real rest is found in honest conversation with Jesus. He knows where you are. As you spend time with him today, thank him ahead of time for being more powerful, more creative, and more loving than you can fathom. Trust him to change your struggles into purpose.

Lord, teach me to find both rest and purpose in you.

Kim Crabill, TV host, author, ministry leader, Christian counselor

WAITING TO BE WANTED

My heart says of you, "Seek His face!"
Your face, LORD, I will seek.

PSALM 27:8 NIV

Have you fallen in love with God lately? Has his gentle presence called to your soul, causing you to pause and come running, anxious to talk with him? He's like that, you know. His voice is quiet, and it's easy to let the cares and pressures of the day drown him out. We waste hours fretting over problems at work and frustrations at home. We agonize over relationships and situations beyond our control. But underneath it all, God is waiting for you to turn to him.

He won't push himself on you, won't demand that you come talk with him. Instead, he waits for you to remember that he is the answer to everything on your mind and the anxieties of your heart. Take a moment to quiet your soul. Accept his invitation to talk with him. Always remember that God is waiting to receive your love today. He rejoices to spend time with you. Nothing settles and calms you like sitting at his feet, so come to him today. He is waiting to be wanted.

Lord, when life's pressures rise, remind me to take a moment and be quiet before you.

Kim Crabill, TV host, author, ministry leader,
Christian counselor

THINKING WITH HEAD AND HEART

It is with your heart that you believe and are justified, and it is with your mouth that you profess your faith and are saved.

ROMANS 10:10 NIV

As a teacher, mother, sister, and friend, I am often asked for advice on a decision or help in solving a problem. For many years, my consistent reminder to everyone, from young children to teens to adults, has been, "Always remember to think with your head *and* your heart." I believe that while actions, opinions, and others' viewpoints may be important, compassion for those impacted by decisions and actions should always be of special consideration in your thought process.

As Ephesians 4:32 urges, "Be kind to one another, tenderhearted, forgiving one another, even as God in Christ forgave you" (NKJV). Kindness and compassion should always be your guide.

Heavenly Father, thank you for giving me a heart filled with compassion and wisdom so that my words and actions glorify you.

Gail Lawler, organizational development consultant

WATCH YOUR WORDS

Let your conversation be always full of grace…so that you may know how to answer everyone.

COLOSSIANS 4:6 NIV

Why should you be friendly to a coworker who says cutting things about you and gossips behind your back? Isn't that being hypocritical? You may struggle with different situations that lead to a similar question, but in the end, the answer is the same: it is absolutely not hypocritical. There are so many times that you will want to give as good as you get, but when you choose to grit your teeth or bite your tongue, you are choosing wisdom.

The Proverbs writer said that gracious words are sweet to the soul and healthy to the body (16:24). A soft and gentle answer makes for peace (Proverbs 15:1). When you smile and choose kind words over the ones you want to say, you are not being hypocritical. You are simply obeying the command of Jesus to treat others as you want to be treated. Always remember that the right actions lead to right feelings. Obedience to Jesus is always better than following your own not-so-reliable emotions. Be the kind of person today who carries kindness and respect wherever you go.

Lord, help me to choose wisdom and speak only words that bring honor to you.

Kim Crabill, TV host, author, ministry leader, Christian counselor

July

WELL EQUIPPED

May the God of peace…equip you with everything good for doing his will.

Hebrews 13:20–21 NIV

When you face the day ahead, do you sometimes think, *How in the world can I ever do this?* Maybe God is calling you to apologize to someone or to have the courage to forgive the person who offended you. It feels too hard. Yet here's the thing: whatever we don't feel qualified to handle is always manageable with God.

You have probably heard the saying that God doesn't call the equipped; he equips the called. I think, in fact, that God does call the equipped. We just don't know how equipped we are! The Bible tells us that God has equipped us with everything good for doing his will. Always remember that God will never call you to something you are not qualified to do. It may not be easy, but you are already equipped to accomplish it with him.

Lord, thank you for equipping me with all I need to serve you.

Kim Crabill, TV host, author, ministry leader, Christian counselor

TRY ME!

"Bring the whole tithe into the storehouse, that there may be food in my house. Test me in this," says the LORD Almighty, "and see if I will not throw open the floodgates of heaven and pour out so much blessing that there will not be room enough to store it."

MALACHI 3:10 NIV

As believers, what do we think of someone testing God? In Matthew 4, Jesus specifically says to the enemy, "Do not put the Lord your God to the test." Surprising, then, that the same God invites us to do just that in the book of Malachi. It's the only place in Scripture that God essentially says, "Try me." Have you "tried him" in this area of giving? Now, when so many of us are struggling, does God want our money? Does God *need* our money?

Always remember, God's ways are not our ways, and he doesn't *need* our tithe. Instead, he offers valuable lessons on obedience and stewardship. If you obey the principle of tithing, you'll be amazed at how God will meet your needs and overflow you with blessings. Believe God. Put him to the test and watch him fulfill his promises!

Lord, I come to you with tithes and offerings and wait expectantly as you work your stewardship principles in my life.[15]

Pat Boone, actor, singer, songwriter, author

---

15 Adapted from *Pat Boone Devotional Book*, published by Bible Voice, Inc. Used by permission from Mr. Boone.

LET'S DANCE

Let them praise his name with dancing and make music to him with timbrel and harp.

Psalm 149:3 NIV

As a little girl, I watched people "get happy" at church. They praised our Lord and Savior in the dance. They worshiped, they cried—wigs even flew off—and I always wondered what in the world made them act that way, until it happened to me. I was fourteen, having a stressful week of testing at school, and I prayed, "God, make it snow." It snowed, but school remained open.

I remember sitting in church that following Sunday, thanking God that I had received high marks on all of my assignments. The music started playing, my foot started tapping, and before I knew it, the Holy Spirit took over and I "got happy." It is an amazing thing to feel God and let him in. Let go, let him in, and always remember to dance.

Lord, I praise you with all my heart. I will be glad and rejoice in you. I will sing praise to your name.

Melinda D. Davis, Roses and Rainbows advisory board member, radio network executive

UNPACK YOUR BURDEN

"Come to me, all of you who are weary and carry heavy burdens, and I will give you rest."

MATTHEW 11:28 NLT

We each carry something we call burdens, don't we? What burden are you dealing with today? Is there a secret deep in your heart that you wish wasn't there? Burdens and hurts are quite clever, aren't they? They fight back hard when you try to step out of your comfort zone, trying to convince you it's safer to keep everything hidden inside.

Friend, there can be many reasons you struggle with the decision to be vulnerable. But when you choose to share a hurt or a burden that you've been carrying, you are set free from the shame of that burden. The Bible tells us that in this world we will experience trials and troubles. That includes our burdens. I want you to always remember that God has already overcome your burdens and all he asks is that you be willing to open your heart and release them. Practice discernment today. Listen to who's speaking to you. If God is asking you to take heart and step out of your hurt today, then take courage and do it. I promise you won't regret it!

Lord, give us each the courage to reveal and release the burdens on our hearts.

Kim Crabill, TV host, author, ministry leader, Christian counselor

ONE STEP

I am convinced that nothing can ever separate us from God's love which Christ Jesus our Lord shows us.

ROMANS 8:38 GW

Her lips trembled as she slowly recounted her past seven years of running from the Lord: the drugs, the alcohol, the one-night stands, and the lying and cheating to escape from one broken situation after another. She had even changed her name to hide from those who loved her. "I was raised in a Christian home, and I messed up way too bad," she said. "I could never be forgiven. My family will never want to see me again after all that I put them through."

My heart broke as I listened to this new friend's story. "Oh, honey," I said, "we've all sinned and fallen short. We're all guilty of things that we would classify as unforgivable. But God! No matter how far we've fallen, God still loves us. No matter how far we've drifted away, God is ready to forgive us. He is our Redeemer. We just have to stop running, turn to him, and repent. Always remember that he is waiting for you. Just take the first step."

Heavenly Father, thank you that no matter how far I run from you, it is always just one step back to your loving, forgiving arms.

Candace Kirkpatrick, actor, speaker, talk show cohost

TOUGH QUESTIONS

"I Am Who I Am. This is what you are to say…
I Am has sent me to you."

Exodus 3:14 NIV

Are you searching for a response to someone's tough question this morning? You just don't have all the answers. Well, then, friend, you're not alone. Everyone who strives to do God's work will deal with this at one time or another. Moses had questions when God called him back to Egypt. In Exodus 3, he battled the "what ifs" of his calling. *Suppose they ask me this question or that? What shall I tell them?*

We ask God those same questions, don't we? As you live out your calling today, I hope you'll always remember that God chose you because you have a passion for what he's called you to do, not because you have all the answers. Shift your thinking from what you don't know and focus on what you do know. You serve a God who has an answer to every question imaginable. Step into this day with confidence. God began a good work in you. He will take you and your questions all the way to the finish line.

Lord, how wonderful it is to know you'll provide every answer I need.

Kim Crabill, TV host, author, ministry leader,
Christian counselor

WHAT'S EATING YOU?

"Then you will know the truth, and the truth will set you free."

John 8:32 NIV

Today, are you carrying an invisible bag filled with secrets? What's in there that is eating at you? Is it a hurt from long ago? A tragedy you suffered that led to an addiction? A deep disappointment brought on by unkept promises or smashed-up dreams? No matter how hard you try to pretty up the bag, your secrets still weigh the same, don't they? They eat at you no matter how cleverly you try to deny their existence. Like pesky rodents, they nibble at your confidence and destroy your peace.

Whatever secrets you carry today, bring them out into the light. Jesus promises that if you do, he will set you free. Always remember that freedom is found only in facing the truth. Don't hide behind a busy life or the happy little smile you try so hard to keep in place. Let the miracle of revealing your truth to Jesus and others set you free.

Lord, give me the courage I need to empty my bags of secrets and allow you to set me free.

Kim Crabill, TV host, author, ministry leader,
Christian counselor

WHEN GOD IS SILENT

May our God come and not keep silent.

PSALM 50:3 AMP

Does God seem as distant as the farthest star to you? No matter how many prayers you pray, the heavens are silent, leaving you bruised and confused, wondering what you did wrong. You might be tempted to think that it is somehow your fault or worry that you have offended God or displeased him. I understand because I've been there too.

But let's consider Job for a minute. The Bible says he was a blameless man, and yet, when he cried out to God in his greatest suffering, God was absolutely silent. Had Job done anything to deserve the silence? Not a thing. If God is silent in your life today, my friend, I beg you not to become discouraged. Always remember that his silence doesn't mean he is absent. Hold tightly to your faith. The day came when God answered Job, showing him just how present he'd been all along. You, too, will eventually hear his voice again, and with it will come a relationship that is more intimate than ever before.

Lord, give me a faith strong enough to stand firm in times of testing and silence.

Esther Carpenter, author

NO WAY OUT

"The Lord will fight for you; you need only to be still."

Exodus 14:14 NIV

Moses and the children of Israel stood before the Red Sea, Pharoah's army close behind. They were terrified of the water before them and the enemy behind them. Death was imminent. What were they going to do? Can you relate? Do you feel caught between a rock and a hard place today?

Your physical life may not be in jeopardy, but what about the deadline that's closing in on you, when you are behind? Maybe the past-due bills are piling up, but you lack steady work. You cry to the heavens because, no matter which way you turn, you see no way out. My friend, always remember that God is fighting for you. You may not see a way out, but God has it under control. Like Israel, you need only to be still before him. Trust in the fact that he always keeps his promise. He will fight for you.

Lord, thank you for promising to fight my battles as I trust you to provide what I need.

Kim Crabill, TV host, author, ministry leader, Christian counselor

WHEN WORRY COMES CALLING

"Do not worry about your life."

MATTHEW 6:25 NIV

Some days my mind is bombarded with a million little worries, and I start wandering down the road of "What if?" *What if I don't pass the test? What if I don't get the pay raise? What if the diagnosis is bad?* I'm sure you know what I'm talking about. We all worry about things we can't control. What makes this struggle complicated is that so many times we feel guilty for worrying because, you know, worry is a sin. But here is a secret I want you to always remember: God knows we will worry about our world, our children, and our grandchildren, so he provided a better way for us.

Jesus told us not to be anxious because he has a remedy in place, and it is simply to bring every worry to him in prayer, petitioning his help for what concerns us. Beyond that, he only asks one other thing: that we present our petitions with thanksgiving. This is brilliant because when we start thanking him, our worry melts away in the presence of gratitude.

Lord, in your gentle way, remind me to replace worry with gratitude.

Kim Crabill, TV host, author, ministry leader, Christian counselor

NOT YOUR BATTLE

"You will not need to fight in this battle. Position yourselves, stand still and see the salvation of the LORD."

2 CHRONICLES 20:17 NKJV

There will be days when you feel under attack and overwhelmed by life's circumstances. Stop, take a deep breath, and remember that every breath and battle belongs to the Lord. He truly does care about you and every detail of your life. None of your battles is too small or too large for God to handle. The story found in 2 Chronicles 20 is a fascinating testimony of God's intervention and power when his people respond properly to overwhelming circumstances. Consider the response of King Jehoshaphat and the people of Judah when a vast enemy army was approaching them:

- The king proclaimed a fast.
- The king prayed, confessing Judah's need for God's help.
- The people worshiped and praised the Lord.
- The king appointed men to sing and praise the Lord as they went to face the enemy.

God destroyed the enemy before their eyes. Always remember that God is with you, too. Pray for his intervention and praise him for what he will do.

Father, I give you my stress and anxiety over circumstances. You have never lost a battle, and you won't start now.

Carmen Pate, Roses and Rainbows advisory board member, author, speaker, Bible teacher, mentor of women

NOT ENOUGH

You are altogether beautiful, my darling;
there is no flaw in you.

Song of Solomon 4:7 NIV

The little seagull was broken, one leg entirely gone. While other gulls stalked around on two good legs, he hopped about on only one. He was different—a misfit. Do you ever feel like the gimpy-legged seagull? Do you hear voices from your past (or maybe your present)? *You are my friend, but certainly not my best friend. You sure don't have a talent for that. Who told you that you could accomplish that?* Each statement validates what you already know. You are different. Less than. Not enough.

Friend, I want you to always remember that this is not the way God sees you. Listen to the words he speaks over you: "Fear not, for I have redeemed you; I have called you by name, you are mine....you are precious in my eyes, and honored, and I love you" (Isaiah 43:1, 4 ESV). Lift your head and allow the truth to heal your wounds. God wants you to live in the knowledge that you are not handicapped at all. In his eyes, you are beautiful and whole.

Lord, thank you that no matter my imperfections, in your eyes I am beautiful and whole.

Kim Crabill, TV host, author, ministry leader,
Christian counselor

HEARTS ON FIRE

"Go and make disciples of all nations, baptizing them in the name of the Father and of the Son and of the Holy Spirit."

MATTHEW 28:19 NIV

What's my purpose? I spent many years worrying and obsessing over that question. Something was missing, but I couldn't figure out exactly what. Maybe a career move, new skill, or big vacation to a foreign country would spice things up. I took piano lessons, I read books, I visited new restaurants. Sometimes I sat blithely at mundane jobs, just waiting for the weekend, for retirement, for things to get better. I was missing the bigger picture. Once my heart was set on fire to make disciples, I was changed forever.

Evangelism is not a calendar appointment. You can do it anytime and anywhere, bringing purpose and meaning to the mundane of life. The Holy Spirit and your unique testimony are powerful. Always remember to bring the gospel into every day and watch it change lives.

Dear Lord, please give me boldness to share your lifesaving truth with others.

Melissa Huray, author, podcast host

BE A SPONGE

"Have faith in me, and you will have life-giving water flowing from deep inside you."

John 7:38 CEV

Does your life resemble a dried-out sponge? Has your energy and zest for life been leaking away little by little until all that is left is a hard, flat, unrecognizable object? I have good news for you: A dried-up sponge is revived almost instantly when placed in a basin of water. And you are just like that sponge. Jesus promises the water of life to every dried-up soul that comes to him. He won't revive you with a basin of water or a lovely bubble bath but with the spring of eternal life that wells up from within you.

So if you are feeling dry and lifeless today, ask Jesus to rehydrate you with the water of life. And always remember that no hot spring or artesian well on earth can revive your soul like time spent in Jesus' presence will. Draw close to him, accepting the relationship and eternal life that he offers you. You can be revived and refilled with life today.

Thank you, Father, for the water of life that revives and renews me today.

Kim Crabill, TV host, author, ministry leader, Christian counselor

BREAK FREE

He chose us in him before the creation of the world to be holy and blameless in his sight.

EPHESIANS 1:4 NIV

Have you ever noticed how circus elephants are kept from galloping off? They're kept in place with itty-bitty bicycle chains around their legs! How can such a scrawny chain control such a brawny animal? The elephant is "locked up" by memory. As a baby, he tried to break loose but wasn't strong enough. Burned into the elephant's brain was that the chain was stronger than he was…and he hasn't forgotten that. The grown elephant could escape easily but rarely tries.

Do you wonder why many kids grow up with a warped sense of their worth and a twisted sense of their true identity? Parents, teachers, the media, and others pummel them with the idea that their identity is defined by looks, performance, or success. Even now, you might still be chained by that idea. But God wants to set you free—and his truth is stronger than any chain. Always remember, God says, *You are my child. You are chosen. You are bigger than the chains that bind you!*

Thank you, God, for making me your child. Help me let go of the voices keeping me chained.[16]

Josh McDowell and Kevin Johnson

---

16 Excerpted from *The One Year Book of Josh McDowell's Family Devotions 2* coauthored by Josh McDowell and Kevin Johnson with permission of Tyndale House Publishers.

WORDLESS PRAYERS

We do not know what we ought to pray for, but the Spirit himself intercedes for us.

ROMANS 8:26 NIV

How is your prayer life today? Are the words bubbling up from a full heart, spilling over in praise and joyful song? Or is your spirit heavy with confusion, deep longing, or distress? Are you having trouble coming up with the right words? Your problem is not a new one. When the Roman believers struggled with an anguish too deep for words, the apostle Paul reminded them that the Holy Spirit was able to deliver their prayers to the Father on their behalf. He does the same for us today.

Isn't it a comfort to know that whether you have joyful words or none at all, God's Spirit knows exactly what message to bring to the Father? Always remember that you demonstrate a powerful message of trust every time you pray, especially when you don't have words. Don't let your silent lips stop you from bringing your trouble to God. He understands a mute voice, and he loves the heart that wants to be with him.

Lord, thank you for the Spirit who is continually working on my behalf.

Kim Crabill, TV host, author, ministry leader, Christian counselor

BOLD WORDS

"The LORD himself goes before you and will be with you; he will never leave you nor forsake you."

DEUTERONOMY 31:8 NIV

Cue the big smile: "I'm doing just fine, thanks!" I'd been saying it to myself for weeks, and to others kind enough to ask. I was in a particularly hard season—one I never imagined, but one I created with a life-changing decision. I was standing in church, where I hadn't been in a very long time. A friend who knew my situation smiled and asked, "How are you doing?" I gave the usual answer, this time adding, "I've got a lot of friends I can count on."

My wise friend looked me straight in the eyes and said, "Susan, those friends are here for now, and they do care. Eventually, though, they will leave you. Jesus is also here, and he is someone you can count on. Always remember that he will be with you. He will never leave you." I will never forget my friend's confidence and conviction as she spoke those bold words. I am thankful that I now have that same bold confidence as Christ lives in my life, allowing me to tell others to always remember his presence.

Father, fill my heart with boldness to speak your truth to those who need to hear it.

Susan Young, educator, speaker, writer

EVER LEARNING

Teach me good judgment and knowledge.

Psalm 119:66 ESV

I love to garden. I love indoor plants, vegetable gardens, and flower beds. But just because I love plants doesn't mean I know how to care for them. In fact, my husband used to say that when I would buy a plant it was like putting it on death row! I'm not sure why my plants died. Didn't I water them enough? Did I give them too much fertilizer? Quite possibly, I just loved them to death.

If you also struggle today with something you can't do well but wish you could—gardening, playing the piano, finishing a degree—always remember you have a God to turn to for help. He loves to teach you what you need to know. He will always equip you with all you need to accomplish the thing he has laid on your heart. So don't give up. I still can't say I have a green thumb, but today my plants are surviving. With God's help, you, too, will thrive!

Lord, I lift to you the desires of my heart, asking you to replace my lack with your ability.

Kim Crabill, TV host, author, ministry leader,
Christian counselor

BE THE LIGHT

Arise, my people! Let your light shine for all the nations to see! For the glory of the Lord is streaming from you.

Isaiah 60:1 TLB

When I was in high school, a boy who was legally blind told me that he wondered what the world would be like if he wasn't in it. This boy was very bright academically, but he didn't have many friends. Loneliness and literal darkness filled most of his days. I will never know why he confessed this thought out loud to me specifically, but I have a feeling that it was because my parents raised me knowing Christ and to treat other people with kindness, no matter what.

To this day, it brings me sadness to think that he was so lacking in real friendship that he chose to disclose his darkest thought to a mere acquaintance. I reported my concern to a trusted guidance counselor, who later thanked me and disclosed that he was getting help for undiagnosed depression. You never know who is in darkness and needs the light of Christ through you. Always remember to shine brightly.

Light of the World, help me shine without fear and bring your glory to those lost in darkness due to hardship, grief, and trauma.

Maggie Winzeler, women's wellness writer, business owner

WHICH MEDICINE?

Why am I discouraged? Why is my heart so sad? I will put my hope in God!

PSALM 43:5 NLT

How many times have you tried to soothe your broken heart by eating junk food? The trip got canceled, the promotion went to someone else, or the relationship ended badly, so you try to alleviate your sorrow with your favorite comfort food and an all-night movie marathon. But junk food and binge-watching are temporary fixes. What about after the food is gone? Do you turn to your Father for healing or pull back because he didn't work things out for you?

Disappointment and heartbreak are as old as our world. Sarah couldn't conceive. Leah was forced into a loveless marriage. Job lost ten children. My friend, always remember that every event of your life, both good and bad, is screened by God before it reaches you. Each has a purpose. Instead of medicating yourself with physical distractions, open your Bible and find hope in the promises of God. He will meet you there, and you'll feel a reconnection to the love and purpose he has waiting for you.

Lord, give me faith to trust your heart when I don't understand your ways.

Kim Crabill, TV host, author, ministry leader, Christian counselor

KNOW YOUR MISSION

"We must obey God rather than human beings!"

ACTS 5:29 NIV

Remember those days in grade school when you and your friends dared each other to do something dangerous or stupid? You wanted so badly to prove who you were that it overrode your common sense. Do you still feel caught in that tension today? If so, what can you do about it? Jesus shows us the answer. Before beginning his ministry, he spent forty days fasting in the wilderness, and he became very hungry. Then Satan showed up, daring him to turn stones into bread. Jesus was caught in the tension of proving who he is or sticking with God's plan. Because he knew his mission, he said no to the devil's temptations.

As human beings, we all struggle with insecurity. But when you know who you belong to and what your calling is, you'll find the need to prove yourself diminishing. There will still be days when you desire validation, but always remember to follow Jesus' example and resist temptation. You have nothing to prove. You belong to the God of heaven, and his approval is all you need.

Lord, help me to stay focused on you so I don't fall prey to desiring this world's validation.

Kim Crabill, TV host, author, ministry leader, Christian counselor

SWEET CORRECTION

The Lord disciplines the one he loves.

Hebrews 12:6 NIV

I bowed my head to express my noble-sounding prayer: "Lord, send me to the nations so I can lead people to worship you." Nothing could have been further from the truth in my heart. I felt the Lord speak to me: *You want people to love you, but you have no desire to love them back.* He was right. I had dressed up my selfish heart in things that looked like worship when in reality, I wanted to *be* worshiped. I was wrecked by this truth. I knew I needed to change.

That day I learned that God's correction is sweet, at times painful, but also necessary and a protection over our lives. I repented and told him that I wanted to desire him more than fame. I asked him to heal my insecurities and my need to find significance apart from him. Always remember, true significance and confidence must be rooted in him.

Lord, may I desire you more than anything this world has to offer.

Myshel Wilkins, speaker, worship leader, recording artist

YOU'RE JUST THIRSTY

As a deer thirsts for streams of water,
so I thirst for you, God.

PSALM 42:1 NCV

Do you wish that you were more righteous? That you knew more about God or had done more for him? Do you feel insignificant? Do you worry you have procrastinated to the point that you've missed what God had for you? My friend, let me share with you a truth that will help you identify what you're feeling. The Bible tells us that we thirst after righteousness. The longing inside you that wants more, to be more, is your heart letting you know that you are thirsting for more of God.

Your desire to be more like him and to know him better is your soul's way of crying out for the living water. Always remember that this feeling is not trying to make you lose heart. It's there to inspire you to be more than you could ever imagine. So why not transform that thinking a little? Don't let the negative seep in. Instead, accept the potential that lies before you. Jesus is ready to take you to more.

Lord, thank you for putting a thirst for more of you in my soul.

Kim Crabill, TV host, author, ministry leader,
Christian counselor

UNSHAKABLE

He will sift out everything without solid foundations so that only unshakable things will be left.

HEBREWS 12:27 TLB

There was a time in my life when my closest relationships were getting shaken. I couldn't understand what was happening and felt betrayed, misunderstood, and alone. Yet moving through this challenging time ultimately led me to a deeper understanding of, and relationship with, the one who would never leave me or forsake me. Only by this temporal experience did I come to fully realize what I have eternally in Jesus.

Through any disappointment or grief that we don't think we can bear, Jesus will always be there, helping us through, loving us, protecting us, and ultimately transforming us into his image. These are just some of his many beautiful promises to us. Always remember that when you build your life on God's principles and trust in him, you will surely endure.

Heavenly Father, I trust that you work all things together for my good. Thank you for pruning my life so I can experience your abundant, unshakable kingdom.

Gianna Simone, actor, author, producer

WHO'S IN FIRST PLACE?

"I have treasured the words of his mouth
more than my daily bread."

JOB 23:12 NIV

Do you feel like you are pulled in all directions today—bombarded with people and projects, each demanding immediate attention? I've learned that when I am the busiest, that's when I most need to stop and reexamine my priorities. Am I focused on what *seems* important but missing what I truly need? Jesus' friend Martha had a problem with priorities. She was so busy serving Jesus that she missed out on being with him (Luke 10:38–42).

If you find yourself pulled in too many directions today, you may want to stop and take inventory of your schedule. The work you are doing for God is important, but always remember that he never gives you a schedule so busy that you don't have time to spend with him. Sitting at his feet is the one thing in your life that is truly necessary. Make sure to include him in your daily schedule. I promise you'll be glad you did.

Lord, help me never to be so busy that I neglect spending time with you.

Kim Crabill, TV host, author, ministry leader,
Christian counselor

WHATEVER

Whatever is true, whatever is noble, whatever is right, whatever is pure, whatever is lovely, whatever is admirable—if anything is excellent or praiseworthy—think about such things.

PHILIPPIANS 4:8 NIV

Whatever. You can hear the sarcastic tone in this word that originally meant a lack of restriction (have whatever you want!) and now expresses a lack of enthusiasm ("Sure, OK, whatever"). Since sin starts with a thought—a consideration of various choices—the apostle Paul's "whatever" was more of a cautionary tale than a throwaway word. Always remember: when our minds are centered on God and his goodness, it's easier to steer clear of mental pitfalls that produce sinful choices.

So much of our modern media is a battle for our minds. We must literally guard our minds against all manner of attack! The next time boredom or anger or helplessness give rise to a "whatever" thought, meditate on things that are pure, productive, and good. Don't give sin an invitation into your mind.

Lord, I give my mind to you. Help me to fill it with constructive and faith-building thoughts.[17]

Pat Boone, actor, singer, songwriter, author

---

17 Adapted from *Pat Boone Devotional Book*, published by Bible Voice, Inc. Used by permission from Mr. Boone.

SO MANY DREAMS

"As the heavens are higher than the earth, my thoughts and my ways are higher than yours."

ISAIAH 55:9 CEV

You had so many dreams, didn't you? There was much more to discover. Maybe you wanted to see the world. Experience cultures and climates and nature's beauty. Or maybe your dreams were internal, like unpacking the yet-to-be-discovered potential inside of you, gaining greater confidence, or finding a place to belong and make a difference in the world. But your dreams remain out of reach, and you are starting to lose hope. Should you bury them and just settle for what's easily attainable?

My friend, what if there is another way of looking at unrealized dreams? You know, they could be God's whispered invitation to look beyond your own small dreams to his ultimate dream for you. I want you to always remember that no matter whether you are in a place of struggle or want of success, God invites you to a place of more abundance. You don't need to stop dreaming but surrender yourself to God's dream for you. It is bound to be bigger and better than any of the small dreams you long for now.

Lord, help me to surrender my small dreams in anticipation of your ultimate dream for me.

Kim Crabill, TV host, author, ministry leader, Christian counselor

THE PRAYER CHAIR

Pray without ceasing.

1 Thessalonians 5:17 NASB

I recall the days as a believer when I didn't pray regularly. I lived as I wanted, not asking God what he wanted. But stuck in my memory was the image of my mother, sitting in her wingback chair, praying and reading her Bible every day. She gave me a wonderful example to follow, but I was too busy to pray daily and listen to God's voice.

Only by walking through some difficulties did I come to a point when I began to listen and not jump ahead of God. I have had my own prayer chair for years. Though not a wingback chair like my mother's, it's a special place to pray. As I listen, God speaks to my heart to step out and do as he directs me. What a blessing to live our lives directed by our Lord Jesus. I will always remember my mother's example to keep listening.

Heavenly Father, I come humbly before you today, recognizing that I am a sinner when I go my own way. My desire is to listen, hear from you, and go your way.

Suellen Roberts, media influencer

HEAVENLY SHADE

The LORD is your shade at your right hand.

PSALM 121:5 NIV

When the summer sun is relentlessly baking everything it touches, the shady spot beneath the canopy of leaves becomes very inviting, doesn't it? Well, friend, God promises an even better kind of shade for you from the relentless troubles and demands of life.

When you are tired spiritually or worn to a frazzle emotionally, always remember that your heavenly Father is waiting for you to join him in the shade of his presence. He wants to revive you from the exhausting pressures of the world. Pick up your Bible and spend a few minutes alone with him. Let his words soothe your soul and remind you of the strength, protection, redemption, and love that are yours as his child. Rest well, my friend. The longer you stay, the better you'll feel.

Lord, thank you for reviving my soul as I rest in the shade of your presence.

Kim Crabill, TV host, author, ministry leader, Christian counselor

REGARDING THE IMPOSSIBLE

"I am the LORD, the God over every creature. Is anything too difficult for me?"

JEREMIAH 32:27 CSB

Do you struggle to believe that God can save someone like you? Maybe you have never surrendered your life to God because you can't see how he would want you after all you have done to defy him. Or could it be that you would like to accept his offer, but it is just too hard to let go of that "one thing" you know he will ask of you? Maybe you feel you have failed him too often. "There is no hope for me," you say, and you walk away in defeat.

If this is you, I want you to always remember that what looks impossible to you is totally possible with God, and he has promised that he will save everyone who comes to him, imperfect as we are. Isn't that the most encouraging promise? And my precious friend, it is yours to claim for all eternity if you choose Jesus today. Choosing him is the best decision you will ever make, so receive him and watch him do the impossible in your life. I promise you won't regret your decision!

Lord, help me understand that salvation is a gift, freely offered to all and made possible only through you.

Kim Crabill, TV host, author, ministry leader, Christian counselor

UNCHANGING IN THE CHANGEABLE

"My peace I give you."

John 14:27 NIV

What does Jesus mean when he tells us he has given us his peace? So many things in life disturb us—things in the world around us and things going on inside us. The future is uncertain, and the world makes sure we know that. It offers its own kind of peace in material things, but we know from experience that no amount of money, possessions, fame, or power will ever bring peace. Worry and stress, yes. Peace, no. So how is God's peace different?

Well, as a believer, your life is one with Jesus, and the spiritual gifts he offers are solid and eternal. He promises the true joy of salvation, real faith to win your spiritual battles, and a peace that assures you he is in control no matter what is happening in the world around you. Always remember that since the moment you first believed in Christ, he became your source of peace. He is your hope in happy times and troubled ones. Cling to who you are in Christ and enjoy all the benefits of being a child of God.

Lord, thank you for a peace that isn't dictated by an ever-changing world.

Kim Crabill, TV host, author, ministry leader,
Christian counselor

August

TRAILBLAZERS

In humility value others above yourselves.

PHILIPPIANS 2:3 NIV

I admire so many people who have influenced our culture for the Lord—true trailblazers. Some of my favorite role models are Corrie ten Boom, Edith Schaeffer, Harriet Tubman, Amy Carmichael, and Mother Teresa. I think of the hardships they endured and how they trusted God and stayed faithful to him. They are great examples of weathering the storms of life while accomplishing so much.

When faced with a project I feel unable to accomplish, I think about how these people had far fewer resources than I have today. Yet they prayed and moved forward, trusting in God, taking the steps he asked. Then they gave God the glory. My desire, too, is to hear from God and step out into the unknown, trusting him for all I need. I have seen God work wonders! I believe the saints who have gone before us knew the importance of having a servant's heart, and that is key for all of us. I want to always remember to be humble and serve others just as Jesus did.

Heavenly Father, I am grateful for the godly examples you set before me. May I serve others all of my days.

Suellen Roberts, media influencer

RIGHT ON TIME

It is God who is working in you both to will and to work according to his good purpose.

PHILIPPIANS 2:13 CSB

Growing. Maturing. Being prepared for God's work. That is where you are, right now. Yes, God is using you in a fabulous, very meaningful way even now, but there is so much more in store for you. I want you to always remember that God is using three things to help you get to that ultimate plan.

First, he is going to use where you are today. You may not like it, but right now you are where you are supposed to be. Secondly, he is using the people around you. They may even be people who irritate you a little bit or people who inspire you. Whoever it is, be engaged and get to know them. They hold something that is a part of your growth process. Then finally, just remember the progression. God has a precise timetable, and you are right on time for whatever you're supposed to be doing. Let God use the place where you are and the people around you as you move into the mighty plan he's already declared for your life.

Lord, thank you for loving me and using me as part of your great plan and purpose on this earth.

Kim Crabill, TV host, author, ministry leader,
Christian counselor

A GREATER GOOD

Those who hope in the LORD will renew their strength.

ISAIAH 40:31 NIV

So many people are dealing with pain today. For some, it is a physical pain that is residual, an ongoing part of daily life. For others, the pain is internal—a mental or emotional suffering that isn't easily identified. Maybe this is you today, wondering why God allows you to suffer as you are. You might feel you aren't nearly as useful to God in your present state as you would be if the pain were alleviated or removed altogether. Frustration sets in, and you question why, if he loves you, does he allow such suffering?

Oh, my precious friend, I want to assure you that God takes no pleasure in your pain, but he also knows that it is not wasted. Always remember that your spiritual health and well-being are his number one priority. Your physical or emotional discomfort may be the very thing that God is using to make you spiritually strong. Find hope and peace today in knowing that even though you may not understand his work in your life, you can trust him.

Father God, grant each suffering soul a gracious portion of your sustaining power today.

Kim Crabill, TV host, author, ministry leader, Christian counselor

WORTH THE WAIT

"What no eye has seen, what no ear has heard, and what no human mind has conceived"—the things God has prepared for those who love him.

1 Corinthians 2:9 NIV

The pastor was only a few minutes into his sermon. My boyfriend checked his watch, not for the first time. I knew he wanted to be anywhere but in church, but I thought, *Well, at least he's willing to come with me. Maybe I should just say yes to his proposal.* Then I heard very softly, *Why would you settle for less than what I have prepared for you?* I looked over my shoulder to see who was talking to me. No one.

Again, I heard this gentle voice ask the same question. This time I knew it was the Lord. He continued: *Always remember that every good and perfect gift comes from me. I can do abundantly more than all you can ask or imagine. Why sell yourself short?* I ended the relationship that day and became open to God's plan, knowing that he wanted to fill me to overflowing with all that he is.

Father, never allow me to trade your timing for my deadline. Your plan is worth the wait.

Candace Kirkpatrick has been happily married for 28 years.

CELEBRATING OTHERS

Each one should test their own actions....without comparing themselves to someone else.

GALATIANS 6:4 NIV

In today's world, it's easy to fall into the trap of comparing ourselves to others and competing for success, but if we're not careful, we'll lose sight of the unique purpose God has for us. When we measure our worth based on others' achievements, we are bound to fall short of the person God created us to be. One biblical example of the danger of comparison and competition is the story of King Saul and David in 1 Samuel. Saul's jealousy and insecurity caused him to view David as a rival, ultimately leading to Saul's downfall. Instead of embracing David's gifts and God's plan for him, Saul allowed comparison to consume him.

The Bible assures us that God has a specific plan and purpose for each of us. We are "fearfully and wonderfully made" in his image (Psalm 139:14). Today, let's celebrate the successes of others without letting comparison and competition hinder our journey. I hope you always remember that God's unique plan and calling for you is perfect. You can trust in his timing and purpose for your life.

God, help me resist the temptation to compare myself to others. Give me the strength to walk confidently in the unique path you have for me.

Kim Crabill, TV host, author, ministry leader, Christian counselor

RECIPE FOR THANKFULNESS

Always giving thanks to God the Father for everything, in the name of our Lord Jesus Christ.

EPHESIANS 5:20 NIV

Do praise and thankfulness flow easily from your tongue, or do you have trouble finding much to be thankful for today? Maybe recent events have caused you more tears than smiles. Disappointment cripples your ability to see beauty. This was the case with Mary and Martha at the tomb of Lazarus. Jesus was late in coming, and the sisters spewed their disappointment. But Jesus answered them, "Your brother will live again....Didn't I tell you that if you had faith, you would see the glory of God?" (John 11:23, 40 CEV).

The secret to unleashing God's power begins with believing, but Jesus does something else to bring life in the face of disappointment and death. Jesus raised his eyes and said, "Father, I thank you for answering my prayer" (v. 41 CEV). First, he looked up, and then he gave thanks. If you struggle to find reasons for thankfulness today, I want you to always remember to do as Jesus did. If nothing else, you can look up today and be thankful that God hears you. Proclaim your thanksgiving to God and then watch him unleash his miracle-working power in your life.

Lord, give me a heart that chooses thankfulness in every situation.

Kim Crabill, TV host, author, ministry leader,
Christian counselor

THE BUILDER

Unless the LORD builds the house, its builders labor in vain.

PSALM 127:1 NIV

This verse speaks to us about the condition of our hearts. Were we to take an inventory of our hearts, would it reveal that we are building with wisdom or with flesh and pride? One day, God spoke to me and said, *Charlene, the big is in the little, and the little is in the big*. God was reminding me that he desires a contrite heart, and that if I am basing my success on accolades, then I am being deceived.

What a powerful word from heaven! Let's always remember that God desires a humble heart. James 4:6 tells us that God resists the proud but gives grace to the humble. And John 3:30 reminds us that he must become greater, and we must become less. The big is in the little and the little is in the big.

Lord, please give me a revelation today about the condition of my heart. Let me hear your voice.

Charlene Baktamarian, ministry president, executive producer, TV host

THIS I KNOW

This I know: God is on my side.

PSALM 56:9 NLT

I can promise you there will be times in your life when you won't be able to figure things out. You may be there today. You don't know why God has you where you are or why he is moving you to a new place. Why did he take your job away and not provide another? Why did he take your child from you, or why did he give you a child with such severe disabilities that you feel overwhelmed by the responsibility?

I used to stare out the window and watch the wind blow, knowing in my soul that God was real but having no idea what he was doing. My friend, if you are grappling with this today, I'd like you to always remember to go back to what you do know. Job, when he lost children, health, and possessions, had no idea what God was doing. Though tormented by his circumstances, he chose to focus on what he knew, saying, "I know that my Redeemer lives." You may never understand the why of your situation, but go back and hold on to what you do know.

Lord, when life doesn't make sense, help me to remember what I know to be true in you.

Kim Crabill, TV host, author, ministry leader, Christian counselor

ABUNDANT LIFE

"The thief comes only to steal and kill and destroy; I have come that they may have life, and have it to the full."

John 10:10 NIV

"Mom, are you afraid of Satan?" my seven-year-old son asked me. "And should *I* be afraid of him?"

"You should not be afraid of Satan because you have the Holy Spirit living inside of you," I told him. "Satan should be more afraid of you!" I read John 10:10 to him and explained that while we must be watchful of Satan's schemes at all times, God has promised to be with us. He has our back, and he wants us to focus on *his* truth and promises. These conversations are important as they help prepare our children for battle.

The Bible tells us that demons tremble at the name of Jesus. I teach my son to say Jesus' name whenever he is feeling worried, stuck, or in fear of the enemy. When we focus on God's truth and promises, we can live the abundant life he has for us—a life that is rich in Christ.

Thank you, Father, that I can call upon the name of your Son, Jesus, the name above all other names.

Destiny Yarbrough, minister, executive TV producer, digital media producer

HIDE AND SEEK

You are my hiding place and my shield.

PSALM 119:114 NCV

What games did you like to play when you were little? My favorite was hide-and-seek. I could play for hours, thrilled at the chance to hide in a quiet place and wait for someone to find me. Even today, when the world is too brutal, I often need to find a quiet place and call an adult version of time-out for myself. What about you? Do you ever long for a time-out from the hurts and stresses of your world?

If so, I want you to know it is OK, even necessary, to hide in a secret place God has prepared for both of you, where you can share with him your frustrations, your worries, and your pain. No matter what emotions you are dealing with today, always remember to run to God's hiding place. In your lowest and your highest moments, seek his comfort for your sorrow, strength for your trials, light for your path, and hope in Christ Jesus. Stay long in that secret place, my friend!

Lord, thank you for providing a quiet place for my soul to rest in you.

Kim Crabill, TV host, author, ministry leader,
Christian counselor

THE BLUE DRESS

Be kind and compassionate to one another, forgiving each other, just as in Christ God forgave you.

EPHESIANS 4:32 NIV

I grew up in the Bronx. Initially, I entered middle school with excitement and curiosity, but before long, I faced the hardship of bullying. It started in the lunchroom when one girl began to call me names and sprayed mustard on my new blue dress. I loved that dress. I began to scream and even started hitting her. A fight broke out between us, and we were taken to the office of the dean, who called our parents.

I watched my dad's disappointment as he learned of what happened. He scolded me, but also asked the dean why the parents of the other girl weren't there. "No one showed up for her," the dean explained. My heart sank as the other girl cried and apologized to me. She told me how lucky I was to have a dad. Dad used that experience to teach me the importance of seeking to understand, and he reminded me to always remember to have compassion and forgive those who hurt me.

Lord, may your grace be with me for all of my days.

Melinda D. Davis, Roses and Rainbows advisory board member, radio network executive

CREATE A FOLLOWING

He has sent me to bind up the brokenhearted.

ISAIAH 61:1 NIV

Do you wish to be noticed today? Like your friend with thousands of followers on social media or your colleague who walks into the room and the crowd gravitates toward her? How do they do it? You wish you could be so popular. Well, my friend, you might never be that person or have their following, but did you know you can have a following of your own? Jesus will show you how.

Matthew 4 reports on the beginning of Jesus' earthly ministry. As he healed the sick and suffering, large crowds began to follow him. Healing and hope drew people to Jesus. So many people today are dealing with sins, hurts, and self-destructive behavior. Reach out to them even if you aren't sure how to start. Always remember that love and empathy are the best ways to touch someone with healing. Tell them your story of hope: what Jesus has done in your life. Use your testimony faithfully, and one day you may have the following you wish for.

Lord, help me to spread the message of hope and healing to others rather than thinking of myself.

Kim Crabill, TV host, author, ministry leader,
Christian counselor

WHAT NOW?

Trust in the LORD with all your heart
and lean not on your own understanding.

PROVERBS 3:5 NIV

I sat in my car crying hysterically as I watched the other young mothers take their toddlers into the women's fellowship. *Why me?* I repeated over and over again. *Why didn't they lose their children?* The Lord answered me in a calm voice: *This is not about you.* I was stunned. The Lord went on to explain to me that he does not revolve around my will, but I revolve around his. He makes all things work together for good, even the fires and loss of life. He wanted me to trust him.

Then he shared words of wisdom that changed my life forever. He went on to explain that *Why me?* is not the best question to ask because even if he told me, it wouldn't change a thing. He encouraged me to ask *What now?* because that would get me moving forward. I do this all of the time now. It works! Always remember to stand on the foundation that God's plans for you are good. His character doesn't change because your circumstance does. He is worthy of your trust.

When my world goes dark, help me trust you, the God of light. You will never leave nor forsake me.

Justina Page, author, speaker, actor

BAG THAT NEGATIVITY

We take captive every thought to make it obedient to Christ.

2 CORINTHIANS 10:5 NIV

How easy it is to assume the worst in life, right? You might hit a rough patch in marriage, and before long, you picture yourself divorced. Or you walk into a room, see a dismissive glance, and convince yourself that everyone in the room is talking about you. The trouble with negative thinking is that it gives us a false perception of life. Instead of seeing love, friendship, and beauty around us—which is, often, what actually exists—we allow our minds to imagine all sorts of horrible scenarios that bring us only a darker view of life.

If you are like me and sometimes fall into the trap of assuming the worst, I encourage you to do as Paul taught the people of Corinth. Take those rogue thoughts captive, bringing them into proper focus through Christ. Always remember that Jesus is willing to help you sort out your thoughts. He will give you the ability to replace the negativity with his promises. You are free to choose what you think about today. Choose the truth!

Lord, give me a heart that is willing to fight for truth and your promises.

Kim Crabill, TV host, author, ministry leader,
Christian counselor

WHAT CAN YOU HANDLE?

"Is anything too hard for the LORD?"

GENESIS 18:14 ESV

"God will not give you more than you can handle." What do you think, my friend? Is the statement true? Because I do not find this concept anywhere in Scripture. God does not promise that life will never be more than we can deal with, but what he does say is far better. There is a difference between us handling the situation and letting God handle it. When we try to handle things, it's bound to get messy. That's because we have a short-sighted vision and limited power to control events.

God, on the other hand, has no end of resources at his disposal, and he does promise that no matter what we face, he is in complete control. Nothing is too hard for him. No problem in your life is more than he can handle. Always remember that God is bigger than anything you are facing today. He is directing your path. He allows you to feel helpless, but he never wants you to feel hopeless. He just wants you to recognize your need for him. It draws you to his heart.

Lord, help me to remember on my darkest days that you are handling everything victoriously.

Kim Crabill, TV host, author, ministry leader, Christian counselor

LOVE POWER

God's love has been poured out into our hearts through the Holy Spirit, who has been given to us.

ROMANS 5:5 NIV

Is it easy for you to love everyone? Do you love the folks who treat you badly, the coworker who talks behind your back, the friend who takes advantage of you? Jesus teaches us to especially love those who persecute us—but he doesn't promise us that it's easy!

Remember, only Jesus has ever loved as Jesus loved. As he hung, dying, on the cross, his boundless love poured out toward the very ones who were crucifying him. "Father, forgive them, for they know not what they do" (Luke 23:34 ESV). The only source for this kind of love is Jesus' own Spirit. Is it any wonder he urges our hearts to be filled with this same Spirit? Jesus wouldn't command us to do something he didn't give us the power to do. Drink deeply of what Jesus gave freely and let him love the unlovable through you.

Jesus, my love is flawed and conditional. Please fill me with your Spirit and soften my heart toward others so that when I'm treated badly, I, too, might whisper, "Father, forgive them, for they know not what they do."[18]

Pat Boone, actor, singer, songwriter, author

18 Adapted from *Pat Boone Devotional Book*, published by Bible Voice, Inc. Used by permission from Mr. Boone.

THE BRICK WALL

"Don't worry about tomorrow, for tomorrow will bring its own worries. Today's trouble is enough for today."

MATTHEW 6:34 NLT

I often struggle with anxiety and easily feel overwhelmed. My people-pleasing leads me to say yes to too many things. I carry too much at once, and I stumble because the weight is too great for me alone.

I remember my godfather saying, "Always remember to look at life's problems like a brick wall that needs to be taken down. Don't let the wall intimidate you by looking at all the bricks at once, but address things one at a time, brick by brick." As with most of my godfather's wisdom, this was spiritually backed. God wants us to bring our bricks to him, and he will give us peace about which to address today. He doesn't want us to carry the load alone. He wants to remove our burdens and to give us rest. When I started prioritizing my bricks, I started to feel the anxiety fade. I focused on today's problems, giving them to the Lord and asking for discernment with every brick.

Father, teach me to seek you first each day so I can receive your peace.

Alisha Griffin, actor, model, blogger

BEST INVITATION EVER

Let him lead me to the banquet hall,
and let his banner over me be love.

SONG OF SOLOMON 2:4 NIV

It's exciting to receive an invitation in the mail, isn't it? Whether for birthday parties, weddings, business events, or church functions, invitations assure you there's a place for you at the event. Although some invitations may hold more meaning than others, each one sends a message that you are worthy. But what about the times you weren't invited? You expected to be, but when others started making plans, you found yourself on the outside looking in. It hurts. The sting of exclusion lasts long after the dinner party is over.

Well, my friend, there's one invitation extended to you today that's open for all time. Jesus invites you to come and follow him, to be one of his friends. The invitation also includes peace, rest, salvation, and an eternal destiny more beautiful than you can imagine. Always remember that no matter how many times you are not invited to earthly social functions, you can be assured that Jesus will always invite you. He has made you permanently worthy.

Lord, thank you for extending to me the best invitation ever.

Kim Crabill, TV host, author, ministry leader,
Christian counselor

MISSED MEALS

You prepare a table before me.

PSALM 23:5 NIV

We all have days when we think we are too busy to eat, right? Then suddenly we find ourselves feeling sluggish and irritable. That's when a good, hot meal can perk us up within minutes and prepare us to handle the rest of the day. Neglecting time with God is almost like missing a meal. God's Word is our spiritual food, and when we find ourselves frustrated and angry, we need to stop and ask ourselves, *Have I had my quiet time today?*

It's amazing how the presence of God can completely change our mood and attitude. One worship song or a few verses of Scripture can take us from the absolute worst mindset to a place of peace and joy. Friend, I hope you'll always remember to seek out intimate moments with the Lord. There you will learn to hear his voice clearly and receive his direction for your life. You are never too busy for that!

Lord, thank you for the blessing and honor of the quiet moments spent sitting at your table.

Kim Crabill, TV host, author, ministry leader, Christian counselor

CHOICES AND VOICES

"This is the way; walk in it."

ISAIAH 30:21 NIV

There are going to be times when you have no idea what to do. You will have many voices in your head, each trying to tell you what to do, how to do it, where to go, and more. Your friends and coworkers will have their opinions too. "Take this job. It has great benefits." "Don't move to that neighborhood. Too much crime." "Come to our church; it's the best."

Maybe you're in this situation now or maybe you just want to tuck this thought away for later. Either way, this is what I want you to always remember: when you don't know what to do, ask God to teach you his way. He promises wisdom to those who ask. Certainly, there will be times when you are not sure which decision is best. But you can depend on God: that he will lead you, teach you, and guide you in every step that you take.

Lord, thank you for the promise that you will always guide me in what to do when I ask.

Kim Crabill, TV host, author, ministry leader,
Christian counselor

DADDY'S SHOES

Yet I still belong to you;
you hold my right hand.

PSALM 73:23 NLT

When I was a child, I loved to step into my daddy's worn leather work boots and pretend I was big and strong like him. But my small feet were completely lost in their depths, and I was soon stumbling about, off-balance and breathless. I wasn't big enough or strong enough to walk in his boots. As adults, we sometimes do the same thing with God. When it appears that he is inactive, we try to help him out. Maybe you are dealing with this struggle today, wishing God would move on your behalf. It is tempting to try to slip into his shoes, but you weren't made to take over his work. Attempting to do so is exhausting and will accomplish nothing.

God would much rather have you give him your hand so that he can support and restore your spiritual balance. Whenever you feel frustrated and impatient, always remember that God has a reason for what you perceive as delayed action. Hold tight to the hand he offers, trust his timing, and let him wear the shoes!

Lord, help me to be patient in times of waiting and to hold tight to your hand every day.

Esther Carpenter, author

FACE THE SUNRISE

"Here on earth you will have many trials and sorrows. But take heart, because I have overcome the world."

John 16:33 NLT

Did you buy into the myth that accepting Christ means you will enjoy a problem-free existence? Are you now surveying your life and feeling a bit disillusioned and deceived? Well, my friend, that myth someone tried to sell you is just that: a myth. The truth is, when Jesus was on earth, he didn't sugarcoat anything. He spelled out exactly what to expect—that in this life, you will have troubles and trials. Peter said something similar when he told the early believers that after they'd suffered a while, then God would establish them, strong and steadfast (1 Peter 5:10).

If you're struggling with the trouble or sorrow of life today, always remember that you won't suffer forever. God is working out an eternal plan for you, one that is trouble-free. You have an everlasting relationship with Christ and eternal glory with him. Compared to eternity, your troubles here are only for a short time. Set your face toward the sunrise of a day when there is only eternal glory and joy. Keep on keeping on.

Lord, help me keep my sights on eternity while dealing with problems and sorrows down here.

Kim Crabill, TV host, author, ministry leader, Christian counselor

HEADS OR TAILS

I wait for the Lord, my whole being waits,
and in his word I put my hope.

PSALM 130:5 NIV

Have you ever been with friends who couldn't decide what to do until finally, someone dug out a coin and suggested, "Let's flip for it!" Well, just as there are two sides to a coin, the decisions you face have two choices. You can decide to do the thing that looks best to you, or you can do what God is asking you to do. Abraham gives us a good example of this. He was settled in Canaan, the promised land, until a drought hit, and his place of blessing became one of famine.

What do you do when you receive the opposite of what you expect from God? You move! At least that's what Abraham did. Rather than waiting on God, he left Canaan and traveled south to Egypt in search of something better. His physical move typified his spiritual one. Perhaps God has you in an unexpected place today and you are confused by it. If so, I hope you'll always remember that God is faithful to do what he says, but he works on his schedule and not yours. Be still before him, and you will make the right choice every time.

Lord, help me to remember to seek your face for the decisions I need to make.

Kim Crabill, TV host, author, ministry leader,
Christian counselor

NEVER EARNED, NEVER LOST

Nothing in all creation will ever be able to separate us from the love of God.

ROMANS 8:39 NLT

I was caught in a performance trap, always striving to earn God's acceptance. It was as though I had a spiritual checklist that had to be completed every week: read my Bible daily, check; pray morning, evening and at mealtime, check; don't miss church, check. You get the idea. These things are all good, but I felt that if I failed to do these so-called "spiritual" things, God might not accept me into his forever family.

When sharing my dilemma with a pastor and mentor, he said, "Always remember, Carmen, Christ's love can never be earned and can never be lost." Of course, this was not a new revelation, but for me it was like hearing truth for the first time. Now I serve the Lord out of joy and thankfulness for all he did for me on the cross and all he is doing through me now. I no longer serve out of duty and drudgery, worried if I have done enough. Oh, the freedom we have through God's grace and love!

Lord, thank you for accepting me by faith alone in Christ Jesus, and not by works.

Carmen Pate, Roses and Rainbows advisory board member, author, speaker, Bible teacher, mentor of women

PROMISE AND POSSIBILITY

We now have this light shining in our hearts, but we ourselves are like fragile clay jars containing this great treasure.

2 Corinthians 4:7 NLT

Do you ever sit in the middle of a mess you've created and wonder what it is that God sees in you? Well, my friend, the answer to that question is in the Word of God, and it should cheer you up because believe it or not, he sees a person of promise and possibilities, one you cannot begin to picture. I know that all you see are your flaws and faults, but throughout history, God has used imperfect people to be his showpieces of grace. Think of Moses the murderer, Peter the impetuous ear-chopper, and Gideon the fraidy-cat. Each of them had flaws that would have made God pass over them if he were looking for perfection.

God chooses you as you are right now, but he also sees you as his finished product. He knows the potential you have within you, and every day he chisels away a little at a time. You may not feel perfect today, but always remember that God sees your heart for him, and in that heart lies the possibility of a masterpiece.

Lord, thank you for taking me as a flawed human and turning me into a showpiece of grace.

Kim Crabill, TV host, author, ministry leader, Christian counselor

WHY WISDOM?

The fear of the Lord is the beginning of knowledge,
but fools despise wisdom and instruction.

Proverbs 1:7 NKJV

"You have wisdom beyond your years." My mom said it to me a thousand times. I was an adult in a kid's body, forced to handle too many grown-up situations. I didn't ask for wisdom. I'd have preferred stability—plus what every teen wants: trendy clothes, cash, a car. But Mom and marriage didn't work out too well. There was Bob, my dad Zeno, and finally David. She married David when I was in high school. They frequently traveled on business, leaving me home alone. The economy tanked, and the business and marriage crashed. After they separated, David staggered in drunk one night. I was just fifteen when I demanded that he leave for good.

Mom's phrase? I hated it then, but I hold it dear now! I'll always remember her words that commended my wisdom. I'd love to hear them from her just once more. Today I know that my life then prepared me for my life now. Back then, I wished I hadn't grown up so fast, but now I realize that wisdom is a sacred gift. Mom recognized it; God fertilized it; I've embraced it.

Dear Lord, fill me with your wisdom. Use my life story for your glory.

Beth Townsend, Christian television personality, author, speaker, life coach

THE CRUCIAL CHOICE

"'Love the Lord your God with all your heart and with all your soul and with all your mind.'"

MATTHEW 22:37 NIV

Have you ever wrestled long and hard over something you knew Jesus wanted you to give up? Some hard-earned savings to a needy family, perhaps, or an hour's worth of your valuable time? Maybe a relationship you knew wasn't God's plan for you? A rich young man in Jesus' day struggled with this problem. He was restless about his guarantee of eternal life and thought Jesus might have a solution. Jesus listened patiently, then went to the heart of his problem: "Sell all your possessions and give the money to the poor....then come, follow me" (Luke 18:22 NLT). The poor boy was heartbroken. Jesus had asked him to give up what he loved most, and instead of choosing Jesus, the young man walked away.

Is there anything you love more than Jesus? In your darkest hour, when you are counting the cost, I want you to always remember that nothing is worth more than your soul. Whatever Jesus asks of you is worth relinquishing to him. When you do, you will have a restful heart and riches beyond imagination stored away in heaven.

Lord, help me to put you first in my life, knowing that whatever the cost, it will be worth it.

Kim Crabill, TV host, author, ministry leader, Christian counselor

TUNNEL VISION

"Only I can tell you the future before it even happens. Everything I plan will come to pass, for I do whatever I wish."

Isaiah 46:10 NLT

Oh, God! What in the world are you doing? I mean, have you just left me here? Have you abandoned me like everyone else has? Are you angry with me too? Do any of these questions sound familiar? Have you ever felt so alone you wondered if even God himself had left you? I know I struggled with those questions, especially in my younger years. I felt like God was taking me through one dark tunnel after another with no light at the far ends.

The only thing I could do was trust who I knew God to be, believing he had a plan that was beyond what I could see. Friend, if this is you, I hope you will always remember that God's ways are best for you every time. He knows the end from the beginning and everything in between. When you don't understand what he is doing, just trust in who he is. Hang in there. One day it will all make sense.

Lord, help me to trust you to bring me safely through the darkness and back into the light.

Kim Crabill, TV host, author, ministry leader, Christian counselor

BE YOU

I am Your unique creation, filled with wonder and awe. You have approached even the smallest details with excellence.

Psalm 139:14 voice

I was getting ready to shoot a new movie called *Mother's Day*, directed by the renowned Garry Marshall. At the end of a video chat with Garry, I asked if he wanted to share anything else with me. He said, "Just be you!" He stressed the importance of how valuable my authenticity was. His words gave me a confidence that carried over to my performance and conveyed a valuable life lesson: God made us on purpose for a purpose.

We aren't one in a million or one in a billion—we are one in a forever! There's nobody like you, and God has a special purpose he intends for only you to fulfill. Not only is your existence meaningful to God, it is also meaningful to many others you encounter. To show up totally authentic takes profound courage and love. Always remember the unique, rare treasure you are and the love you have to offer to so many.

Heavenly Father, help me to see myself and others the way you see us and to grow in understanding your profound love for me. Please continue to bring into my path people whom I may edify, encourage, and love.

Gianna Simone, actor, author, producer

WHAT ARE YOU LOOKING AT?

"We do not know what to do, but our eyes are on you."

2 Chronicles 20:12 NIV

Are you facing a difficult battle today? Financial hardship maybe, or the loss of a loved one? A troubled relationship or a scheming coworker who is causing friction and keeping your stomach in knots? When I am feeling overwhelmed and powerless in the face of what's happening in my life, I like to remind myself of the story of Jehoshaphat from the Old Testament. One day he and his people came under attack from a much bigger, stronger army than he had. With no way of protecting his people, Jehoshaphat called on the Lord, saying, "We do not know what to do, but our eyes are on you."

My friend, when you have no idea what to do, follow Jehoshaphat's lead by focusing on God and waiting in confidence for him to act. Always remember that God promises victory for you. He has a plan in place. Your job is to trust him to work out the plan. Although waiting is not easy when a battle is raging, remember Jehoshaphat. Take your problem to God and let him fight for you.

Lord, help me keep my eyes on you every day and in every situation.

Kim Crabill, TV host, author, ministry leader, Christian counselor

FATHERLY LOVE

See what kind of love the Father has given to us, that we should be called children of God; and so we are.

1 John 3:1 ESV

When I was a child, my mother would send us to greet my father when he arrived home from work. He always gathered us in his arms with a big hug. I found myself as an adult still going to the door to greet him to enjoy the safe embrace of my daddy's hugs. Looking back, I marvel at how he never said, "I'm too tired." He managed to leave his day outside, making our family his focus.

The Bible verse above says that God not only loves us but he has also adopted us into his family, calling us his children. In relationship with my heavenly Father, do I truly believe I am his child? Do I run to him excited to be with him? Just as I ran to my earthly father, confident in his love, I want to always remember I can run to my heavenly Father, knowing he is never too tired or busy to care about my concerns. Take comfort in that kind of unconditional love by our heavenly Father.

Father, help me to always remember your unfailing, unconditional love for me.

Barbara Parker, women's ministry leader, educator, audiologist

September

LOST!

The heart is deceitful above all things and beyond cure.
Who can understand it?
"I the LORD search the heart and examine the mind."

JEREMIAH 17:9–10 NIV

Surely you've heard the endless debate about who gets lost more often, women or men. The conventional wisdom is that men are lost more often because of their unwillingness to ask for directions. But always remember that, male or female, we are spiritually like lost sheep unless we're tethered to Jesus.

Imagine a compass that points south rather than north. Sounds silly, but that's what the human heart is like when it hasn't been *redirected* from selfishness and sin. Scripture reminds us that "as [a man] thinketh in his heart, so is he" (Proverbs 23:7 KJV). So if our hearts are deceitful and misdirected, they're bound to lead us off course. That's why Proverbs 3:5 reminds us not to lean on our own understanding but to acknowledge God in all of our ways. God's Word is a surefire cure for whatever ails us—and a safeguard for all of us "lost" souls.

Lord, help me to pursue your will and your ways so that I'm protected from my own deceitfulness and wanderings.[19]

Pat Boone, actor, singer, songwriter, author

---

19 Adapted from *Pat Boone Devotional Book*, published by Bible Voice, Inc. Used by permission from Mr. Boone.

CRYING THE BLUES

Why are you down in the dumps, dear soul?
Why are you crying the blues?

PSALM 42:11 MSG

Psalm 42 describes a cycle of "crying the blues" and praising God. When I first encountered this in the Psalms I thought, *I expected the Holy Spirit to pick more stable people to write the Psalms. These psalmists have mood swings that could give a person whiplash.* Then I lived a bit longer and discovered that this cycle of blues and praise is real life.

I believe God inspired psalms of lament and put them in his Book as priceless reminders of what is true about our unruly longings, our chaotic circumstances, our dismay at the wickedness of this world (it will not endure), and about the rock-solidness of our God (he endures forever). When we always remember these most real realities, we will emerge from the blues with praise on our lips, as the psalmist did.

Thank you for preparing me through the Psalms for elation and dejection, boom and bust, tranquility and chaos. Help me keep my eyes on you no matter my circumstances.

Sue Kline, writer, editor, writing coach

RESULT OF A TESTIMONY

Because of his words many more became believers.

John 4:41 NIV

Is God asking you to be more vocal in your testimony? Do you have a stirring deep inside your soul to share some of the hurts you have walked through? Maybe you feel he is saying that by speaking up, you can be free from the shame, guilt, and regret that haunts your past. But you are hesitant. What will others think if they see the real you?

My friend, if God is urging you to share your story, then please be brave and share it. I know that being vulnerable can be very scary, especially when you aren't sure how others will receive your words. But always remember that God is with you in every part of your story, both the living and the telling of it. He will take the things that perhaps others meant for harm and use them for your good and for his glory (Genesis 50:20). He wants you to take the comfort you have received from him and use it to encourage and comfort someone else (2 Corinthians 1:3–4). Just think! Your story can be used to save others if you just choose to share it.

Lord, give me the courage to share my testimony and be a blessing to others.

Kim Crabill, TV host, author, ministry leader, Christian counselor

BLESSED ARE THE PEACEKEEPERS

"Blessed are the peacemakers,
for they will be called children of God."

MATTHEW 5:9 NIV

I did it again. I got caught in another late night of doom scrolling on social media, horrified at how mean some of my Christian sisters and brothers can be in comment sections. From experience, I know that trying to change a stranger's mind over the internet seldom works. The anonymity of digital media can bring out the worst in humanity, even in response to compassionate language and thoughtful viewpoints from Scripture or lived experiences.

Jesus reminds me daily that my job isn't to change the world's mind but to show up with love, humility, mercy, compassion, and empathy for others, especially those who are rough around the edges or have been pushed to the margins. Peacekeeping doesn't mean keeping quiet to avoid disruption but rather acting with thoughtfulness, wisdom, and restraint. In a world with so much animosity, reactivity, polarizing viewpoints, and dehumanizing of people who are different, always remember that God sees the hard work of loving and respecting others.

Dear God, guide my words and actions to be those of peace and wisdom during times of divisiveness, hatred, and despair.

Maggie Winzeler, women's wellness writer, business owner

LAUGH A LITTLE LONGER

She can laugh at the days to come.

PROVERBS 31:25 NIV

When was the last time you truly had a belly laugh that bubbled up from deep within and filled your heart with joy? Take a moment to reflect on that today. What prevents all of us from experiencing such pure expressions of laughter and joy? Laughter is a gift, a powerful force that can light up even the darkest moments. In the Bible, we see how laughter and joy are intertwined with faith and hope. Psalm 100:2 reminds us to "come before him with joyful songs" (NIV). Proverbs 17:22 tells us that "a cheerful heart is good medicine" (NIV).

Even during times of trial, laughter can bring unexpected blessings. Laughter is a reflection of the joy that comes from trusting in God's goodness and provision. If it's been a while since you felt that bellyache-inducing laugh, don't wait for the perfect moment—laugh anyway! Always remember, that kind of laughter is a priceless gift from God; it can serve as a reminder that even in difficult times, there is still room for his joy.

Lord, fill me with your joy that I may radiate your light and share your love and laughter with all whom I meet.

Kim Crabill, TV host, author, ministry leader, Christian counselor

THE HUMBLE FAST

"Is not this the kind of fasting I have chosen: to loose the chains of injustice and untie the cords of the yoke, to set the oppressed free and break every yoke?"

ISAIAH 58:6 NIV

It was one of those days that started early at breakneck speed. Too rushed to eat, I felt myself move through the various stages of hunger, first experiencing physical discomfort and loud stomach rumbling, then getting lightheadedness and a headache, and finally feeling full-on *hangry*. I hadn't planned on fasting.

Fasting is something the children of Israel became very familiar with. They understood that God honored prayers of intercession, especially when the prayers were coupled with self-sacrifice and fasting. But always remember, fasting is not only about food. Fasting is also a wonderful act of worship that can lose its effectiveness if it becomes just another ritual or, worse, a means of attracting attention. The prophet Isaiah highlights the beauty and necessity of marrying fasting with works of compassion. This practice encourages humility and a sense of utter dependence on the Lord, which makes us aware of the needs of others too. What a wonderful way to honor Jesus' sacrifice!

Father, I believe you'll break barriers in spiritual places as I fast and pray in faith, seeking a closer walk with you.[20]

Pat Boone, actor, singer, songwriter, author

---

20 Adapted from *Pat Boone Devotional Book*, published by Bible Voice, Inc. Used by permission from Mr. Boone.

STUCK!

Jesus grew in wisdom and stature,
and in favor with God and man.

LUKE 2:52 NIV

We all experience feeling stuck sometimes, don't we? In those times we just want to say, *God, hurry up!* Is that where you are right now? You know the plan God has for you, but nothing is happening. I remember when my boys, just two and three years old, begged for the keys to the car so they could drive. They were sure they could manage the vehicle. As a parent, I knew a lot of growing and maturing needed to happen first. Right now, God is growing and preparing you, too, for the thing you are so excited about.

My friend, when you become tired of waiting on God, always remember that even Jesus had four areas he needed to grow in before he could carry out his Father's plan. Scripture says he grew in wisdom, in stature, and in favor with God and man. Take a look around you. How is God growing you mentally, spiritually, physically, or socially? Maybe God put you right where you need to be to grow in one of these ways. He hasn't forgotten you after all. The keys to your dreams will one day be yours.

Lord, thank you for revealing the plan for my life when I am ready and not before.

Kim Crabill, TV host, author, ministry leader,
Christian counselor

WORDS IN THE WILDERNESS

"I took care of you in the wilderness,
in that dry and thirsty land."

HOSEA 13:5 NLT

Have you ever been in a crowd of people and felt completely alone? You observed facial expressions and listened to conversations swirling around you, but nothing could penetrate the bubble you were in. You were in a wilderness all your own. Friend, let me remind you that faith begins in the wilderness. When fear and confusion surround you, lift your eyes to the face of God.

Don't think so much about what is going on around you or even within you. Focus instead on what you read in the Word. Hold on to the message of the Gospel. Always remember that if you want to hear from God and know that he is with you, just open his Word and start reading. That Word is living, active, God-breathed, and it will meet you right where you are, even in the wilderness. He will never leave you alone.

Lord, give me faith and a word that will sustain me in my wilderness experiences.

Kim Crabill, TV host, author, ministry leader,
Christian counselor

HOW GOOD HE IS!

God made him who had no sin to be sin for us, so that in him we might become the righteousness of God.

2 Corinthians 5:21 NIV

Thomas should've been celebrating. He made it to eighth grade with no grade lower than an A. Instead, he was scowling over his first B. You'd think he'd been sentenced to summer school! Thomas had gotten an A-minus once, back in sixth grade, and rather than applauding the five A's, his parents zeroed in on the single A-minus. He vowed never to get another "bad" grade. This was his only hope of feeling accepted by his parents.

The great thing about God is you don't have to be a whiz at anything to get him to accept you. Your real worth never varies with your grades or popularity. Even if you never succeeded again, God would accept you. God says you're as valuable as the life of his Son, Jesus. Once you know this, you are not only OK with "failing," but also do better when you succeed. No need to pant like a puppy to get people to like you. Always remember, you don't have to do anything to earn God's love.

God, thank you for accepting me the way I am. Help me to extend that acceptance to others![21]

Josh McDowell and Kevin Johnson

21 Excerpted from *The One Year Book of Josh McDowell's Family Devotions 2* coauthored by Josh McDowell and Kevin Johnson with permission of Tyndale House Publishers.

TREASURES IN SUFFERING

Bless the Lord, O my soul...who heals all your diseases.

Psalm 103:2–3 ESV

Are you dealing with illness or debilitating fatigue today? Maybe you've been diagnosed with a physical ailment and are struggling to make a full recovery, praying desperately for strength to endure until your body heals. Your struggle may be a silent one of emotional or mental origins. The inability to cope keeps you under the covers, oblivious to the beauty around you. Illness of any kind is hard to bear. It reminds me of the woman in Jesus' day who spent twelve years and all her money on one doctor after another but received no help. Then she heard Jesus was nearby. He was her last chance. So she reached out, touched him, and was completely healed (Mark 5:25–34)!

Maybe you long for that touch. I've longed for it too, but God doesn't always grant immediate healing. I want you to always remember that he often heals us slowly, taking the time to draw us close and teach us things we couldn't learn any other way. Be patient with yourself. Once on your feet again, you will treasure the lessons suffering taught you.

Lord, thank you for the lessons I learn in the valley of illness—physical or otherwise—and the joy of restored health.

Kim Crabill, TV host, author, ministry leader, Christian counselor

DIVINE INTERFERENCE

Casting all your care upon him; for he careth for you.

1 Peter 5:7 KJV

I was scheduled to fly to Manhattan on September 10, 2001, for a meeting the next morning in one of the Twin Towers. As applications engineer, my job was to provide technical support for our sales department in meetings with clients and to provide support for equipment in the field. But a sudden equipment failure in Miami changed my itinerary. My flight to Manhattan was cancelled and replaced with an afternoon flight to Miami on the eleventh.

I was watching television in my living room on the morning of September 11 when the first airplane slammed into one of the towers. I couldn't believe my eyes. As I was processing this event, the second plane struck the other tower, and the world was changed forever. Somehow, outside of my foresight or control, God had changed my flight arrangements that day. I don't know why he spared my life instead of the lives of all the people who tragically died that day. But ever since, I've known that God cares about every aspect of my life. I must always remember to trust his changes to my plans.

Lord, help me to remember that you care for me. I trust you completely and give you the praise.

James Page Jr., pastor

ALREADY DONE

LORD, our Lord, how majestic is your name in all the earth!
You have set your glory in the heavens.

PSALM 8:1 NIV

It was three o'clock in the morning, and the lines on the road were blinding. The weight of the world crashed down, but still, I had miles to go. It was a five-hour drive to the hospital where my daughter had had her seventh open-heart surgery just weeks before. I gripped the steering wheel but clung to the robe of Jesus. The dark sky seemed to swallow us whole. I kept one eye on the road and the other on the rearview mirror. It was there I saw her—my little girl—struggling to breathe, fighting the fluid that pooled the lungs from a heart that seemed to be failing.

We arrived at the hospital, and the doctors gently told us the news. "Her valve stopped working. We need to go back in." Shaken, I called my pastor. "How can anyone have an eighth open-heart surgery?" I asked. His answer filled me with hope and taught a lesson I will never forget. He told me, "One of the best ways to battle is to always remember what God has already done."

Lord, when I feel scared, help me to fix my eyes on you and remember what you have already done.

Jenny Muscatell, Roses and Rainbows advisory board member, radio host, author

AN ILLUMINATED PATH

He broke the power of death and illuminated the way to life.

2 TIMOTHY 1:10 NLT

Do you ever feel apprehension about what the future might hold? The unknown sometimes feels intimidating because we can't see the path ahead. My friend had an experience that showed her just how little she needs to fear the unknown. It was almost midnight when she closed the door to the brightly lit bathhouse and stared into the darkness. The huge trees surrounding her obliterated the light of the few stars not hidden by clouds. She could not see the path to her cabin that had been so obvious in daylight. Then, as her eyes refocused, she saw a row of tiny, solar-powered lights placed strategically along an otherwise invisible path through the woods. Step by step, she followed those little lights, and they led her safely to her cabin.

Life is sometimes like a midnight trek through the woods, isn't it? We worry about stumbling over rocks, about dangers and diseases that lurk in the shadows. But always remember, Jesus provides all the light we need to walk safely through each day. With him, we can navigate the unknowns.

Lord, thank you for providing the light I need for this moment. I trust my future to you.

Kim Crabill, TV host, author, ministry leader, Christian counselor

PERSONAL WHAC-A-MOLE

"Stop striving and know that I am God."

PSALM 46:10 NASB

Life was hard when I was a Christian and my husband was an atheist and alcoholic. I always thought that our life would be "all that" if God would just save my husband. Then, miraculously, the Lord saved him in a London hotel room during an important business trip. Problems solved, right? Au contraire!

God knew the plans he had for my husband, Stu, so there was much refining to be done. Our problems were mountain-sized! We likened our lives to the arcade game Whac-A-Mole; as one issue was resolved, another popped up. I called my sister Anne and cried, "I must not be praying hard enough or the right way!" Anne calmly replied, "Enough! You are striving, and you need to *stop*. God promises that *all* things work together for good for those who love him and are called according to his purpose" (see Romans 8:28). My sister's brutally honest response reminded me to always remember who God is and how he worked for me. I needed that reminder! It was time for what I call my 3 C's: confession, contrition, and change.

Lord, you are God. You are sovereign, and your promises are true. Help me to believe and to trust you always.

Trish Fuhlendorf, pastor's wife

MADE FOR A PURPOSE

We are his workmanship, created in Christ Jesus for good works, which God prepared beforehand so that we would walk in them.

EPHESIANS 2:10 NASB

For as long as I can remember, my dad has enjoyed woodworking, spending hours creating furniture and home decor. Each item he crafts for a purpose. The Bible calls us God's "workmanship." God has been intentional in creating us exactly the way we are, with distinct passions, interests, personalities, and abilities. Our specific attributes will help us complete the good works he has planned for each one of us before we even think of them. He knows where we will be, whom we will connect with, and how.

Sometimes the good works are grand—giving money to a mission trip, serving at church, or buying a homeless person lunch. At other times, they are as simple as smiling at a stranger or striking up a conversation with someone at the grocery store. Always remember that there are opportunities each day to walk into the good works he has planned for us. You never know the difference you could make!

Dear God, thank you for planning good works for me to walk in today. Help me to be a blessing to others.

Ella Hartt, Roses and Rainbows advisory board member, songwriter, singer, storyteller

OFFER WHAT YOU HAVE

They gathered them and filled twelve baskets with the pieces of the five barley loaves left over.

JOHN 6:13 NIV

Do you feel like you don't have much to offer Jesus today? You didn't receive a great education, aren't exceptionally good-looking, or have no special talent. Maybe you came from the wrong side of the tracks. Still, it's not true that you have nothing to offer.

Think of the little boy who brought his lunch to Jesus. He could have looked at his two little fish and five loaves and drawn the logical conclusion that there was no point in offering his food to the disciples. It could never feed five thousand people. He could have said, "If only I had more to offer." Instead, he asked, "What if I just give Jesus all that I have?" Always remember, my friend, that just like the little boy, you have something to give: a heart for Jesus.

Lord, give me faith to offer what little I have to you.

Kim Crabill, TV host, author, ministry leader,
Christian counselor

EYES FORWARD

"See, the former things have taken place, and new things I declare; before they spring into being I announce them to you."

ISAIAH 42:9 NIV

"What's done is done." Those words ring with a finality that is unnerving. Sometimes, it is hard to accept the fact that the past is history. It can't be changed no matter how badly we want to do so. If you struggle today with a past that can't be changed, hear God's words through his prophet Isaiah: he said that the former things have taken place just as he said they would, but now he has new things to bring into being.

My friend, God knows all about your past with its mistakes and regrets, and he's willing to let them stay in the past. You may wish to change your past, but God wants you to focus on what is ahead, the good things he has planned for you. Always remember that no matter what the mistakes, doubts, regrets, or sins of your past have been, God still finds you worthy of the new and better things he has in mind for you.

Father, help me to let go of past regrets and focus on the hopeful possibilities of the future.

Kim Crabill, TV host, author, ministry leader, Christian counselor

A GODLY HOME

This is how the holy women of old made themselves beautiful. They put their trust in God and accepted the authority of their husbands.

1 Peter 3:5 NLT

I recently played Janelle Moore, a godly wife, in the movie *The Forge*. At the conclusion of the movie, she faced a choice about the order of leadership in the home. 1 Corinthians 11:3 says, "I want you to know that the head of every man is Christ, the head of woman is man, and the head of Christ is God" (NKJV).

Too many films, TV shows, and even statements in church glorify disorder. Comments like "happy wife, happy life," "she's the neck that turns the head," or "we know who the real boss is" are complete departures from what our Father wants for marriages. Always remember that God has placed each of us—as husbands and wives—in very important roles. I strive to be a wife who does not deviate from the position God has assigned to me. Your family's order of leadership may differ from what the world expects, but it will align with what God desires.

Father, give me courage to follow your perfect plan for godly households.

BJ Arnett, actor, TV host

USED UP?

The LORD is my shepherd; I have what I need.

PSALM 23:1 CSB

Are you feeling kind of used up today? I mean, let's just face it, the demands and stresses of everyday life can make us feel empty and rather drained. Simple, necessary things like sleeping or downtime can escape us, leaving us feeling frazzled and with nothing left to give. But the feeling of emptiness is not all bad. Think of it as a call to return to rest. God uses people and events to lead us gently back to him. Friends may remind us of his goodness. Situations may reassure us that no matter where we are, he is already there. He is in control.

Wherever you are today, I hope you'll always remember that God has an endless supply of refreshment ready for you to enjoy as you learn to rest in his presence. He will meet every need you have. When you start to feel used up and empty, just reach for the one who will provide everything you need. Take a deep breath and find rest in him.

Lord, thank you for drawing me back to yourself when I get sidetracked by the demands of life.

Kim Crabill, TV host, author, ministry leader,
Christian counselor

NOT WHAT I EXPECTED

"I know the plans I have for you… plans to give you hope and a future."

JEREMIAH 29:11 NIV

I was thirty-five when I married Larry, eager to start a family. I loved my career but dreamed of being a mother. Extremely healthy, I figured I'd become pregnant whenever it suited me. From the day I married, I heard God's whisper over and over: *You will have many children.* I never expected to deal with infertility. Years of treatments followed—everything except in vitro fertilization. Finally, I was pregnant! Then I miscarried at five months. Multiple adoption attempts fell through, then I miscarried again. Yet the whisper of God persisted: *You will have many children.*

I never did have children of my own. But in hindsight, I see God's promise beautifully fulfilled. I do have many children—a wonderful stepdaughter, a grandson, godchildren, women I mentor, aspiring young Hollywood professionals. I see the purpose of God's plan. Have you sensed God telling you about your future? Maybe it's still being fulfilled. Or perhaps his plan for your life, like mine, looks different from what you expected. But always remember, his plan will bring you greater fulfillment and joy than you could ever imagine.

Lord, thank you for your perfect plan for my life, a future filled with hope.

Nancy Stafford, actor, author, speaker

IN LONELY PLACES

You are close beside me. Your rod and your staff protect and comfort me.

Psalm 23:4 NLT

Do you ever wish you just didn't have to do life alone? If only there was someone you could count on to be there, listen, and maybe help you figure out how to handle the hard knocks that come your way. You know, you already have someone waiting to guide you safely around every obstacle in your path. Jesus sees your spirit sinking because of a failed project, a slanderous comment, or the loneliness of singleness. He sees when your body wants to give in to temptation, whether it be laziness, angry words, or self-pity. When your soul wavers, you will hear your Shepherd calling you back to the truth of his Word—his rod and staff are comforting and protecting you.

My friend, whatever you are dealing with today, know that you don't have to handle life on your own. Jesus is always available to provide all the direction and protection you need, along with his love. You are never, ever alone.

Thank you, Lord, for your presence that is with me, protecting me night and day.

Kim Crabill, TV host, author, ministry leader, Christian counselor

FINDING MY TRUE IDENTITY

You are no longer strangers and aliens, but you are fellow citizens with the saints and members of the household of God.

EPHESIANS 2:19 ESV

"You're too dark and ugly," said my classmates. I was hurt and ashamed. Over time, my mother could see self-hatred luring me to be someone other than myself. My mother, a native of West Africa, said, "Pack your bags; we are going to Ghana." When we arrived, I marveled at all the beauty radiating from the same shade of skin as mine. No one was ashamed of their heritage. Just watching these confident people made me come alive simply because I saw myself as what I now perceived as truly beautiful.

My mother's powerful lesson in identity transferred to my understanding of my spiritual identity. When a person is ignorant to the beauty of who God made them to be, they will wrestle with lies that seek to create a false identity. I saw the truth, and it set me free to love the way God made me. Always remember when you read God's Word to look for who you are in Christ. Do not accept a false identity.

Lord Jesus, help me to accept the truth that I am fearfully and wonderfully made by you.

Myshel Wilkins, speaker, worship leader, recording artist

YOUR TO-DO LIST

As we have opportunity, let us do good to all people.

GALATIANS 6:10 NIV

What does God want me to do today? How do I know his will for my life? Well, friend, what do you have planned for today? Do you need to buy groceries? Do you need to pick up your kids at school? Do you have a budget meeting or appointments with clients? Are you serving at a senior center? Whatever you have written on your to-do list today, do that. Ephesians 2:10 says God has created us as his masterpieces to move around this earth, doing the good things he has already planned for us to do.

It is always God's will to give hope to another. Many people are dealing with sorrow, frustration, or fear. You can be the person who shares God's presence and peace with just a smile or a kind word. So when you look at yourself in the mirror each morning, always remember this one thing: today is your unique opportunity to encourage someone. Wherever you go, trust Jesus and speak life into those around you. Then every day, you will be doing his will, and every day will be a great day!

Lord, as I go about my work for today, give me opportunities to bless others.

Kim Crabill, TV host, author, ministry leader,
Christian counselor

DESERT TRAINING

Water will gush forth in the wilderness
and streams in the desert.

ISAIAH 35:6 NIV

Did you wake up this morning feeling forgotten, like you're not in a place where God can use you? If you did, you're not the only one. This feeling stretches back to the days of Moses. After leaving his homeland to escape punishment for killing a man, Moses lived in the desert year after year, herding sheep. Then one day, Moses encountered a burning bush and heard God calling his name (Exodus 3).

Moses answered God's call with "Here I am" (v. 4), and the next thing he knew, God had given him an assignment. Suddenly, all his years of waiting made sense; the desert was training territory. God had a plan after all. If you are in a desert place today, just keep faithfully herding your sheep. Always remember that you may be learning the final lesson necessary before God comes calling your name.

Lord, help me to practice patience in my desert experiences, allowing you to train me into a servant you can use.

Kim Crabill, TV host, author, ministry leader,
Christian counselor

MOUNTAIN CLIMBING WITH JESUS

I will raise my eyes to the mountains;
from where will my help come?
My help comes from the LORD.

PSALM 121:1–2 NASB

I've always admired the endurance and strength of mountain climbers, perhaps because my own attempts to scale a steep hill leave me exhausted. Sometimes life seems like one looming mountain after another, doesn't it? You may grow weary in the climb as you drudgingly take the next step, and you may be tempted to give up. Always remember, the moment you move your eyes from the mountain to the loving eyes of Jesus before you, your perspective will change and your strength will be renewed.

We know that life's journey will include a lot of mountains to climb and valleys to cross. As you look ahead, you don't have to dread the obstacles. Instead, focus on Christ who goes before you, walks beside you, and guards you from behind. Agree with the Psalmist David and say, "I know the LORD is always with me. I will not be shaken, for he is right beside me." Friends, you truly have nothing to dread or fear. Simply enjoy the presence of Jesus.

Lord, thank you for mountain climbing with me. May I never forget to keep my focus on you.

Carmen Pate, Roses and Rainbows advisory board member, author, speaker, Bible teacher, mentor of women

HAPPY WHERE YOU ARE

I have learned to be satisfied with whatever I have.

PHILIPPIANS 4:11 CEV

Have you ever invested hours in a job or a project that you loved only to have it pulled from your hands and given to someone else? You watched others enjoy what was once yours, and you felt your jaw tighten. How do you deal with those emotions? Can you graciously bow out, relinquish the limelight, and accept that your work is done? John the Baptist is a good example of this very thing. When Jesus showed up on the scene, the crowds left John to follow Jesus, and John's disciples became concerned.

John wasn't worried. "He must become greater; I must become less," he said (John 3:30 NIV). John was content with the assignment God had given him. Sometimes relinquishing a job or project makes you feel replaced and unneeded. In those times, it's important to always remember that God has the right to give and take from all areas of your life, even your jobs and acts of service. Instead of mourning the loss, thank him for using you to fulfill part of his good plan and purpose.

Lord, help me to be content with wherever you place me, knowing it is the best place to be.

Esther Carpenter, author

HARSH REALITIES, AMAZING OUTCOMES

"You intended to harm me, but God intended it all for good."

GENESIS 50:20 NLT

As you take stock of your reality today, do you feel bewildered, wondering what on earth is going on? Joseph would certainly be able to understand your uncertainty. God's work in his life is a thing of beauty, but I doubt Joseph thought so as he was living it out. His story is one of extreme highs and lows: one day deeply honored by his father, the next betrayed, deserted, and sold into slavery by his brothers. One day promoted to lead servant, the next punished for doing the right thing.

I'm sure Joseph was confused, but he chose to believe God was working for his good in each situation, and that fact stabilized him (read Genesis 30–50). Like Joseph, you cannot see the next chapter of your story, but God can. When it's difficult to make sense of what's happening to you, always remember that God is working all the details of your story together for good. Commit to following him today, believing that he's at work in your situation. The outcome of his plan will be amazing!

Lord, when I am confused by what is happening, remind me that you are in control of the whole story.

Kim Crabill, TV host, author, ministry leader, Christian counselor

FUELED BY PRAYER

"Do not fear, for I am with you."

Isaiah 41:10 NIV

God, what should I do? Can you recall a time when a decision opened the door to a crisis of belief? We've all been there at some time. Over the years, I've learned that prayer is the key. God is waiting to listen, act, and commune with us. He desires ongoing communication with his children day and night. God doesn't want us to call on him just during times of crisis. Oh, he is there when we need "crisis counseling," but he longs for us to come to him with *everything*.

Growing up, I remember my grandmama praying for parking spots. Sometimes, Grandmama parked close to the front; other times, she ended up in what she called "the boondocks." Then she'd say, "Honey, God is in control and knows best." My grandmama continually displayed an ongoing, living, breathing, prayer-fueled relationship with Jesus. She taught me to always remember to trust God in the little and big decisions of life.

Lord, remind me that you are always there to light the way. Prompt me to take everything to you in prayer and to trust you no matter what. Thank you for calling me to an intimate relationship through prayer.

Candace Kirkpatrick, actor, speaker, talk show cohost

GOT KNEELING PADS?

God is our refuge and strength,
an ever-present help in trouble.

PSALM 46:1 NIV

Teens driving—every parent's nightmare! I'll always remember the first time our youngest child pulled out of the driveway—*alone*. There was no one to remind her to slow down or to point out that she was too close to the car ahead of her. A look of independence adorned her face. Inwardly, I experienced the bittersweet battle of freedom versus fear—freedom from carpooling and fear of the liberty my daughter now had at her disposal.

With four teenage drivers in our home, I needed "kneeling pads." One morning, after our third son left for school, he called me. His trembling voice said, "Mom, I hit a deer." I expected to see the car's front end smashed, with antlers stuck in the grill. To my amazement, only a tiny dent was visible. My son said, "I have no doubt God's angels protected me!" Joy ignited in my heart as I realized God had answered my prayers. Not only did God protect him, but my son also experienced God's love through that protection.

Lord, remind me to use my "kneeling pads" and to pray without ceasing. I praise you for your love, grace, and mercy.

Carla McDougal, ministry leader, author

YOU DELIGHT GOD

"The LORD your God…will quiet you with His love, He will rejoice over you with singing."

ZEPHANIAH 3:17 NKJV

For years, nothing upset me more than when a relationship with someone I cared about became strained. I would worry endlessly, wondering what I might have done wrong. Do you worry over tenuous relationships, afraid of disappointing a friend? Are you stressing over what they might be saying about you behind your back? Human relationships are important, but I've discovered that focusing on what others think of me causes me to miss a higher priority: focusing on what God has to say about me.

If you are worrying over earthly relationships today, ask God to help you refocus. Forgive what needs to be forgiven. Forget unkind remarks. Turn your back on negative thoughts. And always remember that God's arms are open to you. He delights in you and calls you to a life of purpose. Forget human negativity. Run into the arms of the one who takes great delight in you. Listen to him sing his songs of joy over you. And rest.

Lord, when I get hung up on human relationships and opinions, draw me back to you.

Kim Crabill, TV host, author, ministry leader, Christian counselor

October

MUST I PRAY?

"You will pray to him, and he will hear you."

Job 22:27 NIV

How do you feel about praying out loud? Do your prayers spill easily from your lips in any situation, or are you like a lot of people who prefer to pray silently, where none but God can hear their thoughts? Praying aloud can make us feel vulnerable. We worry that our prayers aren't pretty and organized, not well-thought-out, and not spiritual enough. We are afraid people will judge our prayers and find them wanting.

But can I let you in on a little secret? God loves random prayers, disjointed ones, and even messy prayers spoken in anger. Whatever is in your heart is what God wants to hear, whether spoken silently or aloud. That's the thing to always remember, my friend. Jesus doesn't care if your prayer is perfect. He just wants to hear the prayer of a sincere heart. Those are the prayers he loves to answer.

Lord, thank you that your ear is always ready to hear the prayers of your people.

Kim Crabill, TV host, author, ministry leader, Christian counselor

GOD DOESN'T WASTE ANYTHING

God causes everything to work together for the good of those who love God.

Romans 8:28 NLT

As a prodigal daughter, I chose abortion for two of my children. Even writing that now brings tremendous sorrow and regret for choices that can't be undone. I returned to the Lord in brokenness and with a contrite heart. I surrendered fully to God. Soon after, I received a call at work, where I held an executive position with a major retailer, from a pastor I barely knew.

"There is a position open for an executive director at Living Alternatives pregnancy center," he said. "I realize you have a good job, but I felt God telling me to call." I broke down in tears. I knew what God wanted. I confessed to the pastor my sin of abortion. I assumed the conversation would end there. Instead, the pastor said, "Remember, God doesn't waste anything. It seems to me you would be perfect for the job."

Lord, thank you for making beauty from the ashes of my life.

Carmen Pate, Roses and Rainbows advisory board member, author, speaker, Bible teacher, mentor of women

YOU CAN FLY!

When your endurance is fully developed, you will be perfect and complete, needing nothing.

JAMES 1:4 NLT

You knew stepping out in faith to follow God probably wouldn't be easy, but you didn't know it would be this hard. Why are there so many unforeseen hoops to jump through and hurdles to overcome? If you feel frustrated by the struggles in your life, let me remind you of another creature who struggles greatly with change. You may have heard that if you release a butterfly from its cocoon too soon, it will be unable to fly because its wings haven't fully developed. The struggle to emerge naturally is just what the butterfly needs to be able to fly once it does break free.

It is the same with you and me. Difficulties are a necessary part of life. Without them, our growth would be stunted, and we wouldn't be able to fly as God wants us to. If you are weighed down by the struggles in your life today, I want you to always remember that the obstacle causing you such struggle will one day be the thing that enables you to fly.

Lord, help me to endure difficulty with grace and determination, knowing it is for my ultimate good.

Kim Crabill, TV host, author, ministry leader, Christian counselor

BESTIES WITH JESUS

The Lord would speak to Moses face to face, as one speaks to a friend.

Exodus 33:11 NIV

When I first committed to going deeper into a relationship with Christ, it was hard to get my mind around what that was supposed to look like. Do you find this to be true for you as well? I mean, Jesus isn't physically present beside you on the couch. He isn't strapped into the passenger's seat of the car as you run errands. So what does a relationship with him look like? Well, my friend, think for a minute. What makes your earthly friendships work? Isn't it spending time together, talking about everything under the sun, really listening?

Why not try the same things with Jesus? A spilling of your thoughts to him does wonders for your heart. He is the best listener. His friendship is the only one that will never fail you. He is the only one who will bring restoration to the broken pieces of your life and healing when you have a broken heart. Always remember, Jesus works in you through relationship, yours and his. The stronger it is, the better you will be.

Lord, give me the desire for a deeper relationship with you every day.

Kim Crabill, TV host, author, ministry leader, Christian counselor

YOUR WORDS MATTER

Out of the same mouth proceed blessing and cursing.

JAMES 3:10 NKJV

Certain days are forever embedded in my memory, and this was one of those days. Residents were slumped in their wheelchairs as I walked down the hallway toward my mother's room. The hospice care nurses had done all they could. My mother's life hung by a thread. As I walked into the room, family members were gathered around her bed while she slept. They tried to wake her, but she didn't move.

Before leaving, after giving Mom all of the comfort they knew how, they said to her, "Kathleen is here." I walked around to the other side of the bed, took Mom's sweet hand, and said, "I'm here, Mom!" She then opened her eyes and said, "You look like a million dollars!" I will never forget her words, the last ones she spoke to me. Her words prompt me to always remember that we need to choose our words carefully. The right choice of words will bless our hearers.

Lord, my prayer is to walk in kindness with every word I say. Help me be a blessing to all those I encounter.

Kathleen Hardaway, author, speaker

BE READY

A gift opens the way and ushers the giver
into the presence of the great.

PROVERBS 18:16 NIV

After graduating college, I woke up believing I was going to work for Ted Turner, the media giant. My mom, witnessing my confidence, bought me a car that day to drive from Chicago to Atlanta. She said, "If you get the job, you'll need a car. Baby girl, you have to always remember to be ready." I arrived at the CNN center, filled out an application, and requested to deliver it myself to human resources. Unbeknownst to me, one of Mr. Turner's five secretaries was on a leave of absence when I submitted my application. I was dressed to interview, and they hired me on the spot.

The job I had applied for paid $12,000 annually; the job I was hired for started at $25,000. My mom had insisted I take three years of typing and accounting in high school. Well, typing 75 words per minute and balancing books added real value, so soon they bumped my annual salary up to $40,000. I'm so grateful my mom taught me to be ready for what God will do.

Lord, thank you for giving me gifts that make room for me in this world. Help me to cultivate my gifts and learn to be ready for your opportunities.

Maura Gale, speaker, actor, author, podcaster

THE RIGHT WAY OUT

"Do not lie. Do not deceive one another."

LEVITICUS 19:11 NIV

Do you ever feel like deception is your only way out? You tried it before and it seemed to work out fine, so why not again? It is true: God sometimes allows our deception to gain us a temporary advantage. Abraham made many decisions in Egypt that were not guided by godly motives. In fact, sometimes it almost seemed like God wanted him to practice deception to keep himself out of trouble. In Genesis 12, Abraham's fear caused him to spout off a lot of falsehoods, and in the middle of those falsehoods was an element of truth.

Because Sarah was so beautiful, Abraham told her to tell the Egyptians she was Abraham's sister, not his wife. Sarah was indeed a beautiful woman, and the Egyptians would not have thought twice about killing a man to add another beautiful woman to their harem. She was also Abraham's half-sister, so there was an element of truth to his deception. But here's the thing. You may try to justify telling a half-truth to save your marriage, gain financial success, or restore your reputation, but lies and deception are never acceptable to God. I hope you'll always remember that in God's eyes, telling half the truth is always a whole lie.

Lord, give me courage to tell the truth at all times, even when it hurts.

Kim Crabill, TV host, author, ministry leader, Christian counselor

THE WAITING ROOM

I waited patiently for the Lord;
he turned to me and heard my cry.

Psalm 40:1 NIV

For many years, I've dealt with health issues that have progressively become worse. After hundreds of hours researching and thousands of dollars for doctors, I still had zero results. I became obsessed with healing, and this affected everything in my life. I prayed but still struggled. Finally, a good friend told me that I wasn't looking to God for healing; I was looking to myself. He told me to always remember that we need to surrender fully to the Lord as the Great Doctor, putting him first, and praising him while we wait. Then we will be open to receiving healing and answers.

Through this journey, I've learned that in every test, there is a temptation. Do we choose to stress, get upset with the Lord, and do it our own way, or do we give it to the Lord and have faith despite the circumstances? Our view of God and the faith we have in him can save us from anxiety and doubt so we can receive what he has for us. Place your hope in him, expect him to answer, and praise him in the waiting room.

Lord, I will praise you while I wait.

Alisha Griffin, actor, model, blogger

THE IMPOSSIBLE CALL

I can do everything through Christ, who gives me strength.

PHILIPPIANS 4:13 NLT

Have you ever invited someone into your life and then wished you hadn't? In Genesis 16, Sarah found herself in such a situation. God promised that she and Abraham would have a son, but there was just one problem. Sarah was barren. Rather than waiting on God, she took matters into her own hands, giving her servant, Hagar, to her husband as a surrogate mother. The results were disastrous, including a jealous Sarah and a spiteful servant. And it was all because Sarah didn't believe God would do what he said he would do.

Sometimes, God asks us to do things that seem impossible too. Maybe that is where you are today. Perhaps he is asking you to write a book, learn a new skill, or do something else that is overwhelming. Whatever feels impossible today, please don't seek alternate answers. Always remember that God will help you to finish what he has given you to do. The challenge is to let him work out the details of the calling he has placed on your life.

Give me faith to believe that what looks impossible to accomplish I can complete with you.

Kim Crabill, TV host, author, ministry leader,
Christian counselor

START CLIMBING

"Physical training is good,
but training for godliness is much better."

1 TIMOTHY 4:8 NLT

I am not a person who likes to climb mountains. It's just not something I aspire to do. Unfortunately, that doesn't mean I am exempt from climbing spiritual mountains. I have certainly done my share of those over the years. You see, the Bible never promised that we would always walk along on easy, level ground. God puts mountains before us because they provide the spiritual exercise we need to grow in him. The muscles you gain from the climb are shaping you into who he wants you to be.

If you fear the mountain before you today, always remember that God will never ask you to climb it alone. His presence will go with you, and his hand will guide you every step of the way. So put on your spiritual shoes, my friend, take a deep breath, and begin the climb. One day the mountain in front of you will be so far behind you that it will barely be visible. But the person you have become while climbing that mountain? *That* is what is most important. Always seek to climb with God.

Lord, give me the strength and the willingness to climb with you each mountain before me.

Kim Crabill, TV host, author, ministry leader,
Christian counselor

FRIENDS WELL-CHOSEN

The righteous choose their friends carefully, but the way of the wicked leads them astray.

PROVERBS 12:26 NIV

You know that feeling of leaving a party with a smile still on your face? Or having coffee with a friend and talking for hours? I love spending time with friends—the people we open up to about our feelings and not just give the standard "Good" reply after "How are you?" The people who make us feel rejuvenated, loved, and heard. I remember the first time I opened up to a close friend about a challenge I was facing. Simply sharing made me feel better, clearer, and more peaceful.

Because of the trust gained and memories we've made, that friendship has lasted for years. My friend has never asked me to compromise my convictions; instead, we share the same fundamental beliefs about God and how we want to live our lives. We become like the people we spend most of our time with. Always remember: Jesus chose his twelve disciples and friends intentionally, and so should we. We should seek to befriend people who uplift us, stand by us, are honest with us (even when it's hard), and who point us to Jesus.

Dear Lord, thank you for friends who bring joy to my life. Help me to always choose my friends wisely.

Ella Hartt, Roses and Rainbows advisory board member, songwriter, singer, storyteller

THE OVERCOMER

You, dear children, are from God and have overcome them, because the one who is in you is greater than the one who is in the world.

1 John 4:4 NIV

Have you ever left church feeling lighter, content, optimistic? And then you walked right into the world and felt defeated, discouraged, depressed? Always remember, we are living in "occupied territory." Satan's kingdom is all around us. We seem to be surrounded by his deeds. Large-scale wars and small personal skirmishes abound. God's truth has been replaced by outlandish lies, and the lines of sin versus virtue are blurred for our young generation.

And yet there is one who is greater than all of Satan's evil—and he lives in us! God's Holy Spirit fills us with overcoming power. As his children, we enjoy full protection from the evil ruler of this world. Better than a bodyguard, the Holy Spirit shields us from the flaming arrows of the enemy. The next time you feel hopeless or even attacked, picture the "greater than" sign you learned in elementary school math, and picture Jesus standing next to it.

Lord, thank you for protecting me from the Evil One by your Holy Spirit. I may falter once in a while, but with you in my corner, I'm winning the fight.[22]

Pat Boone, actor, singer, songwriter, author

---

22 Adapted from *Pat Boone Devotional Book*, published by Bible Voice, Inc. Used by permission from Mr. Boone.

TO FOLLOW OR TO GUARD

Above all else, guard your heart,
for everything you do flows from it.

PROVERBS 4:23 NIV

Have you ever done something you really wanted to do, even though a little voice in your mind told you not to? Things didn't turn out so well for you, did they? There's a popular slogan thrown around today that sounds good, but it is detrimental to your spiritual health. You've heard the saying "Follow your heart" before, haven't you? The idea appeals to our emotions, but it goes directly against Bible principles.

Solomon, the wisest man who ever lived, was advising his sons when he told them to guard their hearts above all else. Their hearts determined the course of their lives. Our hearts are naturally prone to evil, so God's slogan for us today is "Guard your heart." You see, friend, if you want to end up in a good place, you need to make decisions based on Scripture rather than on what your emotions are begging you to do. Emotions are not reliable; God's Word is. A heart driven by emotions will come to ruin, but a heart carefully guarded will result in life and peace.

Lord, help me to follow your heart and not my own so that I can experience true life and peace.

Kim Crabill, TV host, author, ministry leader,
Christian counselor

EVEN IF

I would have lost heart, unless I had believed
that I would see the goodness of the LORD.

PSALM 27:13 NKJV

So many times we want to show God that we have faith that he will do the impossible for us. We pray and believe and look for the answer with great anticipation. But what about when the answer doesn't come? I worked with a young woman once who struggled for years to get pregnant. She prayed. She believed. She even got pregnant. She rejoiced. God had answered! And then she miscarried.

Her hopes dashed and her heart broken, she began to take her frustration and anger out on Christ. I introduced her to the words of three Hebrew boys who were brought before the king to be thrown into a fiery furnace. "God…is able to rescue us.…But even if He does not…we are not going to serve your gods" (Daniel 3:17–18 AMP). What about you, my friend? When you don't understand his ways and nothing makes sense, I hope you will always remember that even when you can't see it, you must still serve God. He still has a plan…and it's a good one.

Lord, help me to remain true to you even when your answer is no.

Kim Crabill, TV host, author, ministry leader,
Christian counselor

THE NARROW GATE

"Enter by the narrow gate....For the gate is narrow and the way is hard that leads to life, and those who find it are few."

MATTHEW 7:13–14 ESV

As an undergraduate, I attended a party school where we drank a lot and stayed out late. During my sophomore year, it was harder to maintain my grades, and some of my friends were of questionable character. Most importantly, I did not always like the person in the mirror, and I knew something had to change. A favorite professor told me I would become more like those I spent time with, so I should always remember to choose my circle of influence wisely. I began my junior year at a new campus making new friends.

Scripture never promised a life of all fun and games. In fact, it says just the opposite. Though the road is difficult, we don't have to face it alone. Scripture encourages us to find other believers to help us along the way. The world will try to entice you with excitement and easy living. Choose your circle of influence wisely. Find people who will hold you accountable for your beliefs and lift you up in times of trouble.

Father, connect me with those you have chosen for my circle of influence. I want to enter by the narrow gate.

Barbara Parker, women's ministry leader, educator, audiologist

JUST FIX IT

To bestow on them...a garment of praise
instead of a spirit of despair.

ISAIAH 61:3 NIV

For years, I begged God: *Just fix everything that hurts. Just touch me and make it all better.* Do you ever feel like this? Jesus knows all about the trials and struggles you face: health issues, financial worries, loneliness, a rocky marriage, and so much more. He knows your life is hard sometimes. That's why he reminds you to take heart because he has overcome the world.

While God sometimes gives the gift of an instant miraculous healing, he often does something much better by allowing you to walk through the transformation with him. With each tiny step you take, he will help you to overcome by using the truth of his Word. Always remember that Jesus is so much bigger than your current troubles. As you lean into him, you will be able to endure until the pain has been transformed into joy. Cling to that truth, my friend, when facing things that cause you to want to lose hope.

Lord, give me the faith that holds on to hope and chooses joy in the face of despair.

Kim Crabill, TV host, author, ministry leader,
Christian counselor

YOU CAN BE OK

"Come to me, all you who are weary and burdened, and I will give you rest."

MATTHEW 11:28 NIV

You're not OK. It felt like God speaking to me right there from the passenger seat of the car. My life was in chaos, on the verge of being completely destroyed. I tried to convince myself that I was OK, but God said I wasn't. Friend, always remember that God will be honest with you, no matter where you are or what season of life you are in. He loves you too much to let you believe a lie.

But wait…let me tell you the rest of the story. Upon giving me the truth, God immediately delivered a message of hope to my soul. *You're not OK, Kim, but you can be*. God has the same message for you today. All he asks is that you bring your burden to him. He will give you rest like only he can provide. Maybe you're not OK today, but that doesn't mean you can't be OK tomorrow.

Lord, thank you for inviting me to bring my burdens to you and receive what I need to be OK.

Kim Crabill, TV host, author, ministry leader, Christian counselor

CAN'T NEVER COULD

In the fear of the LORD there is strong confidence.

PROVERBS 14:26 NASB

"But Daddy, I can't!" How many times has a parent heard this? When my husband was a young boy, feeling less than confident about his abilities to do things, his father would say, "Son, 'can't' never could do nothin'!" To that young boy, the phrase was the boost he needed to feel assurance from his father that he could do anything he was asked to do.

My husband's father was a man of strong faith. As the young boy grew, conversations with his father helped him understand that his own faith in God would help him navigate his tasks and develop confidence. When my husband was just eighteen, his father died suddenly. He greatly missed his father, but his faith and wisdom stayed with him. Now, even as my husband turns to God as his source for strength and confidence, he says he can still hear his father saying, "Son, always remember, 'can't' never could do nothin'!"

Lord, in the times when I lack confidence, help me remember that with you, I can have complete assurance for my tasks.

Susan Young, educator, speaker, writer

LONG-RANGE FRUIT

At the proper time we will reap a harvest if we do not give up.

GALATIANS 6:9 NIV

Are you sitting with a furrowed brow, wondering if your life is making a difference? Maybe your kids aren't heeding your advice, or you aren't sure your tactful, nonthreatening way of sharing your faith is being noticed. Is God using anything you are doing to bring about something good? My friend, when you feel discouraged about the lack of fruit from your labor, stop and consider whether you are confusing obedience with success. Spiritual effort rarely brings instant gratification. Your contribution is only a small part of God's much bigger plan.

As 1 Corinthians 3:6 describes it, one person plants a seed, another waters the soil, but it is God who takes all that we do and makes a soul blossom and grow. Always remember that what you are doing does make a difference, whether you see it or not. Just because you don't notice any big results doesn't mean God isn't working. Keep planting those seeds; you are making a difference.

Thank you, Father, that when I do the work you assign to me, I can leave the results with you.

Kim Crabill, TV host, author, ministry leader, Christian counselor

UNITED TO CHRIST

Your love, LORD, reaches to the heavens,
your faithfulness to the skies.

PSALM 36:5 NIV

The other day, my friend told me she and her husband were separating. I nearly fell off my chair. I was there to listen and offer support even as I processed the shock. We all know of some tragic breakup of a long-term marriage or a union that's in trouble now. We sympathize with the heartbreak our friends are going through, and our own hearts break.

In these situations, we lose faith in people we thought we could trust. But we can take comfort in the fact that Jesus will never divorce his bride. Could you even imagine such a thing? Jesus will never leave you or forsake you. He gave himself for you and cherishes you (Ephesians 5:25, 29). We can lean into the security that this provides. In a world where even the most important relationships can break, there is one relationship we can count on that will never waver.

Lord, thank you for the perfect union I have with Jesus. I thank you for the eternal love and protection he gives me.[23]

Pat Boone, actor, singer, songwriter, author

---

23 Adapted from *Pat Boone Devotional Book*, published by Bible Voice, Inc. Used by permission from Mr. Boone.

ODD ORDERS

He will certainly care for you.

MATTHEW 6:30 NLT

Have you ever felt confused about some commands in Scripture? Believe me, I wonder about them too! Take today, for instance. During my quiet time, I read 1 Peter 5:7: "Cast all your anxiety on him because he cares for you" (NIV). A few years ago, I would have said, *But how? How do I pick up my anxieties and throw them on you, Lord?* Maybe you are wondering the same thing. If so, I hope you'll always remember that you accomplish this by a simple prayer.

Think about your anxieties, write them down (be specific), and then put them in a letter to the Lord. *Dear Lord, into your hands I place my worries, my cares, my troubles. Into your wisdom I place my path, my direction, and my goals. I give over to you all things that make me anxious today.* That's how you cast your anxieties on him. Try that today, my friend. Why should you do it? Because he truly does care for you.

Lord, thank you that when I have questions about your Word, you are faithful to answer me.

Kim Crabill, TV host, author, ministry leader, Christian counselor

GOD IS STILL IN CONTROL

Royal power belongs to the LORD.
He rules all the nations.

PSALM 22:28 NLT

We see the chaos in the world. We read the headlines. Who would want to be in charge of this universe? It gives me great comfort to know that God does, and he is in control. Still, I don't know about you, but some days, it seems like God took a long lunch break, and I think he needs help from me. I don't mean in fixing things but in worrying about all that seems so wrong. And sometimes I find myself crying out to the Lord with advice on what he should do!

Oh friends, the Scriptures are full of reminders that put me in my place. For example, God existed before anything else, and he holds all creation together (Colossians 1:17). Also, the life of every living thing is in his hand, and the breath of every human being (Job 12:10). The reality is, we don't have a clue compared to our all-wise, all-powerful, everywhere-present God. Always remember to let him rule while you rest in his sovereign control.

Lord, I am so grateful that you are in control and that your plans cannot be thwarted.

Carmen Pate, Roses and Rainbows advisory board member, author, speaker, Bible teacher, mentor of women

SEEDS, SEEDS EVERYWHERE

"A farmer went out to sow his seed."

LUKE 8:5 NIV

Reading the parable of the sower recently, something new hit me: this sower is wildly extravagant! Some might say he is wildly wasteful. But God alone fully knows the power of his words (seed) and that frees him to be wasteful, confident that even though some words fall on deaf ears, many will take root and bear fruit in the world he sent his Son to save.

God's extravagance is meant to infect us with a similar extravagance. We must always remember how much truth we've been given to speak into this lie-infested world. How much grace to hold up to the meanness. How much love to outshine the hate. And yet, I think of the times I've felt the urge to say something on social media that might plant a "God seed" amid all the foolishness, but then I falter. I tell myself, *Facebook is so trivial*. But a truly extravagant sower would throw that seed at Facebook—or wherever—and leave the rest to God. Always remember that you will never run out of seed when God is your seed-source.

Dear God, fill me with more of your extravagance so that I may sow seeds of your transforming love wherever I go.

Sue Kline, writer, editor, writing coach

NO NEGATIVITY HERE

We do this by keeping our eyes on Jesus.

Hebrews 12:2 NLT

What have I done? What was I thinking? Shame on me! Are these words on repeat in your mind today, making you miserable? Are you dealing with self-reproach that stems from a recent failure, perhaps, or maybe an accusation that you can't forget, spoken long ago by a loved one or a friend or a teacher? These words can race around in your head, peppering your mind with condemning thoughts.

If this is you today, I have good news for you. Galatians 5:1 tells you to "stand firm" and not be "burdened again by a yoke of slavery" (NIV) because in Christ you are free. Rather than allowing negative thoughts of shame, guilt, and regret to weigh you down, remind yourself of the truth that in Jesus you are a new creation. Always remember that God will never place negative, condemning thoughts in your mind. Jesus came to set you free to live joyfully in him. So run free, my child. Don't let shame, guilt, and regret hold you back any longer.

Lord, thank you for freedom in Christ that lifts the burden of negativity and condemnation from my soul.

Kim Crabill, TV host, author, ministry leader, Christian counselor

FORGIVEN!

You will not reject a broken and repentant heart, O God.

Psalm 51:17 NLT

What do you do when you have committed the same sin for the thousandth time? Or maybe you are guilty of a great transgression. Regardless, you can hardly bring yourself to ask for forgiveness because who deserves that kind of mercy? Oh, you have no trouble telling others that God forgives their sin whenever they ask for it. But you are kinder to them than to yourself. King David struggled with this issue. He put off coming to God for forgiveness when he had taken Uriah's wife and then had Uriah killed in battle. But God longed to have the relationship restored, so he sent Nathan the prophet to nudge David toward repentance (2 Samuel 11–12).

My friend, instead of focusing on how imperfect you are or how often you sin, gaze instead into the forgiving eyes of the heavenly Father who loves you. Always remember that God clears you of guilt every time you ask him. He wants you to come and talk to him. He wants you to live free of guilt so that you can shout along with David, "You forgave me! All my guilt is gone" (Psalm 32:5 NLT).

Lord, I praise you for your forgiveness that covers my sins and failures.

Kim Crabill, TV host, author, ministry leader, Christian counselor

NEW CLOTHES

You who were baptized into Christ have clothed yourselves with Christ.

GALATIANS 3:27 NIV

Picture yourself approaching Jesus in your worst pair of paint-spattered jeans or your oldest gardening outfit. The stains of your sins blaze glaringly, and you're unable to hide your raggedy behavior. Jesus surveys your messiness and, with a kind smile, places a hand on your shoulder. *Your sins are forgiven*, he says. *Now put on the new clothes I have for you. They look like mine and will be a reminder that you belong to me.*

Isn't it wonderful to know Jesus loves you that much? No matter how unworthy you feel today, always remember that Jesus loves to see you dressed in your new garments. He is proud of the new person he has made of you. Take a long look at yourself through Jesus' eyes. You are clean, free, beautiful, and satisfied because he has made you new.

Lord, thank you for throwing away my ugly sin garments and dressing me in beautiful clothes of righteousness.

Kim Crabill, TV host, author, ministry leader,
Christian counselor

ONE OPINION MATTERS

"The Lord God will help Me; therefore I will not be disgraced; therefore I have set My face like a flint, and I know that I will not be ashamed."

Isaiah 50:7 NKJV

"Bimbo." "Not convincing." "I've heard it all before." "Dumb!" I set my phone down after scanning through a few nasty comments left on a video I had posted online about the release of my first book. As the harsh words recycled through my mind, I became more despondent and distracted. Finally, I bowed my head to pray and heard the Holy Spirit say, *Stop feeding on garbage*. I was reminded of the importance of using social media only as a tool and how quickly it could pollute my mind and render me ineffective for the kingdom if I wasn't careful.

Always remember that God's opinion is the only one worth worrying about. Once you have a clear vision of the Lord's call on your life, don't let anyone discourage you.

Lord, please make my path straight and help me boldly and confidently carry out your mission.

Melissa Huray, author, podcast host

TRAUMA AND TRUST

We are God's masterpiece.

EPHESIANS 2:10 NLT

Do you ever notice the people who walk by you day after day? Do you wonder what's on their minds and, more importantly, what's in their hearts? The statistics regarding people with trauma in their lives are unbelievable. Sometimes that trauma irritates us. Anger and bad attitudes are around every corner, often the result of people trying to drown out the pain in their hearts.

But what about those you pass each day who appear happy and fulfilled, blending in with the crowd? It's important to remember that some of them also carry deep wounds. I know this on both a professional and personal level because, at the height of my depression, acting OK became my lifestyle. What about you, friend? Perhaps, deep in your heart, all you see is your past hurts, but I want you to always remember that God sees the treasure you are—a masterpiece he is still creating. Try allowing others into your heart. Trust them with your pain. Before long you'll discover that God is using your pain to give hope to someone else.

Lord, heal my hurts and then use me to bring healing to those around me who need your love.

Kim Crabill, TV host, author, ministry leader,
Christian counselor

MILESTONES WITH GOD

Then I recall all you have done, O LORD;
I remember your wonderful deeds of long ago.

PSALM 77:11 NLT

I was getting up there in age. Single. Too long, in my opinion. *Did God forget to write my love story? Did my prayers fall on deaf ears?* During this season, I stumbled across Psalm 77. It was a great example of a person in distress who then recounted God's past faithfulness to carry him through a difficult time. You can hear the psalmist's tone going from depressed to hopeful.

As I read God's Word daily, it was like I could hear him say, *I haven't forgotten you either.* This became the inspiration to create a journal entry: "My Milestones with God List." I wrote a list of key dates and events. These entries marked past times when God had tangibly shown up for me in moments of faithfulness, answered prayers, protection, rescue, and even miracles. To this day, I still treasure this list of remembrances. I found that when you always remember the times when God was faithful, they will carry you through the times when you need encouragement.

Dear God, help me never to forget the great things you have already done for me in the past.

Cheryl McKay, screenwriter, author, producer

PEACE STEALERS

You will keep in perfect peace those whose minds are steadfast.

Isaiah 26:3 NIV

Have you wrestled with any peace stealers lately? You know, those pesky feelings of restlessness, fear, and the like that want to take you down the road of negativity. You may be an unhappy employee, struggling with the monotony of your less-than-ideal job, and discontent threatens to rob you of your peace. Or you could be on the other end of the spectrum. Maybe you have chosen to serve your country, and change is on the horizon. Where will you be sent next? Where will you live? Why must you say goodbye again?

Uncertainty and reluctance plague you as you grapple with the unknowns. My friend, whether you are struggling with the monotony of life or the unknowns of the future, always remember that peace is found in surrendering your circumstances to your heavenly Father. Instead of stressing over the present, focus on the sovereignty of the God who knows every detail of your future. As you set your mind on him, those pesky peace stealers have no choice but to leave.

Lord, when circumstances try to steal my peace, help me to remember to lean hard on you.

Kim Crabill, TV host, author, ministry leader, Christian counselor

NEVER GIVE UP

"Oh, that you would bless me and enlarge my territory!"

1 Chronicles 4:10 NIV

Years ago, I was working for a local TV station in Tulsa. I knew it was my calling, yet I had some hard days. At times I wanted to quit. Yet I learned to press in and persevere. I started praying the prayer of Jabez (from 1 Chronicles 4:10) every day. After six years at that station doing local programming, I was promoted to the number one TV market, New York City, doing international programming. I saw how God answered that prayer and expanded my territory in a tangible way I never expected.

Staying faithful in tough times isn't easy, but it reaps great rewards. Galatians 6:9 tells us, "Let us not become weary in doing good, for at the proper time we will reap a harvest if we do not give up" (NIV). Continue to have faith and believe, and you will see God do above and beyond your hopes, dreams, and imaginations.

Father, encourage me when I want to give up. Expand my territories so that I will be a blessing.

Chris Luppo, TV producer, media consultant, speaker, author

November

FAITH WALK

"I will guide you along the best pathway for your life.
I will advise you and watch over you."

Psalm 32:8 NLT

I was at a crossroads of two seemingly great opportunities, both in alignment with my life goals. I kept playing out in my mind which choice would be best and where each one could lead. Despite my in-depth scenario attempts, I still wasn't sure. So I chose to seek advice. I called my wise and faith-filled friend of many years and explained my situation to him. He gave me some of the best advice I've ever received: "Just make a choice and then let the chips fall where they may." This simple concept of confident trust lifted the burden of indecision right off me and gave me the push I needed to move.

Sometimes we must take that first step in faith, knowing God works out everything for our best. Always remember that he is our constant companion and guiding light. With our focus on him, we will surely be moving in the right direction.

Heavenly Father, you are such a wonderful leader! Thank you for always watching over me and for guiding me to green pastures and still waters.

Gianna Simone, actor, author, producer

SAY YES TO THE BEST

Everything is permissible for me,
but not all things are beneficial.

1 Corinthians 6:12 AMP

Let's face it; many of us can be stuck in the mode of saying yes to too many things, can't we? We love to be helpful, we aim to please others, and we try to fix things. We hate to be perceived as selfish, unsociable, or self-indulgent. But my friend, if you find yourself saying yes to too many things, it might be a good idea to ask God first before you say yes or no. There are many opportunities out there that are right and good, but they may not be the thing that God wants you to be doing.

Think for a minute. What is on your plate today that you wish you had said no to when asked? Always remember that God may be calling you to say no to something today so that you can say yes to something that is a better fit for you tomorrow. You can be free from the indecision and stress of wondering what's the right use of your time. Before you commit to the next thing, stop and send up a prayer of seven little words: "God, shall I say yes or no?"

Lord, give me wisdom to commit only to what you want me to do.

Kim Crabill, TV host, author, ministry leader,
Christian counselor

BREAK THE SILENCE

The LORD's unfailing love surrounds the one who trusts in him.

PSALM 32:10 NIV

Do you carry hurts and disappointments in the shape of abuses, addictions, and unfulfilled dreams, all of it begging for your attention? They want their day in court, but you keep stuffing them down, afraid to break the silence for fear of what will happen. If this is you, my friend, you'll relate to the writer of Psalm 32. He fought this same battle until he found his voice and took his troubles to God's listening ear. And what did he find? Not judgment. Not criticism. Not a cold shoulder. He found unfailing love.

Let me assure you that you don't need to be afraid to break the silence with God. Always remember that he is eager to hear from you. He's an utterly trustworthy confidant. Read the rest of Psalm 32 and find the courage to open your mouth and spill out everything into his listening ears. You may find yourself surrounded with songs of praise and shouts of deliverance!

Thank you, Father, for the unfailing love and forgiveness that you offer every day.

Kim Crabill, TV host, author, ministry leader, Christian counselor

DARKNESS TO LIGHT

"I know the plans I have for you," declares the LORD, "...to give you hope and a future."

JEREMIAH 29:11 NIV

Sometimes life just doesn't make sense. Bad things happen to good people—you or someone you know. Everything happens at once, and you're on a rollercoaster of emotions. A couple of years ago, it felt just like that for me. While I have always been known as someone with a sunny demeanor and positive outlook, it was not the case during that difficult season. In the middle of the day, I found myself with my covers up to my head, tears streaming down my face.

Feeling stressed, confused, and frustrated, I remembered Jeremiah 29:11. In the midst of my darkness, God was speaking to me, bringing light to my situation. Things did not change overnight, but I now had a clear reminder that God was with me. Whenever you feel like you are in the dark, always remember that God is light, and he can be your hope.

Lord, help me find your light when I'm in darkness. Please bring your hope to my situation.

Ella Hartt, Roses and Rainbows advisory board member, songwriter, singer, storyteller

GOD WILL RESCUE YOU AGAIN

"Call upon Me on the day of trouble;
I will rescue you, and you will honor Me."

Psalm 50:15 NASB

When you look back on your life and see the many times God has rescued you, it changes your perspective on the circumstances you face today. Maybe you feel like your back is up against a wall, and you are about to give up. But God has proven himself to you again and again. And your response when he does has probably been to praise him and to tell others of your wonderful Savior.

As someone who has been around for many decades, I can tell you that my list of "The times God rescued me" is very long. And I can tell you that each time he rescued me built my faith. You see, as a member of God's family, because of your faith in Jesus, you have special privileges that are not known to those who have not trusted our Savior. When you honor God with your life, he hears your prayers for help, and he will rescue you again and again. And sometimes he delivers you from things you don't even know about!

Lord, I've learned to never give up on life because you have never given up on me.

Carmen Pate, Roses and Rainbows advisory board member, author, speaker, Bible teacher, mentor of women

A SONG FOR EVERY OCCASION

Sing to the LORD a new song.

PSALM 149:1 NIV

Did you ever notice that some people have a song for every occasion? If you're in the same room for any length of time, you soon discover whether they're feeling happy or blue, energized or slogging through the day. You can gauge their frame of mind by the songs they sing. What song are you singing today, either aloud or in your mind? Is it a feel-good song, or have circumstances dictated that you sing one of sorrow, regret, or longing?

Did you know God wants you to sing a new song to him today? He even specifies the genre—a song of praise—because he knows you will benefit from continually giving glory to him. If you are in a difficult season, always remember that no matter what mood your spirit is in today, a song of praise can only make it better. That's why God wants us to have a song of praise for every occasion. What will yours be today?

Lord, please give me a heart that loves to sing praise to you in every season of life.

Kim Crabill, TV host, author, ministry leader,
Christian counselor

DRESS TO THE NINES

Put on every piece of God's armor so you will be able to resist the enemy.

EPHESIANS 6:13 NLT

How much time do you need to get dressed in the morning? Are you compelled to painstakingly attend to every detail of your appearance and attire, or are you the minimalist who hates to be bothered by too much time in front of the mirror? While making sure that our physical appearance represents our King, God has also given us clothing he wants us to wear to protect our spiritual selves. The design is brilliant. Every piece will fit you perfectly and has its own purpose for defeating the enemy. With the clothing God provides, you can live a truthful, righteous, peaceful life of faith.

Isn't God so good to have thought to provide these clothes for you? Doesn't it show so clearly his heart of love? When you face discouragement, doubt, and temptations, always remember that if you are dressed in the six pieces of God's designed armor as described in Ephesians 6, you have all the protection you need. He wants you to live confidently and walk courageously as you fight the enemy and fulfill your Father's plan for you.

Thank you, Father, for providing everything I need to live victoriously in this world.

Kim Crabill, TV host, author, ministry leader, Christian counselor

SELF-SUFFICIENCY OR CHRIST-SUFFICIENCY?

See that you do not refuse him who is speaking.

HEBREWS 12:25 ESV

I have a friend who is known for saying, "You will never know that Jesus is all you need until Jesus is all you have," and I always remember that. The opposite of self-sufficiency is Christ-sufficiency. I pray often that God will always keep some significant unmet need in my life so that I'm always dependent on him. Someone once called this prayer courageous, but it is not. It's a prayer of fear and awe—awe of a holy God. For God has the power to give us what we deserve, whether good or bad. I have come to fear, with reverence and awe, the God who is, for he is a consuming fire.

To be Christ-sufficient doesn't primarily mean that we surrender our minds. It means that we surrender our wills. Many think that surrendering the will diminishes the intellect, but it's just the opposite. The sharpened mind leads us through the process of surrender. Only thinking people advance themselves toward either self-sufficiency or Christ-sufficiency. Christ commands us to surrender to him as Lord and to do so regularly. The result is transformative…and mind boggling!

Lord, shake the heavens and the earth; remove the things that can be shaken from my life so that what remains is all in you.

Stu Fuhlendorf, senior pastor, author

TALENTS AND FLAWS

To all who mourn in Israel,
he will give a crown of beauty for ashes.

ISAIAH 61:3 NLT

Do you sometimes look at your life and think it is nothing to brag about? Others have a well-ordered life, complete with glowing talents and a room full of accolades. You, on the other hand, have too many mistakes, a few too many sins, and not enough successes. But did you know that you are just the kind of person God is looking for? That's right, my friend. God has always used flawed individuals who thought they had nothing to offer him.

He can and does use people with their successes, talents, and gifts, but he also uses the broken and the burdened. Sometimes that kind of heart best fulfills his good purposes. Don't lose hope today because you feel too flawed for God to use you. Always remember that it is most often in your pain that people will connect to you. It is where they find hope for themselves. Offer up all that you are to God—your flaws, mistakes, sins, foolishness, and weakness. He can transform them into lovely examples of his mercy and grace.

Lord, give me the courage to offer up my flaws, trusting you to transform them into beauty.

Kim Crabill, TV host, author, ministry leader,
Christian counselor

LIVE IN LOVE

God is love. Whoever lives in love lives in God, and God in them.

1 John 4:16 NIV

Recently, I had the opportunity to spend some time with my good friend, Dyan Cannon. Our conversation turned serious as we discussed the current times in which we are living. We talked about the sense of chaos and unrest among people these days and how we, as believers, can make an impact on our world. Her advice was emphatic and one I'll never forget: "We have to live in love," Dyan said. "We must embody love in the grocery store, in our offices, wherever we go."

Dyan went on to say, "This world can often be a lonely and desperate place, filled with struggles. We tend to seek answers externally, but they are not out there. We find the answers by turning inward to experience the presence of God. When we align with God's teachings rather than the world's, we possess the ability to live in love. Always remember," said Dyan, "the only love that will truly fill and complete you is God's love."

Father, help me to seek you every day. That way, I can navigate each day prepared to share your love wherever I go and with everyone I encounter.

Kim Crabill, TV host, author, ministry leader, Christian counselor with Dyan Cannon, actor, producer, director, screenwriter

VALUE THE DIFFERENCES

We have different gifts, according to the grace given to each of us.

ROMANS 12:6 NIV

Years ago, I managed a team comprised of experts from all areas of our company. It was an excellent group, but occasionally there were disagreements among individuals. In managing these differing opinions, I had to remember that every individual has unique skills and talents that can contribute to his or her success personally and professionally.

While the best teams are comprised of different talents, skills, knowledge, and attributes, bringing about a successful outcome with many differences can be extremely challenging. Right-brained and left-brained thinkers come from different perspectives. Imagine an artist and an accountant designing a brochure! But I found in my work situations that we could achieve amazing results if each member would truly value, appreciate, and use the different talents and ideas of others. The kingdom of God works in the same way—we all have unique gifts to use and roles to fulfill for his purposes. Years ago, my team gave me a picture that simply said, "Value the Differences." They must have heard it once or twice from me! Always remember to "value the differences."

Heavenly Father, thank you for my individual gifts. Help me to value my gifts and those of others and use them for your glory.

Gail Lawler, organizational development consultant

PORTRAITS OF JESUS

Follow my example, as I follow the example of Christ.

1 CORINTHIANS 11:1 NIV

Our lives are constantly drawing a picture of Jesus for those around us. Who popped into your mind when you read those words? Who do you think is a good example of Jesus today? More important, what impression of Jesus do others walk away with after spending an hour with you? The apostle Paul encouraged the believers in Corinth to imitate him as he imitated Christ. He wasn't claiming personal perfection but rather a close relationship with Christ, which led to the right behavior. If you aren't sure how well you're representing Jesus, then I urge you to hang out with him more often. The more you sit with him, the more accurate your representation will be.

On the other hand, if you skip spending time at Jesus' feet and focusing solely on serving him, people will see a lot of you but very little of Jesus. Sure, you will never portray Jesus perfectly, but always remember, it isn't about perfection. It's about Jesus being visible through your imperfection. And that, my friend, will create a picture of someone others will love to spend time with.

Lord, help me to spend time with you so I can portray you accurately to others.

Kim Crabill, TV host, author, ministry leader,
Christian counselor

FROM DESPAIR TO DELIGHT

Whom have I in heaven but you? And there is nothing on earth that I desire besides you.

PSALM 73:25–26 ESV

After a miscarriage a year after my daughter was born, doctors informed me I wouldn't get pregnant again. My husband and I had planned on a big family, and to me, this devastating news proved God wasn't doing his part. Was he really the good father I thought he was? Devastated, I marinated in self-pity longer than I'd like to admit.

God allowed me to wallow for a time but didn't let me stay there. He taught me the most important lesson I've ever learned: knowing him is far better than any gift he could possibly give me. He is worth everything, and in spite of my sorrow and disappointment, *he is enough*. I long to know him far more than I long for any earthly thing. "There is nothing on earth that I desire besides [him]" (Psalm 73:25 ESV). I can never forget the power of his goodness to me; I will always remember how he gently brought me to trust in his sovereignty over my life.

Lord, let me always trust that your will for me is good. You alone know exactly what I need.

Kate Battistelli, author, speaker, podcaster

PITY PARTY CANCELLED

He lifted me out of the slimy pit…
and gave me a firm place to stand.

Psalm 40:2 NIV

Dashed hopes and smashed dreams happen to everyone, but what do you do when they happen to you? It's easy to fall into the pit of self-pity, but that wallow only makes you feel worse. The best remedy for self-pity is to look outward rather than inward. Who needs help today? It could simply be the elderly woman across the street who's struggling to weed her flower bed. It may be the person who isn't tall enough to reach the item on the top shelf at the grocery store. So many folks can use a helping hand.

I promise that if you reach out to another, focusing on them and their needs rather than your own, you will find the pit of self-pity turning to solid ground. Always remember that God is using every event, including your smashed dreams, to give you a chance to do the kingdom work you've been longing to do. Don't give in to that pity party. Allow your ruined plans to be the catalyst for another person's joy.

Lord, thank you for providing a way for me to turn smashed dreams into royal successes.

Kim Crabill, TV host, author, ministry leader,
Christian counselor

WHERE AM I?

You discern my going out and my lying down;
you are familiar with all my ways.

PSALM 139:3 NIV

"You are here." Those three little words on the mall directory relieved my fatigue and frustration. I knew my destination, but before getting there, I had to know where I was. Has life left you feeling a little lost and fatigued lately? You will get to where you want to be by knowing *who* you are in addition to *where* you are. In Isaiah 42:1, God said, "Here is my servant, whom I uphold, my chosen one in whom I delight" (NIV). Jesus was proclaimed the Chosen One, but you have been chosen too.

When God chooses you, he loves you and delights in you every day. You never leave his mind, escape his sight, or flee from his thoughts. He has taken into account all your struggles and sins. He knows and understands you better than you understand yourself. When you feel lost, always remember that you have immediate access to God's enduring strength, wisdom, and rest. He knows right where you are and is always ready to remind you of who you are in him.

Lord, thank you for your presence and direction every day.

Kim Crabill, TV host, author, ministry leader, Christian counselor

IS NOW THE TIME?

I know that there is nothing better for people than… to do good while they live.

ECCLESIASTES 3:12 NIV

Do you feel God nudging you to do something today? He might be asking you to send an encouraging note to a struggling friend. Maybe you feel an urge to pick up the phone and call someone who has been on your mind, but you are afraid of interrupting their busy schedule. I know that indecision quite well, my friend. I struggle with "Should I or shouldn't I?" scenarios too. We don't want to bother anyone.

But the Bible tells us now is the time. The time to encourage. The time to do good. When you are in a moment of indecision, always remember that God's timing is perfect. The moment he puts something or someone on your mind, that is the time to act. Don't worry about being a bother; you need only to obey his voice. Your words may be just what that person needs to carry them through a hard day or to propel them to the finish line.

Lord, help me to always heed your voice when you prompt me to do something for you.

Kim Crabill, TV host, author, ministry leader, Christian counselor

JOIN THE CROWD

Faith is confidence in what we hope for and assurance about what we do not see.

HEBREWS 11:1 NIV

Are you engaged in a tug-of-war with hope today? Your circumstances suggest there is no reason for you to fight anymore; you are beyond the point of rescue. Still, you hesitate to let go because a flicker of hope is pulling you forward, promising a reward if you hold on. Whenever I find my hope faltering, I turn to the great cloud of witnesses in the Bible: people who never lost hope even in the direst of circumstances. They remind us that we, too, can accomplish the plans and purpose God has in mind for us.

God designed us to be inspired by the lives of others. Read Hebrews 11. It is full of uplifting accounts of those who remained faithful and held on to hope in the darkest of times. I hope you will always remember that in God's Word, you will find strength in the stories of those who have gone before you. After all, you do want to be included in that crowd one day!

Lord, give me faith that steadfastly trusts in you to revive my faltering hope.

Kim Crabill, TV host, author, ministry leader, Christian counselor

SLEEP WELL

Be ye angry, and sin not:
let not the sun go down upon your wrath.

EPHESIANS 4:26 KJV

I stormed out of the room with my pillow in hand and my cover dragging behind me. "What are you doing?" James asked cautiously as he followed close behind. "I'm sleeping on the couch!" I shouted, infuriated that he even asked. James responded in a calm resolute voice, "Then I am too."

I didn't expect that. He came back with his pillow and explained to me that we would never let the sun go down on our anger toward each other and would never sleep apart unless it was absolutely necessary. If there was a problem, we would talk it out until we got a resolution, even if it took all night. And it did. But the issue got resolved, and we woke up peacefully on the couch in each other's arms. James had to be strong for me in my weakness. Always remember that problems happen in every relationship; it's how we respond that makes all the difference.

Lord, give me grace and strength to support others in their weaknesses. Help me to seek reconciliation over separation.

James and Justina Page, pastor and elect lady

BEHIND THE DOUBT

Hope deferred makes the heart sick,
but a longing fulfilled is a tree of life.

PROVERBS 13:12 NIV

Are you struggling with doubts about God's presence in your life today? Is his apparent lack of action in your circumstances causing confusion and something akin to feelings of abandonment? Welcome to the story of Thomas, the disciple who struggled with doubts too. He loved Jesus deeply, and the pain he felt at Jesus' death was distressing and disorienting. When the other disciples announced that they'd seen Jesus, Thomas responded with doubt (John 20:24–25). He refused to allow hope to enter because, if they were wrong, he'd only hurt worse. He chose to protect his heart.

Then one day Jesus answered his doubt by showing up and letting Thomas touch the evidence (John 20:26–29). When he did, Thomas's joy was uncontainable. My friend, God understands your tendency to doubt when life becomes confusing and deferred hope causes deep pain, but he wants you to hold on to trust. Always remember that his work on your behalf may be invisible, but he is working nonetheless. When it appears he has abandoned you, he is only preparing you for a season of joy.

Lord, give me faith that overcomes doubt and anticipates blessings.

Kim Crabill, TV host, author, ministry leader,
Christian counselor

STRENGTH FOR TODAY'S STRUGGLE

Be strong in the Lord and in the strength of his might.

EPHESIANS 6:10 ESV

Are you feeling like you want to give up today? Are things beginning to be too hard to bear? Are you wondering why you thought you could take on such a challenge? Take heart, for the Lord is with you in today's struggle. God promises to give you strength and comfort in times of trouble and discouragement. In Isaiah 41:10, he said, "Do not fear, for I am with you; do not be dismayed, for I am your God. I will strengthen you and help you; I will uphold you with my righteous right hand" (NIV).

We can also find inspiration from the story of Job. Despite facing immense suffering and loss, Job chose to remain faithful to God and was rewarded for his perseverance. Just like Job, we can choose to trust in the Lord's plan for our lives even when things seem bleak. Always remember that God's love and grace are sufficient for you. He never gives you more than he can handle.

Father, give me the strength to persevere through challenges and the faith to trust in your plan. Allow your peace and comfort to be my guiding light in times of disappointment and darkness.

Kim Crabill, TV host, author, ministry leader,
Christian counselor

TIME AFTER TIME

Whoever does not love does not know God,
because God is love.

1 John 4:8 NIV

I come from a musical family. Piano players, vocalists, and more filled our family growing up, and music was an integral part of our family gatherings. My dad had a captivating voice and was known to sing oldies with verses that spoke to God's everlasting love for each of us. If you have not spent much time listening to old religious classics, I encourage you to do some research and listen to a few.

Music enriches the soul. My dad has gone on to glory, but I will always remember how he expressed his love for us in such a beautiful way. Love is from God; God is love (1 John 4:8).

Lord, may your grace touch my soul to live in love, express love, speak love, and receive love.

Melinda D. Davis, Roses and Rainbows advisory board member, radio network executive

WATCH HIM WORK

"Humanly speaking, it is impossible. But with God everything is possible."

MATTHEW 19:26 NLT

Are you sitting in bewilderment, studying the messed-up puzzle pieces of your life and wondering how on earth God could ever use you? Discouraged, you let out a huff of frustration, and your shoulders droop because you know God's using you for his kingdom is impossible. My friend, no matter how tempting it is, please don't give in to that lie. The things that seem impossible to you are no big deal to the God of the universe.

All those hurtful repulsive bits of you that shout condescending messages don't intimidate him in the least. He surveys the mistakes, hurts, and abandoned dreams and then proclaims, "I can work with this!" The truth is that what you or others see as spiritually catastrophic, God stands ready to put to good use. He invites you to change your view of him. As you watch him do his thing, always remember that you serve the God for whom all things are possible. Let him work through you, providing the faith and strength you need to believe. You may be on the verge of becoming God's greatest miracle!

Lord, thank you so much that you can take my messed-up life and create something miraculous from it.

Kim Crabill, TV host, author, ministry leader, Christian counselor

UNASHAMED

Do not be ashamed of the testimony of our Lord.

2 TIMOTHY 1:8 NASB

We were in shock and saddened when my father was diagnosed with cancer so young. The doctors said he didn't have long to live. Dad was an incredible blessing to us all. His joy in life was his walk with the Lord and his family. He walked his talk. He always encouraged us to live out our faith. In his final days in the hospital, Dad seemed to hang on. With the family out of the room, I had some time alone with him.

As he lay there, though he wasn't responsive, I felt compelled to talk to him. At that moment, I believe the Holy Spirit reminded me of some of Paul's final words to his son in the faith, Timothy. I told him, "Dad, thank you for your love, and thank you for your testimony. I will never be ashamed of the gospel. I will take the baton from you, and I will run the race." Always remember to live out your faith and run your race. How are you running, my friend?

Lord, allow me to be a godly witness so that my children will run their race for you.

Kathleen Hardaway, author, speaker

GOD OF COMPLETION

He who began a good work in you will carry it on to completion.

Philippians 1:6 NIV

Hey there, my friend! How about rejoicing with me? Today is a new day, just waiting for us to fulfill the purposes of God. OK, I know you might struggle with the idea of rejoicing, particularly if you are sitting here measuring your strength against the job God has called you to do. Even King David struggled with God's calling. On one occasion he tells us he "was worn out from sobbing" (Psalm 6:6 NLT), yet another time he states that when he prayed for help, God answered him and freed him from all his fear (Psalm 34:4).

Always remember that being human means you will sometimes feel worry and stress. That's why I wanted to remind you today that God is doing a good work in you. You can be confident that he will complete all that he has planned for you to do. So don't stop. Keep going, my friend. This is your day!

Lord, thank you that you are always faithful to fulfill the good purposes you have for my life.

Kim Crabill, TV host, author, ministry leader, Christian counselor

CALL THE DESIGNER

The God of Israel....He is the Creator of everything that exists.

JEREMIAH 10:16 NLT

I stood before the window with my new drapes, extremely frustrated. No matter how hard I tried, I could not arrange the panels to match the picture before me. I needed help, so I called the woman who'd made them. She arrived and, with a flick of her hand, effortlessly put each panel in its proper place. How could she so easily do what I could not? Because she had created them.

My friend, you, too, have a creator to call on for help when life becomes twisted and tangled. He has ordered every detail of your life. It is nothing for him to heal your disease, restore your income, mend your marriage, or whatever it is that you need. No matter what is or isn't happening in your life, no matter how hard you try to set things right, always remember that God is the creator. Only he knows how to take the messy broken pieces of your life and make them into a thing of beauty. Take courage and invite the Master Designer in to straighten out the situation for you.

Lord, thank you for stepping into my brokenness and making it beautiful.

Kim Crabill, TV host, author, ministry leader,
Christian counselor

THE BLESSINGS OF THANKFULNESS

I will give thanks to you, LORD, with all my heart;
I will tell of all your wonderful deeds.

PSALMS 9:1 NIV

I am a model and an actor. The Lord has placed me in a dark industry for a reason, and I know I will face testing and battles. I fight comparison, vanity, coveting, and anxiety in myself, and I often find myself comparing my journey with others, especially on social media. I think most of us can relate to this. We see that person going on their third vacation, that woman who got the promotion, or that one we feel is prettier.

Those thoughts are a part of Satan's plan to destroy us by discouragement. He knows what God wants most from us is thankfulness. If we don't take those thoughts captive, they will block us from our blessings and rob our joy. My manager, a wonderful man of God, told me to always remember that God wants to give big gifts to his children. He always wants to give us more, but our gifts are determined by thankfulness for what we have. Being thankful is what God designed us for. His joy and his blessings will then overflow to others.

Thank you for the greatest gift ever given: Jesus!

Alisha Griffin, actor, model, blogger

BEYOND STATISTICS

All the days ordained for me were written in Your book.

PSALM 139:16 NIV

Shortly after my mother was diagnosed with cancer, a terrible fear gripped my soul. I would look at my little boys and pray, *Lord, just let me live to see them grow up*. That cloak of fear wrapped itself tightly around me, and I viewed the world in a completely different way. It took a long time to recognize it, but when I did, I began to call on God for discernment. It was then that I discovered something so profound that I want you to always remember it: you are not bound by this world's statistics.

You may be poring over charts, reports, and statistics, knowing things don't look favorable, but may you always remember that the Lord has already determined the length of our days. Ecclesiastes says there's a time to be born and a time to die. Nothing will change that statistic. So, my friend, look up! Live each day guided by God's promises; they never fail.

Lord, keep me from giving in to the fear that wants to rob me of your joy.

Kim Crabill, TV host, author, ministry leader, Christian counselor

FOR EXAMPLE

"My Father, if it is possible, may this cup be taken from me. Yet not as I will, but as you will."

MATTHEW 26:39 NIV

When someone says "submission," do you think of a timid man, muttering, "Yes, dear!" as his shrew of a wife bellows her demands? This is usually the kind of picture today's culture has of submission. Grown men and women resist the very thought of being submissive. We see it as a sign of weakness, and we're strong independent creatures, right?

That is, we resist it until we read today's verse. Even the Holy Trinity gives us this startling picture of submission. Always remember that Jesus, tortured emotionally and physically, understood the sort of death he faced, but even in his agony, he submitted himself to his Father. What an example he set for us! No matter what we face, Jesus has been there ahead of us. He extends a hand to help us through, to his glory and our blessing! The more often we follow his example, the easier it becomes to submit to his authority.

Father, help me to be like Jesus. Thank you for his example of submitting even unto death. Help me to submit to the "little deaths" I might face today.[24]

Pat Boone, actor, singer, songwriter, author

24 Adapted from *Pat Boone Devotional Book*, published by Bible Voice, Inc. Used by permission from Mr. Boone.

YOU BELONG

Even if my father and mother abandon me,
the LORD will hold me close.

PSALM 27:10 NLT

"You cannot put a price tag on solid family relationships," the woman stated, deep emotion on her face. How do those words sit with you today? Does a smile light your face as you think of your own loved ones, or does a tear form in the corner of your eye as you wonder what on earth that would feel like? The truth is, some of us grieve the fact that we will never know the stability of a strong family dynamic. If you stand on the outside looking in, a lump of jealousy in your throat, I want you to know that your grief is legitimate. But you don't have to carry it alone.

The psalmist struggled with feelings of family rejection and abandonment. In his pain he found that the Lord was there, holding him close. Whenever you mourn the absence of a close, happy family, always remember that you can go to God for comfort. He understands your longings. He will comfort your soul and remind you that you do belong to a family—the family of God.

Father God, thank you for the special love and tenderness you show to the rejected heart.

Kim Crabill, TV host, author, ministry leader,
Christian counselor

YOU SEE ME

She gave this name to the LORD who spoke to her:
"You are the God who sees me."

GENESIS 16:13 NIV

I recently participated in my first road race since before I had kids. It was an 8K, nothing close to the marathons I used to run, but it felt like my way of victoriously reclaiming life after nearly a decade of breastfeeding babies and toddlers, being pregnant on and off, enduring multiple losses, and recovering from a near-death emergency.

I realized the day beforehand that the race was on the anniversary of my third son's funeral. On race day, I unexpectedly saw the building where I almost died after his loss. All the air left my lungs in an overwhelming moment, but I kept running. I looked toward the road ahead and saw someone holding a poster that said, "This is your victory lap!" My mood shifted to gratitude. I began to sob. God always sees me—at the graveyard years ago and as I run with newfound strength into the future. Always remember that God always sees you.

God, I adore you for being the one who collects each one of my tears. I praise you for seeing me in the unseen-by-the-world moments.

Maggie Winzeler, women's wellness writer,
business owner

December

SPARKLY OR GLAZED?

In all things Jesus has first place.

COLOSSIANS 1:18 NCV

"It's Christmas time!" Do those words make your eyes sparkle, or do they glaze over with exhaustion at the mere mention of our nation's busiest season? I mean, added to your regular workload are the school plays, social functions at work, acquiring and sending out the perfect family photo, and the buying and sending of gifts. How will you do all this and still enjoy the season? Daniel shows us the way. Before his values and priorities were ever challenged, he "purposed in his heart" that he wouldn't be swayed from his convictions (Daniel 1:8 KJV).

You can do the same if you first identify what you want this Christmas to mean to you and your family. What are your Christmas values? Always remember that God's desire is for you to celebrate the gift of his Son, not stress yourself to the point of exhaustion. So check your schedule, my friend, and see what you value most. Then cross the rest of the items off your list and enjoy a restful month of celebrating Jesus, the best gift ever!

Lord, help me to keep my heart in tune with you through this sometimes chaotic season.

Kim Crabill, TV host, author, ministry leader, Christian counselor

BAD TIMES, GOOD FRUIT

The fruit of the Spirit is love, joy, peace, patience, kindness, goodness, faithfulness, gentleness, self-control.

Galatians 5:22–23 NASB

We never know what's going to come our way in life. Sometimes the unexpected will change life forever. That happened to me when my husband had a massive stroke. He was an active man, a deacon in our church, retired from an amazing career with Billy Graham, and enjoying his family. Everyone admired and respected him. Though our lives did change, God gave me true love, peace, and joy in the thirteen years I cared for my husband until he went to be with the Lord.

People would comment about how hard it must be, and I would say, "No, surprisingly, it isn't. God gives me all I need, and I have true joy in managing his care." The response I got from my husband each day was all I needed. The light of Jesus shone from his eyes and in his reactions, however limited. Always remember, God knows our difficult situations, and he can turn them around so we have his love, peace, and joy.

Father, thank you that you are in control of all things. Make me grateful for all you have done during the hard times. Help me trust you always.

Suellen Roberts, media influencer

MIND AND MUSCLES

The heart of the discerning acquires knowledge,
for the ears of the wise seek it out.

PROVERBS 18:15 NIV

So you have a dream. Good for you! No doubt you're dedicating countless hours to training and refining your skills, whether you're pursuing athletics, music, art, or business. Keep going. Keep practicing. Stay intentional. But don't forget about the other areas of your life, particularly intellectual and relational ones. If you're a student pursuing sports, don't let schoolwork slide down the list of priorities. If you're in the business world climbing the ladder, don't push family time to the side.

I understand the temptation to focus solely on one thing—for me, it was sports. However, I discovered that pursuing a master's degree opened doors in my career, even within the sporting world. Education equips you with valuable tools, enhances your discipline, and prepares you for life after sports (or music, or parenting), which can come sooner than you expect. Keep working toward your aspirations and dreams, but I hope you'll always remember that building your mind and investing in relationships are just as vital as building your muscles or special skills.

Lord, please direct my priorities to follow the path you have set for me so that I'll become the person you created me to be.

Michael Curry, former NBA player/coach
and college coach

CHRISTMAS PRESSURE

There was no place for them in the inn.

Luke 2:7 ESV

We Americans go all out for Christmas, don't we? Almost without realizing it, we're swept up into a world of busyness and festivities. In our quest to find the perfect gift, the best Christmas décor, or the tastiest food for the party, we sometimes allow pressure to creep in and steal our peace, don't we? Well, friend, sometimes pressure is unavoidable, but we do have a choice in how we handle it.

Joseph and Mary knew about Christmas pressure. God allowed a crazy census to happen right when Mary was due to give birth. How would she and Joseph make a trip that was uncomfortable in the best of circumstances but almost unthinkable now? And when they finally reached Bethlehem, no bed awaited the weary travelers. Talk about pressure! But there's no evidence of panic in their story, and neither does there need to be in yours. When the pressure builds, always remember that Christmas isn't about perfect circumstances or the best finger food. It's about God's gift to you—the birth of One who can replace your pressure with peace.

Lord, help me to remember to choose peace over pressure during this busy Christmas season.

Kim Crabill, TV host, author, ministry leader, Christian counselor

WHEN THE GOING GETS TOUGH

The God of all grace, who called you...will himself restore you and make you strong, firm and steadfast.

1 PETER 5:10 NIV

Sometimes life starts feeling a bit unbearable, doesn't it? We can have such overwhelming pain or embarrassment that we feel our heart is about to explode. Sometimes the weight of the world can make us feel as though we're struggling to walk through fast-drying cement. In moments of such great difficulty, we can draw strength from the experiences of Elijah, the prophet who faced immense challenges yet remained steadfast in his trust in God.

In the book of 1 Kings, we see three principles that Elijah implemented: he relied on God's provision and timing, he maintained an eternal perspective, and he sought comfort and strength through prayer. My friend, as you face the challenges of today, always remember that God's desire is for you to press on with courage and perseverance. He assures all of us of his constant presence and unwavering support. When the going gets tough, let's cling to the one who is stronger than all, our God, who is our deliverer and our sustainer.

Heavenly Father, in times of struggle, grant me the grace to rely on the strength that comes from your grace and wisdom.

Kim Crabill, TV host, author, ministry leader,
Christian counselor

EMPOWERED!

"You will receive power when the Holy Spirit comes upon you. And you will be my witnesses, telling people about me everywhere."

ACTS 1:8 NLT

For years, I tried to do life without the aid of the Holy Spirit. It was a powerless and exhausting rat race—a lot like trying to function without legs: with a lot of ingenuity and effort it is doable, but a fully functioning body makes things so much easier! Becoming Spirit-filled takes your calling to the next level and brings assistance from God that you didn't even know you needed. No amount of human effort, preparation, or training will ever replace the incredible third person of the Trinity.

Ten years ago, a prayer team laid hands on me, and one week later I had a powerful encounter. The Holy Spirit became the most awesome teacher, comforter, and advocate I'd ever known. Pressure to perform and to figure things out vanished, and I was finally running like the wind. Always remember: you can accomplish powerful work through the Holy Spirit.

Dear Lord, please fill me with the Holy Spirit and help me to be sensitive to his leadings.

Melissa Huray, author, podcast host

THE WANDERER

"It is time to bring back the Ark of our God,
for we neglected it."

1 Chronicles 13:3 NLT

Do you ever wander away from close fellowship with God? You know how it is. Life gets busy. One thing leads to another until you realize you have stopped asking God for direction. You've started going your own way, relying on yourself instead of God. This is an age-old human struggle. The people of Israel wandered away from God's heart many times. During one of those seasons of poor choices and disobedience, the ark of God was captured by the Philistines (see 1 Samuel 4). When David became king, he announced that it was time to bring the ark back to Israel where it belonged (1 Chronicles 13).

Has God been nudging you lately, reminding you to come back to his heart? If so, always remember that God is only a prayer away. You can reposition your heart and find close communion with him again. He wants to see the ark of your life in its rightful place again.

Lord, I am prone to wandering from you. Thank you for your love that draws me back.

Kim Crabill, TV host, author, ministry leader,
Christian counselor

ALREADY EQUIPPED

All Scripture is God-breathed and is useful....so that the servant of God may be thoroughly equipped for every good work.

2 Timothy 3:16–17 NIV

Are you facing doubts today? Do you find yourself questioning your abilities and feeling overwhelmed by your circumstances? I know how easy it can be to listen to the voices that say you can't, but as believers, we have access to a higher truth. In times of uncertainty, remember the words of Philippians 4:13: "I can do all things through Christ who strengthens me" (NKJV). Trust in the promise that nothing is impossible with God (Luke 1:37) and lean on his wisdom rather than your own understanding (Proverbs 3:5).

No matter what challenges may come, know that God has already equipped you with what you need to overcome them. Rely on him, and you will fulfill the calling he has placed on your life. God's plans for you are good and purposeful. He sees you as you are presently, but he also sees your potential. My friend, confront your doubts and always remember that God's strength will sustain you through every challenge. Have faith that he will make a way where there seems to be no way.

Lord, thank you that I can do all things through Christ who strengthens me. Help me to not be swayed by doubts or circumstances.

Kim Crabill, TV host, author, ministry leader, Christian counselor

LEAN IN

"Ask me and I will tell you remarkable secrets you do not know about things to come."

JEREMIAH 33:3 NLT

Is this what life's going to be from now on? That question popped into my mind often during a certain season, always following my discovery of another obstacle to what I wanted to do. My husband was going through a period of illness and hospital visits. And while I truly loved being able to take care of him, our situation came with restrictions, giving rise to my internal complaint. Maybe you've had times of similar frustration—times when you couldn't do what you wanted, longed to go on vacation, felt stuck in a job or a relationship or the "mundane-ness" of life…and you couldn't see things changing anytime soon.

My complaining went on until I heard the words *Lean in*. I felt God whispering in my spirit, *Lean in to me and I will show you how to experience joy, how to draw out every bit of goodness in those mundane moments.* Of course, frustrations still popped up, and I still complained sometimes. But when I really leaned into Jesus, he showed me the joy tucked into each moment, the things I could never have seen on my own.

Jesus, remind me always to seek you that I may see the good you have placed before me.

Karen Lombardo, Roses and Rainbows Ministry

EMBRACE YOUR FUTURE

Forgetting what is behind and straining toward what is ahead, I press on toward the goal.

PHILIPPIANS 3:13–14 NIV

When you were a kid, did it seem like your mother had eyes in the back of her head? You couldn't figure out how she could possibly see what was going on behind her, but somehow she did. Those days are long gone now, but maybe you have developed the same feature of focusing on what lies behind you in your past rather than looking ahead to the possibilities and dreams of the future. You're stuck in the land of regret and all that could have been.

A backward focus keeps you from seeing God's promises for your future. Always remember that nothing bad from your past can keep God from using you today. He is still able to carry out his good plans and purposes for your life. Ask him to open your eyes to all that he has for you today and for your future. Catch his enthusiasm and move forward with joy.

Lord, help me keep my eyes fixed on future possibilities rather than my past mistakes.

Kim Crabill, TV host, author, ministry leader, Christian counselor

YOU ARE FOREVER FAMILY

"His father saw him, and his heart went out to him; he ran and hugged his son and kissed him."

Luke 15:20 NET

For a season of my life, I turned my back on the Lord and lived a life that dishonored God and shamed my family. My sweet grandmother never turned her back on me. Instead, she reminded me that I would forever be part of the family and would always have her love. She wasn't condoning my sin. My grandmother's love and grace were a stronger message to my sinful heart than any scolding could have been. She reminded me of God's love and his desire for me to know him more and love him in return.

When I became a believer, the Holy Spirit convicted me. I felt the shame and brokenness I had caused others. I repented and turned to the Lord, grateful for his mercy and grace. As a Christian, you are part of God's forever family. You sometimes fail, but that doesn't change your relationship with the Father. Your fellowship will need to be restored, and that may require his loving conviction and discipline until you repent, but always remember that God will forever be your Father.

Father, thank you for your grace that assures me I am forever yours.

Carmen Pate, Roses and Rainbows advisory board member, author, speaker, Bible teacher, mentor of women

FEELING INVISIBLE

"This day in the city of David there has been born for you a Savior."

LUKE 2:11 AMP

Christmas is a season of peace on earth, goodwill to all, and joy to the world. At least that's what is emblazoned on every church sign, greeting card, and item of Christmas decor. Does the burden you carry tell a different story? Do you dread social events because they only point out your feelings of inadequacy among your peers? Well, my friend, I want you to know God has a special place in his heart for the one who feels invisible.

When he announced the arrival of his Son, God didn't send the angels to the super-spiritual Pharisees or the ultra-wealthy citizens of Bethlehem. God decided instead to come to shepherds, the invisible of the day. His message was clear: "A Savior has been born to you" (Luke 2:11 NIV). God has no favorites; his Son came for every person, and that includes you. Always remember that you don't have to be important in the eyes of the world to be used by God. After all, he chose shepherds to deliver the message our whole world rejoices over today.

Lord, thank you for choosing to send your messages through anyone willing to be used by you.

Kim Crabill, TV host, author, ministry leader, Christian counselor

A WHISPER FROM HEAVEN

After the fire came a gentle whisper.

1 Kings 19:12 NIV

We have reached the season when Christmas music fills the air, no matter which way we turn. Lyrics of "Joy to the World" and "Deck the Halls" mix with "I'll Be Home for Christmas" and "Frosty the Snowman." Amid the hustle and bustle, we sometimes forget to listen for Jesus. Where will you listen for him today? In the church choir? He might be there. In the blare of the mall's Christmas marching band? He might be there also.

But he isn't only in the music. When you sit down for a meal at a restaurant, is Jesus in the sigh of a weary server? He might be. In the exhausted eyes of the young mother who is trying to hold the family together? Maybe. Elijah might have expected God to speak to him in dramatic, impossible-to-miss ways, but God didn't thunder down from heaven. He whispered. As you walk through the next few busy, noisy weeks, pay attention to the people you meet. And always remember to listen for the still small whisper of God. Be expectant. Be ready to be surprised.

Lord, give me ears to hear your still, small voice as it directs my steps to meet others' needs.

Kim Crabill, TV host, author, ministry leader,
Christian counselor

HE QUALIFIES THE UNQUALIFIED

A gift opens the way and ushers the giver
into the presence of the great.

Proverbs 18:16 NIV

Are there times when you don't feel worthy or qualified? I've felt this way. In fact, when I was invited to participate in this book, I felt unqualified. Another time, I was asked to speak at the United Nations Bible study in New York City. That was intimidating! I didn't think the leader was even confident in me as a speaker. Yet I shared my testimony and what was on my heart, and I was surprised by the power of the Spirit's anointing and the audience's response. So many people talked to me afterward and told me how they were encouraged and blessed. Even the leader was excited and invited me to come back.

Sometimes we just need to say yes and see how the Holy Spirit will show up and move through us. It may not be convenient; it may stretch us beyond our comfort zone. But it will be worth the risk. I love Psalm 138:3: "When I called, you answered me; you greatly emboldened me." Always remember that when we are weak, he is strong (2 Corinthians 12:10).

Father, embolden me and give me confidence to do great and mighty deeds in you.

Chris Luppo, TV producer, media consultant,
speaker, author

EXCESS BAGGAGE

Let us throw off everything that hinders and the sin that so easily entangles.

HEBREWS 12:1 NIV

For many people, wintertime comes with a collection of boots, mittens, and bulky coats. Sometimes trying to get somewhere quickly is difficult because these things hinder our progress. Our spiritual lives experience winter seasons from time to time too. We want to go places and do things for God, but we have all this extra stuff hanging on that hampers our best efforts.

Is anything hindering your progress right now? Doubt? Worry? Feelings of unworthiness? Is life too busy? Maybe things have gotten so bad that you think God can't fix the mess. Friend, if you find yourself burdened with excess baggage, Hebrews 12 is a great place to go for encouragement. So many others before you have fought this same battle, and how did they disentangle themselves? By turning to Jesus, the one who helps us identify and get rid of the things that bog us down. I hope you will always remember that God's intention is for you to live and work in freedom. Let him disentangle you so that you are free to run again. He will turn the heaviness of winter into the lightheartedness of springtime.

Lord, help me to shed all that entangles me so I can live with a light heart.

Kim Crabill, TV host, author, ministry leader, Christian counselor

PRUNED

"He cuts off every branch in me that bears no fruit, while every branch that does bear fruit he prunes so that it will be even more fruitful."

John 15:2 NIV

Remember in *The Wizard of Oz* when Dorothy picked an apple off a tree and the tree smacked her hand? It seems silly to say, but we're not so very different from that tree! As we mature spiritually, we may find ourselves abandoning old pursuits, old habits, even old friends. We might even grieve who we used to be before we felt affirmed by God rather than man, before we felt accountable for our actions and sorry for our sins. Like Dorothy's overly sensitive apple tree, we don't like being pruned.

Always remember, though, that God is doing a good work in you. Sawing off branches may not feel good, but it creates strong and sturdy trees. As head caretaker in his orchard, Jesus moves among the trees (us), pruning back many branches. God has a vested interest in the harvest and in stimulating new growth and healthier trees. Next time you think you're having a setback, consider that you may be getting pruned. Bloom and resolve to stay fruitful!

Lord, I'm willing to undergo your expert "trimming," knowing that you're bringing forth new fruit and more growth for eternity. I know I can trust you with my life.[25]

Pat Boone, actor, singer, songwriter, author

25 Adapted from *Pat Boone Devotional Book*, published by Bible Voice, Inc. Used by permission from Mr. Boone.

PICKLEBALL, ANYONE?

Do you not know that you are the temple of God and that the Spirit of God dwells in you?

1 Corinthians 3:16 NKJV

How are you feeling today? Taking care of our body and spirit is crucial since unhealthy living can take a toll on both. I know because I struggled with an eating disorder for most of my life. Now I know that nurturing and nourishing my body holistically is far more important than striving to look thin and buff on the outside. Healthy living is about treating our bodies as what they truly are: temples of the Holy Spirit!

Striving to live a healthier lifestyle includes eating a balanced diet filled with fruits, vegetables, whole grains, and lean protein. If possible, incorporate physical activity like walking or pickleball each day, and try to get enough sleep to allow your body to rest and recover. Remember, seek your doctors' recommendations before making any health changes. Always remember that our bodies are a gift from God entrusted to us for his glory. Let's strive to steward our health with gratitude and diligence, recognizing that by caring for ourselves, we are better equipped to serve others and fulfill God's purpose for our lives.

Father, grant me the wisdom and strength to prioritize my health so that I may glorify you in all I do.

Kim Crabill, TV host, author, ministry leader, Christian counselor

GOD OF THE GIANTS

"I come against you in the name of the Lord Almighty."

1 Samuel 17:45 NIV

What do you face today? What giant seems insurmountable? Is it depression? Debt? Loneliness? Just as David stood before Goliath, bravely facing his towering foe, we, too, will confront challenges that feel overwhelming. In those moments, it's essential to remember David's example of resourcefulness and faith. David didn't approach Goliath empty-handed; he picked up five smooth stones (v. 40), symbols of his trust in God's provision and readiness to meet the giant. Similarly, Samson used the jawbone of a donkey to achieve victory (Judges 15:15–17), demonstrating that God can use the simplest tools for mighty purposes.

When facing our personal giants, we can take inspiration from these stories. We can find what is at hand to help us. We can be assured that God equips us for the battles we face. With faith and courage, you can move forward in your calling, trusting in God's strength. God wants you to always remember that on your own, many things in life will seem impossible to overcome, but you are not alone. Just like David, you face your giants with God.

Lord, help me face my giants with courage, knowing that you have equipped me for every battle. Guide me to use what is at hand to walk confidently in your calling.

Kim Crabill, TV host, author, ministry leader, Christian counselor

HAMMERING OUT GOD'S PLAN

I call to God Most High,
to God who fulfills his purpose for me.

Psalm 57:2 CSB

Are you being called to follow God's path even though it seems difficult, unpopular, and even impossible? Noah surely faced ridicule and uncertainty as he obediently picked up a hammer to build an ark to save his family and pairs of animals from the impending flood. Despite the challenges, Noah's unwavering faith in God's plan stood as a testament to his trust in the Almighty.

Just as Noah trusted God's wisdom and sovereignty, we are also called to have confidence in the divine guidance we receive. Though the road may be rocky, embracing God's plan with faith and obedience leads us to experience his unfailing provision and faithfulness in our lives. Following God's will often leads to unexpected blessings. Always remember that God's plans are designed for our good and his glory. By faithfully obeying his call, we can continue to witness the miraculous unfold in our lives.

Father, help me to trust in your plan for my life. Show me how to obey and "pick up my hammer," knowing that your plans are always for my good and your glory.

Kim Crabill, TV host, author, ministry leader,
Christian counselor

ALONE BUT NEVER ABANDONED

He heals the brokenhearted and binds up their wounds.

PSALM 147:3 NIV

Feeling abandoned can cut deep, especially when someone we love and trust hurts our feelings. It's natural to feel alone in those moments, but we have something greater to rely on: the truth that we're never truly abandoned. In Isaiah 41:10, God promises, "Do not fear, for I am with you; do not be dismayed, for I am your God. I will strengthen you and help you." During times of feeling abandoned and hurt, we can turn to God for comfort and guidance. We can spend time in prayer, opening our hearts to him and allowing his peace to fill us.

We can seek solace in his Word by meditating on Scripture passages that remind us of his constant presence and faithfulness. Additionally, we can choose to surround ourselves with supportive believers who can offer encouragement and prayer. Always remember that God's love for you is unfailing even when others fail you. In times of hurt, turn to him, for he is the healer of all wounds and the restorer of all brokenness.

Lord, when I feel abandoned and hurt by others, help me to remember that you are always with me and that I can find comfort in your presence.

Kim Crabill, TV host, author, ministry leader, Christian counselor

MORE THAN A BABY

"He will reign for ever and ever."

REVELATION 11:15 NIV

My holiday wreath is adorned with four things: a crown of thorns, a nail, a crown, and a scepter. It reminds me that Christmas is not the most important holiday. Easter is! You see, creation began with two perfect humans communing with God. Then they sinned, disobeying God. The result is that we are all born physically alive but spiritually dead. That first sin had to be paid for before we could have full spiritual life with God. We all had to be forgiven, and Scripture says forgiveness of sin requires the shedding of blood (Hebrews 9:22).

So the baby we celebrate at Christmas was born for one reason: to die for our sins. Christmas is not only the birth of our Savior but the celebration of the beginning of the end of sin and death. The angels announced that our peace with God would be restored by the baby in the manger. That's why, for me, the most important item on my wreath is a crown for our King. Always remember, this baby will reign first in our hearts, then as the King of kings!

Lord, thank you for the baby born to die and be our King.

Shelia Erwin, author, ministry leader, Bible teacher

GROWING UP

Grow in the grace and knowledge of our Lord and Savior Jesus Christ.

2 Peter 3:18 NIV

"What do you want to be when you grow up?" You remember that question, don't you? As a child, your answer probably varied. You had big dreams, and anything was possible. Now as an adult, you look back and maybe feel some regret: *Why didn't I grow up faster? Why am I not further along in life?* We ask the same questions about our spiritual lives, too, don't we? We wish we had more knowledge. We long to be more mature.

If this is you, I want you to always remember that growing spiritually is not so much about growing up as it is about growing in love. It is about a growing dependency on and deeper intimacy with Christ more than a desire to overcome adversity. As we spend time with God, our knowledge and our love for Jesus grows and transforms our minds, bringing the maturity we seek. Christ will be the greatness that grows up in you.

Lord, thank you for the growth that comes from spending time with you.

Kim Crabill, TV host, author, ministry leader, Christian counselor

THE RIGHT MINDSET

Command them to do good, to be rich in good deeds.

1 Timothy 6:18 NIV

Two mindsets are alive and well today. There's just one problem: they are both lies. One version declares the challenge too big and your strength too small. You are too busy, or your hurts run too deep. The other version says that what you are being asked to do is beneath you. The task's insignificance makes you toss it aside because it won't make a difference anyway. Which one do you struggle with, my friend? Maybe a little of both?

Remember how Jesus fed five thousand people with only five loaves and two fish? The crowd was "too big" and the lunch "too little." But the right mindset saved the day. You cannot comprehend Jesus' power or wisdom when he asks you to do something, but he can. When you are tempted to think a job is too big or too small, always remember that Jesus knows the difference your obedience will make. It's time to untangle your mind from the size of the task and focus on the real issue. Are you willing to be obedient to any task he chooses to give you today?

Lord, make my heart willing to accept every job you ask me to do, whether big or small.

Kim Crabill, TV host, author, ministry leader,
Christian counselor

A CHRISTMAS SERVANT

He took the humble position of a slave and was born as a human being.

PHILIPPIANS 2:7 NLT

Do you struggle with all the duties, errands, and expectations that family and friends put on you during the holiday season? Do you feel taken for granted? More like a servant than anything else? Well, my friend, maybe being a servant isn't so bad. You might just need a change of perspective. Jesus didn't come to a royal dwelling or a middle-class hotel. He didn't even come to the low-budget establishment. He was born in the place where animals rest, the dirtiest building in the village.

His humble beginning dictated the rest of his life. He poured all his energy into giving and serving, making no fuss and demanding none of his rights, even though he was God. If you are feeling a little down because your work is taken for granted, always remember that Jesus is a great confidant. He understands your feelings because he was the Master Servant. Just keep following his example.

Lord, give me the humility I need to serve you and others faithfully.

Kim Crabill, TV host, author, ministry leader, Christian counselor

CLOSER THAN CLOSE

The Word became flesh and blood, and moved into the neighborhood.

JOHN 1:14 MSG

Rocket is not a lap cat. Most of the time he is on the move: policing his territory, making sure all loose paper is properly shredded, lecturing the squirrels about stealing bird food, investigating the odd noise from the printer. But when he decides to snuggle with me, he snuggles with his whole being, draping himself to achieve maximum contact. This morning as he assumed the drape position while I savored my first cup of coffee, I thought, "He isn't happy unless he can be closer than close."

And it hit me. That's what the Christmas star points to: no, not a cat, but a baby wanting to be closer than close. Yearning for maximum contact. And not just any bare naked, vulnerable, snuggling baby. That infant was God Almighty. In the flesh. He was inviting us to know him "closer than close." Who can fathom it? Wonder upon wonder. Always remember.

Dearest Jesus, my words feel inadequate to express what my heart feels when I think of you as Emmanuel, God with us, determined to "move into my neighborhood" so that I might know intimacy with the God of love.

Sue Kline, writer, editor, writing coach

PEACE ON EARTH

"Peace I leave with you; my peace I give you. I do not give to you as the world gives."

JOHN 14:27 NIV

Peace is not the first thing we see when we turn on the TV or scroll the morning news. Usually we see disaster, destruction, or decimation. It's all deeply upsetting, often leaving me searching for a cute dog video online or sending a prayer to heaven. Deep down, our hearts yearn for peace in the world and in our personal lives. God showed me that his life-changing peace is found only through an internal experience with the Holy Spirit. It is not fleeting or momentary, like the world's peace. It is forever. It transcends all understanding and guards our hearts and minds (Philippians 4:7) from fears, lies, and worry.

The more time we spend with Jesus, the more it becomes evident. Exercise, deep breathing, and time in nature all bring a sense of peace, but always remember that the everlasting peace we search for is in Jesus. God promises peace on earth one day, but what if today your peace on earth is found by reading your Bible, praying, and trusting God for the peace he has promised you?

Dear God, I trust you with the difficult situations in my life. I want to experience the peace you've given me.

Ella Hartt, Roses and Rainbows advisory board member, songwriter, singer, storyteller

FACING OUR FEARS

Perfect love casts out fear.

1 John 4:18 ESV

What fear is trying to overtake your peace today? Most of us struggle with fear at some point in our lives. Seeking insight, I spoke with my brother Tim, a retired police officer who held various positions in law enforcement for decades. I asked him how he confronted fearful situations without allowing fear to overcome him. He shared a profound point: "I never knew when I'd face a dangerous situation, so I had to continually think through and mitigate any thoughts of fear. My readiness came from faith in God's power and promises."

My brother reminded me that God knows we will face fear, but he has given us a way to overcome it. Staying engaged with God's promises keeps doubt from overtaking us. As believers, we must believe that God is all-powerful and bigger than any fear we could encounter. In addition to this, my brother encouraged me to pray for the peace that surpasses all understanding—a peace that is promised in Philippians 4:6–7. Always remember, friend, that we will all face fear, but because of God's perfect love, we do not have to live fearfully.

Father, help me to run to you and your Word as I prepare to face my fears.

Kim Crabill with Tim Sawyer, retired law enforcement officer

SECOND-RATE GOODS

"Truly I tell you, I have not found anyone in Israel with such great faith."

MATTHEW 8:10 NIV

Secondhand stores and clothes labeled "seconds" make you feel as if you are getting less than the best, don't they? Do you ever feel like you are second-rate? Your job pays the bills, but there is no money left over. Maybe your clothes come from that secondhand store, and you occupy the less prominent pews of the church. Well, my friend, did you know that when Jesus started his earthly ministry, he went first to the land where many gentiles lived? The Jews who were Jesus' nationality did not have anything to do with gentiles. Gentiles were the unclean heathen. Second-rate citizens.

But Jesus loved gentiles as well as Jews, accepting all whose hearts were receptive to his message. He will come to you, too, my friend. If you are feeling second-rate today, I want you to always remember that Jesus does not put that label on you. He loves to come to anyone open to a relationship with him. He makes no distinction between Jews and gentiles, rich or poor. He came to offer love, light, and hope to everyone, and that includes you.

Lord, thank you for showering all of us with your perfect and impartial love.

Kim Crabill, TV host, author, ministry leader, Christian counselor

SATAN 1, WORLD 0?

We know that we are children of God, and that the whole world is under the control of the evil one.

1 John 5:19 NIV

Did you ever spend a little too much time scrolling on social media and find yourself wanting to crawl in a hole afterward? So much sadness, hatred, and anger. Make no mistake, friend: we live in a truly hostile world. It doesn't take a scholar to see rebellion against God. So why does this always surprise and horrify us? Satan has actually been given great power over our planet. Even Jesus refers to him as "the prince of this world" (John 14:30 NIV). But take heart—and be on guard! Satan may be a prince, but we are royalty too—the royal blood of Jesus flows through us.

We can observe the evil all around us without being afraid of its power. We just need to carry our armor wherever we go (see Ephesians 6:10–17). And remember that our King, Jesus himself, taught us to pray, "Deliver us from the evil one" (Matthew 6:13 NIV).

Lord, sometimes I feel outnumbered, but I will not be overpowered by evil. I may be surrounded by Satan's chains, but I am free in Christ Jesus.[26]

Pat Boone, actor, singer, songwriter, author

---

26 Adapted from *Pat Boone Devotional Book*, published by Bible Voice, Inc. Used by permission from Mr. Boone.

ACTIONS TELL ALL

[Christ] is your example, and you must follow in his steps.

1 Peter 2:21 NLT

"Who do you say that Jesus is?" People today spout off all kinds of accurate answers. "Jesus is the Son of God." "Jesus is the only way to heaven." "Jesus is the exact representation of God." All these statements are true, my friend, but stop and think for a minute. Who is Jesus to you? Is he the one you love best, the one you thank every day for all he's given you? Do you love to share your secret hopes and dreams with him?

Living out your profession of who Jesus is requires a heart connection with him. It means sitting before him and asking for a clear vision of what it cost him to redeem you and for wisdom to relate with others as he did. Always remember that when you know who Jesus is, your behavior will resemble his. You will love like he loves. You'll choose to be his servant. Your actions will show to the watching world just who you believe Jesus is.

Lord, help me to know who you are personally so I can share you with a broken world.

Kim Crabill, TV host, author, ministry leader,
Christian counselor

JESUS LOVES YOU

Nothing can ever separate us from God's love.

ROMANS 8:38 NLT

As we conclude our year together, I want to reflect on the words my grandfather imparted to me as a little girl about the love of Jesus. He would say, "There will be times when you feel all alone, when you wonder if anyone truly loves you. When this happens, I want you to always remember that, as much as I love you, there is someone who loves you even more." He reassured me that Jesus would always be there for me, no matter where life would take me. To this day, I have held on to that truth.

I hope you have enjoyed reading the stories of so many of my friends who have shared incredible words to remember. I want you to know that you also have important words to share with those you love. From my heart to yours, I leave you with my own rephrasing of the words from my grandfather that have sustained me all my life: My friend, there will be moments when you feel alone. In those moments, I want you to always remember that, as much as you and your friendship mean to me, there is someone who loves you even more. His name is Jesus, and he will go with you wherever life takes you.

Lord, thank you for your endless and unconditional love that guides, comforts, and keeps me company every day.

Kim Crabill, TV host, author, ministry leader, Christian counselor

ABOUT THE AUTHOR

Kim Crabill is an award-winning author and TV talk-show host, a board-certified Christian counselor, and the president of Roses and Rainbows Ministry, Inc. Her passion is bringing God's healing and hope to hearts and homes worldwide.

Kim's TV program, "COFFEE with Kim," is a testimonial talk show which airs on over one hundred of the largest faith-based networks, reaching millions of homes daily. Kim is the author of numerous books, including her signature work, *Burdens to Blessings: Discovering the Power of Your Story*, *Infinitely More*, and *Living Free*, all winners of Christian Literary Awards.

Though her ministry has TV and radio programming, as well as written curriculum, potentially reaching six hundred million people across the nations, Kim states, "We will not be satisfied until every person feels rescued by God's love and empowered by his purpose." You can contact Kim at www.KimCrabill.org.